Strengthen
MY
SPIRIT

Strengthen
MY
SPIRIT

DAILY DEVOTIONS FROM THE
WORKS OF CHARLES SPURGEON

CHARLES
SPURGEON

BARBOUR
PUBLISHING

© 2004 by Barbour Publishing, Inc.

Compiled by Jennifer Hahn.

Print ISBN 978-1-63609-030-6

eBook Editions:
Adobe Digital Edition (.epub) 978-1-63609-237-9

Published by Barbour Publishing, Inc., 1810 Barbour Drive, Uhrichsville, Ohio 44683, www.barbourbooks.com

Our mission is to inspire the world with the life-changing message of the Bible.

Member of the
Evangelical Christian
Publishers Association

Printed in the United States of America.

INTRODUCTION

Charles Spurgeon is considered the most widely read preacher in history, excluding those of the Bible. He preached his first sermon at the age of sixteen, and by age twenty had delivered over six hundred sermons. Throughout his lifetime, he preached to over ten million people.

This godly pastor was well acquainted with hardship. He endured personal and family illness, as well as the enormous task of leading a church whose congregation also faced numerous difficulties. Spurgeon did not merely instruct his listeners to ask God for the power to withstand adversity, however; he was a living testimony of one who relied on God to be his strength. Missionary David Livingstone once inquired, "How do you manage to do two men's work in a single day?" Spurgeon answered, "You have forgotten that there are two of us."

Strengthen My Spirit is a compilation of lightly edited selections from Charles Spurgeon's sermons and writings, preceded by brief passages of scripture. Each day of the year, his words will encourage you to deepen your relationship with Christ. You may be experiencing trials and hardships: financial distress, a broken relationship, physical illness. . . . Whatever you are facing today, God longs to hear you call out, "Lord, strengthen my spirit."

Day 1

NEWNESS IN CHRIST

---

*Then He who sat on the throne said,
"Behold, I make all things new."*
REVELATION 21:5 NKJV

I do not know, but it is sometimes as well, when one has been plunged in sorrow or feels ashamed of his past life—after having regretted that which is bygone and repented of it and sorrowed over it—to feel as if he breathed another atmosphere and had started on a fresh career. Having thrown away the old sword, he is now about to see what he can do with the new; having put off an old garment, he is desirous to walk more worthily of his vocation with fresh ones that are provided for him. Perhaps the thought of freshness, the fact of new time having dawned on our path, may be a little help to those of us who are dull and heavy, and we may be stirred up to action. If not to action, it may awaken earnest hope that the infusion of a new start into our lives, new vigor instead of the old lethargy, new love instead of the old lukewarmness, new zeal instead of the old deathlikeness, new persevering industry for Christ instead of the old idleness may result. God grant that it may be so!

THE NEW NATURE

Therefore, if anyone is in Christ, the new creation
has come: The old has gone, the new is here!
2 CORINTHIANS 5:17 NIV

Christ has been pleased to make us new men. His saints
are "new creatures in Christ Jesus." They have a new nature.
God has breathed into them a new life. The Holy Spirit,
though the old nature is still there, has been pleased to put
within them a new nature. There is now a contending force
within them—the old carnal nature inclining to evil and
the new God-given nature panting after perfection. They are
new men "begotten again unto a lively hope by the resurrection of Jesus Christ from the dead." This new nature is moved
by new principles. The old nature needed to be awed with
threatenings or bribed with rewards; the new nature feels the
impulse of love. Gratitude is its mainspring: "We love Him
because He first loved us."

This new nature is conscious of new emotions. It loves
what once it hated; it hates what once it loved. It finds blight
where once it sought for bliss, and finds bliss where once
it found nothing but bitterness. It leaps at the sound that
was once dull to its ears—the name of a precious Christ. It
rejoices in hopes that once seemed idle as dreams. It is filled
with a divine enthusiasm that it once rejected as fanatical.
It is conscious now of living in a new element, breathing a
fresh air, partaking of new food, drinking out of new wells not
dug by men or filled from the earth. The man is new—new
in principles and new in emotions.

✓

Day 3

DEEPER DESIRE FOR CHRIST

As the deer pants for streams of water,
so my soul pants for you, my God.
PSALM 42:1 NIV

Now man is new in relationship. He was an heir to wrath; he is now a child of God. He was a bondslave; he is now a freeman. He rejoices in Christ Jesus and feasts to the full. He was the citizen of earth once; he is now a citizen of heaven. He once found his all beneath the clouds, but now his all is beyond the stars. He has new relationships. Christ is his Brother, God is his Father, the angels are his friends, and the despised people of God are his best and nearest kinsfolk. And hence the man has new aspirations. He now pants to glorify God. What did he care about the glory of God once? He now pants to see God; once he would have paid the fare—if it had cost his life—that he might escape from the presence of the Lord. Now he hungers and thirsts after the living God; if his soul had wings and he could break the fetters of this mortality, he would mount at once to dwell where Jesus is. Dear friends, are you new men? If you are, you understand what it is; if you are not, I know I cannot explain it to you. To be born again is a great mystery; blessed is the soul that comprehends it! But he who does not know it will never learn it by the lip; he can only know it by the Spirit of God causing him also to be made a new creature in Christ Jesus.

Day 4
A NEW HEART

> *"I will give you a new heart and*
> *put a new spirit in you."*
> EZEKIEL 36:26 NIV

"Behold," says Christ, "I make all things new." What a wonder it is that a man should ever have a new heart! You know if a lobster loses its claw in a fight it can get a new claw, and that is thought to be very marvelous. It would be very wonderful if men should be able to grow new arms and new legs, but who ever heard of a creature that grew a new heart?

You may have seen a bough lopped off a tree, and you may have thought that perhaps the tree will sprout again and there will be a new limb, but who ever heard of old trees getting new sap and a new core? But my Lord and Master, the crucified and exalted Savior, has given new hearts and new cores; He has put the vital substance into man afresh and made new creatures of them. I am glad to notice the tear in your eye when you think on the past, but wipe it away now, and look up to the cross and say—

> *Just as I am, without one plea,*
> *But that Your blood was shed for me,*
> *And that You bid'st me come to You,*
> *O Lamb, O God, I come.*

"Make me a new creature!" If you have said that from your heart, you are a new creature, dear brother, and we will rejoice together in this regenerating Savior.

Day 5
TRUST HIS SALVATION

*Sing to the LORD a new song, for he has done
marvelous things; his right hand and his holy arm
have worked salvation for him. The LORD has made
his salvation known and revealed his righteousness
to the nations. He has remembered his love and his
faithfulness to Israel; all the ends of the earth
have seen the salvation of our God.*

PSALM 98:1–3 NIV

Courage, my brothers and sisters. We will not entertain any more doubt about Christ's power to save. Rather, by God's grace, may we henceforth believe more in Him, and according to our faith, so shall it be done unto us. If we can only trust Him for those of our friends whose faults seem to us few and light, our little trust will reap little reward. But if we can go with strong faith in a great God and bring great sinners in our arms and put them down before this mighty Regenerator of men and say, "Lord, if You will, You can make them new"; and if we will never cease the pleading until we get the blessing, then we shall see ever-accumulating illustrations of the fact that Jesus makes all things new—and calling up the witnesses of His redeeming power, we shall cry in the ears of a drowsy Church and an incredulous world, "Behold, behold, behold! He makes all things new."

The Lord give us eyes to see it. Amen.

CHRIST'S PRAYER FOR HIS CHILDREN

I pray not that thou shouldest take them out of the world, but that thou shouldest keep them from the evil.

JOHN 17:15 KJV

This prayer of Christ is an ever-precious portion to all true believers, from the fact that each of them has an inalienable interest in it. Every one of us, beloved, when we listen to the words of Christ should recollect that He is praying for us; that while it is for the great body of His elect He intercedes in this chapter and the one preceding it, yet it is also for each believer in particular that He offers intercession. However weak we are, however poor, however little our faith, or however small our grace may be, our names are still written on His heart; nor shall we lose our share in Jesus' love.

Oh poor sinner, do not be doubtful of my Master's power. Do but touch the hem of His garment, and you shall be made whole. Like the poor woman in the crowd, get at it and touch it, and He will surely say unto you, "You are saved." If you will go to Him with this cry,

I'm a poor sinner and nothing at all,
And Jesus Christ is my all in all,

then you will see the blessed reason why Jesus interceded thus: "I pray not that thou shouldest take them out of the world."

✓

Day 7
NEVER FORSAKEN

And they that know thy name will
put their trust in thee: for thou, LORD,
hast not forsaken them that seek thee.
PSALM 9:10 KJV

Fellowship with Christ is so honorable a thing that it is worthwhile to suffer, that we may thereby enjoy it. You have sometimes heard me express a desire that I might be in the number of those who shall be alive and remain, and so shall escape death; but a dear friend of mine says he had rather die, in order that he might thus have fellowship with Christ in His sufferings, and the thought finds an echo in my own breast. To die with Jesus makes death a perfect treasure; to be a follower in the grave with Him makes death a pleasure.

Moreover you and I might be taken for cowards, although we may have fellowship with Him in His glory, if we had no scars to prove the sufferings we had passed through and the wounds we had received for His name. Thus again you see it is for our good to be here; we should not have known fellowship with the Savior if we had not stayed here a little while. I should never have known the Savior's love half as much if I had not been in the storms of affliction. How sweet it is to learn the Savior's love when nobody else loves us! When friends flee, what a blessed thing it is to see that the Savior does not forsake us but still keeps us and holds us fast and clings to us and will not let us go!

Oh beloved brother and sister, believe that your remaining here on earth is for your eternal benefit.

Day 8
CALL TO WIN SOULS

The fruit of the righteous is a tree of life,
and he who wins souls is wise.

PROVERBS 11:30 NKJV

Why is it that saints do not die as soon as they are converted? Because God meant that they should be the means of the salvation of their brethren. You would not surely wish to go out of the world if there were a soul to be saved by you. If I could go to glory before I had converted all the souls allotted to me, I should not be happy. We do not wish to enter heaven until our work is done, for it would make us uneasy if there were one single soul left to be saved by our means.

Tarry then, Christian; there is a sinner to be saved from his sins, a rebel to be turned from the error of his ways, and perhaps that sinner is one of your relatives. Perhaps you are spared in this world because there is a wayward son of yours not yet saved, and God has designed to make you the favored instrument of bringing him to glory. It may be that you are kept here because one of your offspring, by your instrumentality, is yet to be saved. Tarry then for your son's sake. I know how deeply you love him, and for his sake, surely, you are content to be left here a little while, counting it for the best that you may bring in your son to glory with you.

Day 9

ENDURING TRIALS
FOR GOD'S GLORY

*Now for a little while you may have had to suffer
grief in all kinds of trials. These have come so that the
proven genuineness of your faith—of greater worth
than gold, which perishes even though refined
by fire—may result in praise, glory and
honor when Jesus Christ is revealed.*

1 PETER 1:6–7 NIV

A tried saint brings more glory to God than an untried one. I think in my own soul that a believer in a prison reflects more glory on his Master than a believer in paradise, that a child of God in the burning, fiery furnace, whose hair is yet unscorched and upon whom the smell of the fire has not passed, displays more the glory of the Godhead than even he who stands with a crown upon his head, perpetually singing praises before the Father's throne. Nothing reflects so much honor on a workman as a trial of his work and its endurance of it.

So it is with God. It honors Him when His saints preserve their integrity. Peter honored Christ more when he walked on the water than when he stood upon the land. There was no glory given to God by his walking on the solid shore, but there was glory reflected when he walked on the water.

If we could but add more jewels to the crown of Christ by remaining here, why should we wish to be taken out of the world? We should say, "It is blessed to be anywhere where we can glorify Him."

✓

OUR FELLOWSHIP WITH CHRIST

We have fellowship with him.
1 JOHN 1:6 KJV

When we were united by faith to Christ, we were brought into such complete fellowship with Him that we were made one with Him, and His interests and ours became mutual and identical. We have fellowship with Christ in His love. He loves the saints—so do we. He loves sinners—so do we. He loves the poor perishing race of man—so do we.

We have fellowship with Him in His desires. He desires the glory of God—we also labor for the same. He desires that the saints may be with Him—we desire to be with Him there too. He desires that His Father's name may be loved and adored by all His creatures—we pray daily, "Thy kingdom come. Your will be done on earth, even as it is in heaven."

We have fellowship with Christ in His sufferings. We are not nailed to the cross, nor do we die a cruel death, but when He is reproached, we are reproached; and a very sweet thing it is to be blamed for His sake. In our measure we commune with Him in His labors, ministering to men by the Word of truth and by deeds of love.

We have also fellowship with Christ in His joys. We rejoice in His exaltation. There is no purer or more thrilling delight to be known this side heaven than that of having Christ's joy fulfilled in us, that our joy may be full. His glory awaits us to complete our fellowship, for His Church shall sit with Him upon His throne as His well-beloved bride and queen.

Day 11
BLESSED BY GOD

Praise be to the Lord, to God our Savior, who daily bears our burdens. Our God is a God who saves; from the Sovereign LORD comes escape from death.
PSALM 68:19–20 NIV

Are any of you inclined to murmur? Do you think God deals harshly with you? Well, you are what you are by His grace. Though you are not what you wish to be, remember you are not what—if strict justice were carried out—you would be. In the poorhouse you might be—few admire that residence. In the prison you might be—God preserves you from the sin that would bring you there. At the grave's mouth you might be—on the sick bed, on the verge of eternity. God's holiest saints have not been spared from the grave. O God, when we think of what we are not because Your grace has kept us from it, we can only say, "You have loaded us with benefits."

Think of what you are, you Christians. You are God's children; you are joint heirs with Christ. The "many mansions" are for you; the palms and harps of the glorified are for you. You have a share in all that Christ has and is and shall be. In all the gifts of His ascension, you have a part; in the gifts that come to us through His being seated at the right hand of God, you have your share; and in the glories of the Second Coming, you shall partake. See how in the present and in the past and in the future, He loads you with benefits.

Day 12
PRAISE HIM!

I will praise Your name forever and ever.
PSALM 145:2 NKJV

The one occupation of a Christian is to praise his God. Now in order to do this, we must maintain by God's grace a grateful, happy, praiseful frame of mind; and we must endeavor to express that condition of mind by songs of gratitude. Let us make both ends of the day bright with His praise, and throughout the day. We are in a wrong state of mind if we are not in a thankful state of mind. There is something wrong with you if you cannot praise God. "Oh!" a person says. "Even in trouble?" Yes, in every bitter trouble too, for Job could say, "The Lord gave, and the Lord has taken away, and blessed be the name of the Lord."

"But are we never to be sorrowful?" Yes, yet always rejoicing. How can that be? The Lord will teach you! It is a work of grace. Cast down but yet rejoicing in the Lord! He lifts up the light of His countenance upon us, even when heart and flesh are failing us. There is something amiss when our heart does not praise God. When your heart is glad, praise Him with your lips. Do you work alone? Sing. Perhaps, if you work with others, you cannot; then sing with your heart. Habitually praise Him. All our actions, as well as our thoughts and words, should praise Him who always blesses us. You may stop praising God when He stops having mercy on you—not until then.

INSPIRE PRAISE IN OTHERS

*For what you have done I will always praise you
in the presence of your faithful people. And I will
hope in your name, for your name is good.*
PSALM 52:9 NIV

If we praise God ourselves by word and life, we ought to
try to bring others to praise Him too. It is a mark of sincere
thankfulness, desiring others to assist in the expression of its
joy. The psalmist in the sixty-seventh Psalm says, "Blessed
be the Lord. Let the people praise You—yea, let all the
people praise You! Oh, let the nations be glad and sing for
joy!" He also says, "Let the people praise You, O God; yea,
let all the people praise You!"

Do your utmost to be the means, in God's hands, of
bringing others to praise Him. Tell them what He has done
for you. Tell them of His saving grace. In this way you will
be setting other tongues praising God, so that when your
tongue is silent, there will be others who will take up the strain.
Labor for this, every one of you. Labor for the extension of
the choir that shall sing the praises of the Savior. I trust we
shall never fall into that narrow-minded spirit which seems
to say, "It is enough for me that I am saved." No, Master, Your
throne is not to be set up in some little secret assembly in
a back street, and there alone. You are not to reign in some
little corner of a city, and there alone. Let the whole earth
be filled with His praise!

His Poverty, Our Riches

For your sake He became poor.
2 Corinthians 8:9 nasb

The Lord Jesus Christ was eternally rich, glorious, and exalted; but "though He was rich, yet for your sakes, He became poor." It is impossible that our divine Lord could have had fellowship with us unless He had imparted to us of His own abounding wealth and had become poor to make us rich. Had He remained upon His throne of glory and had we continued in the ruins of the fall without receiving His salvation, communion would have been impossible on both sides. Our position by the fall, apart from the covenant of grace, made it impossible for fallen man to communicate with God. In order therefore that communion might be possible, it was necessary that the rich Kinsman should bestow His wealth upon His poor relatives, that the righteous Savior should give to His sinning children of His own perfection, and that we, the poor and guilty, should receive of His fullness grace for grace; that in giving and receiving, the One might descend from the heights and the other ascend from the depths, and so be able to embrace each other in true and hearty fellowship.

Jesus must clothe His people in His own garments, or He cannot admit them into His palace of glory; and He must wash them in His own blood, or else they will be too defiled for the embrace of His fellowship. Oh believer, this is love! For your sake the Lord Jesus "became poor" that He might lift you up into communion with Himself.

Day 15

OUR NEVER-CHANGING GOD

"For I am the LORD, I do not change;
therefore you are not consumed."
MALACHI 3:6 NKJV

What a consolation it is that our God never changes! What He was yesterday, He is today. What we find Him today, we shall find Him forever. Are you struggling against sin? Don't struggle in your own strength: It is God who performs all things for you. Victories over sin are only sham victories unless we overcome through the blood of the Lamb and through the power of divine grace. May we have what we really think we have—no surface work but deep, inner, spiritual life fashioned in us from God—yes, every good spiritual thing from Him who performs all things for us; and I say, whatever struggles may come, whatever temptations may overwhelm, or whatever thunderclouds may burst over your heads, you shall not be deserted, much less destroyed.

In spiritual things it is God who performs all things for you. Rest in Him then. You cannot work to save your own soul; Christ is the Savior. If He cannot save you, you certainly cannot save yourself. Why do you rest your hopes where hopes never should be rested? Or let me change the question: Why do you fear where you should never have hoped? Instead of fearing that you cannot hold on, fear holding on yourself and never look in that direction again. Let your entire reliance be fixed in Him. Cast the burden of your care on Him who performs all things for you.

Day 16
CONTINUAL BLESSING

I will bless the LORD at all times;
His praise shall continually be in my mouth.
PSALM 34:1 NKJV

Others may do what they please and murmur and complain
and be filled with dread and apprehension of the future, but
I will bless the Lord at all times. I can always see something
for which I ought to bless Him. I can always see some good
that will come out of blessing Him. Therefore I will bless
Him at all times.

"And this," says the psalmist, "I will not only do in
my heart, but I will do it with my tongue. His praise shall
continually be in my mouth," that others may hear it, that
others may begin to praise Him too, for murmuring is
contagious, and so, thank God, is praise; and one man may
learn from another—and then begin to praise God with him.
"His praise shall continually be in my mouth."

What a blessed mouthful! If some people had God's
praises in their mouths, they would not so often find fault
with their fellowmen. "If half the breath thus vainly spent" in
finding fault with our fellow Christians was spent in prayer
and praise, how much happier, how much richer we should
be spiritually!

Day 17

BOASTING IN THE LORD

My soul shall make its boast in the LORD;
the humble shall hear of it and be glad.

PSALM 34:2 NKJV

Boasting is generally annoying. Even those who boast themselves cannot endure the boasting of other people. But there is one kind of boasting that even the humble can bear to hear—in fact, they are glad to hear it. "The humble shall hear thereof and be glad." That must be boasting in God—a holy glorifying and extolling the Most High with words sought out with care that might magnify His blessed name. You will never exaggerate when you speak good things of God. It is not possible to do so. Try, dear brethren, and boast in the Lord. There are many poor, trembling, doubting, humble souls who can hardly tell whether they are the Lord's people or not and are half afraid whether they will be delivered in the hour of trouble, who will become comforted when they hear you boasting. "The humble shall hear thereof and be glad."

"Why," says the humble soul, "the God who helped him can help me. He who brought him up through the deep waters and landed him safely can also take me through the river and through the sea and give me final deliverance."

My soul shall make her boast in the Lord. "The humble shall hear thereof and be glad."

Day 18
NEARER TO GOD

Get thee up into the high mountain.
ISAIAH 40:9 KJV

Each believer should be thirsting for God, for the living God, and longing to climb the hill of the Lord and see Him face-to-face. My soul thirsts of the cup which is reserved for those who reach the mountain's brow and bathe their brows in heaven. How pure are the dews of the hills, how fresh is the mountain air, how rich the fare of the dwellers aloft whose windows look into the New Jerusalem! Many saints are content to live like men in coal mines who see not the sun; they eat dust like the serpent when they might taste the ambrosial meat of angels, they are content to wear the miner's garb when they might put on the king's robes, and tears mar their faces when they might anoint them with celestial oil. Many a believer pines in a dungeon when he might walk on the palace roof and view the goodly land of Lebanon.

Rouse yourself from your low condition! Cast away your sloth, your lethargy, your coldness, or whatever interferes with your chaste and pure love for Christ, your soul's Husband. Make Him the source, the center, and the circumference of all your soul's range of delight. What charms you into such folly as to remain in a pit when you may sit on a throne? Rest no longer satisfied with your dwarfish attainments, but press forward to things more sublime and heavenly. Aspire to a higher, a nobler, a fuller life. Upward to heaven! Nearer to God!

DILIGENT SERVICE

Whatever your hand finds to do, do it with your might.
ECCLESIASTES 9:10 NKJV

"Whatever your hand finds to do" refers to works that are possible. Let us not wait for large opportunities or for a different kind of work, but do just the things we "find to do" day by day. We have no other time in which to live. The past is gone, and the future has not arrived; we never shall have any time but time present. Then do not wait until your experience has ripened into maturity before you attempt to serve God. Endeavor now to bring forth fruit. Serve God now, but be careful as to the way in which you perform what you find to do—"do it with your might." Do it promptly; no man ever served God by doing things tomorrow. If we honor Christ and are blessed, it is by the things that we do today. Whatever you do for Christ, throw your whole soul into it. Do not give Christ a little slurred labor done as a matter of course now and then, but when you do serve Him, do it with heart and soul and strength.

But where is the might of a Christian? It is not in himself, for he is perfect weakness. His might lies in the Lord of Hosts. Then let us seek His help; let us proceed with prayer and faith, and when we have done what our "hand[s] find to do," let us wait upon the Lord for His blessing. What we do thus will be well done and will not fail in its effect.

Day 20

THE REDEMPTION OF GOD

I will deliver thee out of the hand of the wicked,
and I will redeem thee out of the hand of the terrible.
JEREMIAH 15:21 KJV

Note the glorious personality of the promise. "I will"—the Lord Jehovah Himself interposes to deliver and redeem His people. He pledges Himself personally to rescue them. His own arm will do it that He may have the glory. There is not a word said of any effort of our own which may be needed to assist the Lord. Neither our strength nor our weakness is taken into the account, but the lone *I*, like the sun in the heavens, shines out resplendent in all-sufficiency. Peace, you unbelieving thoughts—be still and know that the Lord reigns.

Nor is there a hint concerning secondary means and causes. The Lord says nothing of friends and helpers: He undertakes the work alone and feels no need of human arms to aid Him. Vain are all our lookings around to companions and relatives; they are broken reeds if we lean upon them—often unwilling when able and unable when they are willing. Since the promise comes alone from God, it would be well to wait only upon Him, and when we do so, our expectation never fails us. In all times of fiery trial, in patience let us possess our souls.

Day 21
LIFT YOUR PRAISE!

They shall give thanks to the LORD for His mercy,
and for His wonders to the sons of mankind!
PSALM 107:8 NASB

If we complained less and praised more, we should be happier and God would be more glorified. Let us daily praise God for common mercies—common as we frequently call them, and yet so priceless that when deprived of them we are ready to perish. Let us bless God for the eyes with which we behold the sun, for the health and strength to walk abroad, for the bread we eat, for the raiment we wear. Let us praise Him for everything we receive from His bounteous hand, for we deserve little and yet are most plenteously endowed.

But the sweetest and the loudest note in our songs of praise should be of redeeming love. God's redeeming acts toward His chosen are forever the favorite themes of their praise. If we know what redemption means, let us not withhold our sonnets of thanksgiving. We have been redeemed from the power of our corruptions, uplifted from the depth of sin in which we were naturally plunged. We have been led to the cross of Christ—we are no longer slaves but children of the living God. Child of God, can you be silent?

Day 22

CONTENTMENT IN GOD

---

*O fear the LORD, ye his saints: for there is no
want to them that fear him. The young lions do
lack, and suffer hunger: but they that seek the
LORD shall not want any good thing.*

PSALM 34:9–10 KJV

They are very strong, those young lions. They are fierce. They
are voracious. They are cunning. And yet they do lack and
suffer hunger. And there are many men in this world who
are very clever, strong in body, and active in mind. They say
that they can take care of themselves, and perhaps they do
appear to prosper; but we know that often those who are the
most prosperous apparently are the most miserable of men.
They are young lions, but they do lack and suffer hunger.

But when a man's soul lives upon God, he may have very
little of this world, but he will be perfectly content. He has
learned the secret of true happiness. He does not want any
good things, for the things that he does not have, he does
not wish to have. He brings his mind down to his estate if
he cannot bring his estate to his mind. He is thankful to
have a little spending money, but his treasure is above. He
likes to have the best things last, and so he is well content, if
he has food and raiment, to press on his way to the rest that
remains for the people of God. "The young lions do lack, and
suffer hunger; but they that seek the Lord shall not want
any good thing."

Day 23

OVERCOMING THROUGH CHRIST

Who is this King of glory? The LORD strong and mighty, the LORD mighty in battle.

PSALM 24:8 NKJV

Well may our God be glorious in the eyes of His people, seeing that He has wrought such wonders for them, in them, and by them. The saved may well adore their Lord for His conquests in them, since the arrows of their natural hatred are snapped and the weapons of their rebellion broken. What victories has grace won in our evil hearts! How glorious is Jesus when the will is subdued and sin dethroned! As for our remaining corruptions, they shall sustain an equally sure defeat, and every temptation and doubt and fear shall be utterly destroyed.

In the Salem of our peaceful hearts, the name of Jesus is great beyond compare: He has won our love, and He shall wear it. Even thus securely may we look for victories by us. We are more than conquerors through Him who loved us. We shall cast down the powers of darkness which are in the world, by our faith and zeal and holiness; we shall win sinners to Jesus, we shall overturn false systems, we shall convert nations, for God is with us and none shall stand before us. Let the Christian warrior chant the war song and prepare for tomorrow's fight. Greater is He who is in us than he who is in the world.

Day 24
BENEVOLENT FORESIGHT

Thou, O God, hast prepared of
thy goodness for the poor.
PSALM 68:10 KJV

God anticipates our needs, and out of the fullness which He has treasured up in Christ Jesus, He provides of His goodness for the poor. You may trust Him for all the necessities that can occur, for He has infallibly foreknown every one of them. God has marked with prescient eye all the requirements of His poor wandering children, and when those needs occur, supplies are ready. It is goodness which He has prepared for the poor in heart, goodness and goodness only. "My grace is sufficient for thee." "As your days, so shall your strength be."

Is your heart heavy? God knew it would be; the comfort that your heart wants is treasured in the sweet assurance of the text. You are poor and needy, but He has thought of you and has the exact blessing which you require in store for you. Plead the promise, believe it, and obtain its fulfillment. Do you feel that you never were so consciously vile as you are now? Behold, the crimson fountain is open still with all its former efficacy, to wash your sin away. Never shall you come into such a position that Christ cannot aid you. No pinch shall ever arrive in your spiritual affairs in which Jesus Christ shall not be equal to the emergency, for your history has all been foreknown and provided for in Jesus.

Day 25
WAIT FOR THE LORD

Therefore will the LORD wait,
that he may be gracious unto you.
ISAIAH 30:18 KJV

God often delays in answering prayer. If you have been knocking at the gate of mercy and have received no answer, shall I tell you why the mighty Maker has not opened the door and let you in? Our Father has reasons known only to Himself. Sometimes it is to show His power and His sovereignty, that men may know that Jehovah has a right to give or to withhold. More frequently the delay is for our profit. Perhaps you are kept waiting in order that your desires may be more fervent. God knows that delay will quicken and increase desire, and that if He keeps you waiting, you will see your necessity more clearly and will seek more earnestly; and that you will prize the mercy all the more for its long tarrying.

There may also be something in you that needs to be removed before the joy of the Lord is given. Perhaps you may be placing some little reliance on yourself instead of trusting entirely to the Lord Jesus. Your prayers are all filed in heaven; and if not immediately answered, they are certainly not forgotten, but in a little while shall be fulfilled to your delight and satisfaction. Let not despair make you silent, but continue constantly in earnest supplication.

ASSURANCE OF GOD'S FAITHFULNESS

The one who calls you is faithful, and he will do it.
1 THESSALONIANS 5:24 NIV

Heaven is a place where we shall never sin; there will be no tempter to ensnare our feet. There the wicked cease from troubling and the weary are at rest. Heaven is the "undefiled inheritance"; it is the land of perfect holiness, and therefore of complete security. But do not the saints even on earth sometimes taste the joys of blissful security? The doctrine of God's Word is that all who are in union with the Lamb are safe, that all the righteous shall hold on their way, that those who have committed their souls to the keeping of Christ shall find Him a faithful and immutable preserver. Sustained by such a doctrine we can enjoy security even on earth; not that high and glorious security which renders us free from every slip, but that holy security which arises from the sure promise of Jesus that none who believe in Him shall ever perish but shall be with Him where He is. Let us often reflect with joy on the doctrine of the perseverance of the saints and honor the faithfulness of our God by a holy confidence in Him.

Look upon Him as faithful and true, and therefore bound and engaged to present you, the weakest of the family, with all the chosen race before the throne of God. You will have the enjoyments which ravish the souls of the perfect saints above, if you can believe with unstaggering faith that "the One who calls you is faithful and He will do it."

Day 27

THE ENDURANCE
OF CHRISTIANITY

Christt is all.

COLOSSIANS 3:11 KJV

While there are many falsehoods, there can be but one truth; real religion is therefore one. There is but one Gospel—the Gospel of our Lord Jesus Christ. What a wonderful thing it is that Jesus Christ, the Son of God, should be born of humble parents and live as a poor man in this world for the purpose of our salvation! He lived a life of suffering and trial, and at length, through the defamation of His enemies, was crucified on Calvary as an outcast of society.

"Now," they said, "there is the end of His religion; now it will be such a contemptible thing that nobody will ever call himself a Christian. It will be discreditable to have anything to do with the name of the man Jesus, the prophet of Nazareth." But it is a wonderful fact that this religion has not only lived but is as strong as ever. Yes! The religion He founded still exists and is still powerful and constantly extending. While other religions have sunk into the darkness of the past, the name of Jesus is still mighty, and it shall continue to be a blessed power as long as the universe shall endure.

Day 28

A PROMISE FOR
TROUBLED TIMES

---

*"May the LORD value my life and
deliver me from all trouble."*
1 SAMUEL 26:24 NIV

Some people seem to think that Christians are very melancholy, that they have no real happiness. I know something about religion, and I will not admit that I stand second to any man in respect of being happy. As far as I know religion, I have found it to be a very happy thing. I used to think that a religious man must never smile; but, on the contrary, I find that religion will make a man's eyes bright and cover his face with smiles and impart comfort and consolation to his soul, even in the deepest of his earthly tribulations.

I ask you who love Jesus: Does religion ever make you unhappy? Does love for Jesus distress you and make you miserable? It may bring you into trouble sometimes and cause you to endure persecution for His name's sake. If you are a child of God, you will have to suffer tribulation; but all the afflictions which you may be called upon to endure for Him will work for your good and are not worthy to be compared with the glory which is to be revealed in the future.

Day 29

EVERLASTING AND UNCHANGING

His ways are everlasting.
HABAKKUK 3:6 KJV

Man's ways are variable, but God's ways are everlasting. The Lord's ways are the result of wise deliberation; He orders all things according to the counsel of His own will. Human action is frequently the hasty result of passion or fear and is followed by regret and alteration, but nothing can take the Almighty by surprise or happen otherwise than He has foreseen. His ways are the outgrowth of an immutable character, and in them the fixed and settled attributes of God are clearly to be seen. Unless the Eternal One Himself can undergo change, His ways, which are Himself in action, must remain forever the same.

Is He eternally just, gracious, faithful, wise, tender? Then His ways must ever be distinguished for the same excellences. Beings act according to their nature: When those natures change, their conduct varies also; but since God cannot know the shadow of a turning, His ways will abide everlastingly the same. Furthermore there is no reason from without which could reverse the divine ways since they are the embodiment of irresistible might. It is not might alone which gives stability; God's ways are the manifestation of the eternal principles of right and therefore can never pass away. Wrong breeds decay and involves ruin, but the true and the good have about them a vitality which ages cannot diminish.

Let us go to our heavenly Father with confidence, remembering that Jesus Christ is the same yesterday, today, and forever, and in Him the Lord is ever gracious to His people.

Day 30
OUR HOLY GUIDE

And the LORD shall guide thee continually.
ISAIAH 58:11 KJV

Not an angel, but Jehovah shall guide you. God has not left you in your earthly pilgrimage to an angel's guidance: He Himself leads the van. You may not see the cloudy, fiery pillar, but Jehovah will never forsake you.

Notice the word *shall*—"The Lord *shall* guide thee." How certain this makes it! How sure it is that God will not forsake us! His precious "shalls" and "wills" are better than men's oaths. "I will never leave thee nor forsake thee." Then observe the adverb "continually." We are not merely to be guided sometimes, but we are to have a perpetual monitor; not occasionally to be left to our own understanding, and so to wander, but we are continually to hear the guiding voice of the Great Shepherd; and if we follow close at His heels, we shall not err, but be led by a right way to a city to dwell in. If you have to change your position in life, if you have to emigrate to distant shores, if it should happen that you are cast into poverty or uplifted suddenly into a more responsible position than the one you now occupy, if you are thrown among strangers or cast among foes, tremble not, for "the Lord shall guide you continually."

There are no dilemmas out of which you shall not be delivered if you live near to God. He goes not amiss who goes in the company of God. You have infallible wisdom to direct you, immutable love to comfort you, and eternal power to defend you.

Day 31

GOD'S THOUGHTS
FOR HIS CHILDREN

"I remember you."
JEREMIAH 2:2 NKJV

Let us note that Christ delights to think upon His Church and to look upon her beauty. As the bird returns often to its nest and as the wayfarer hastens to his home, so does the mind continually pursue the object of its choice. We cannot look too often upon that face which we love; we desire always to have our precious things in our sight. It is even so with our Lord Jesus.

From all eternity "His delights were with the sons of men." His thoughts rolled onward to the time when His elect should be born into the world; He viewed them in the mirror of His foreknowledge. "In Your book," He says, "all my members were written, which in continuance were fashioned when as yet there was none of them." When the world was set upon its pillars, He was there, and He set the bounds of the people according to the number of the children of Israel. As the breastplate containing the names of the tribes of Israel was the most brilliant ornament worn by the high priest, so the names of Christ's elect were His most precious jewels and glittered on His heart.

We may often forget to meditate upon the perfections of our Lord, but He never ceases to remember us. Let us chide ourselves for past forgetfulness and pray for grace ever to bear Him in fondest remembrance. Lord, paint upon the eyeballs of my soul the image of Your Son.

Day 32

THE DOOR

I am the door: by me if any man enter in, he shall be
saved, and shall go in and out, and find pasture.
JOHN 10:9 KJV

Jesus, the great I AM, is the entrance into the true Church and the way of access to God Himself. He gives to the man who comes to God by Him four choice privileges.

1. He shall be saved. Entrance through Jesus into peace is the guarantee of entrance by the same door into heaven. Jesus is the only door, an open door, a wide door, a safe door; and blessed is he who rests all his hope of admission to glory upon the crucified Redeemer.

2. He shall go in. He shall go in among the divine family, participating in all their honors and enjoyments. He shall go in to the chambers of communion, to the banquets of love, to the treasures of the covenant, to the storehouses of the promises. He shall go in unto the King of kings in the power of the Holy Spirit.

3. He shall go out. We go out into the world to labor and suffer, but what a mercy to go in the name and power of Jesus! We are called to bear witness to the truth, to cheer the disconsolate, to warn the careless, to win souls, and to glorify God.

4. He shall find pasture. He who knows Jesus shall never want. Having made Jesus his all, he shall find all in Jesus. His soul shall be as a watered garden and as a well of water whose waters fail not.

Day 33

OUR ULTIMATE INHERITANCE

He will choose our inheritance for us.
PSALM 47:4 NKJV

Believer, if your inheritance is a lowly one, you should be satisfied with your earthly portion, for you may rest assured that it is the fittest for you. Unerring wisdom ordained your lot and selected for you the safest and best condition. A large ship is to be brought up the river; now in one part of the stream there is a sandbank. Should someone ask, "Why does the captain steer through the deep part of the channel and deviate so much from a straight line?" his answer would be, "Because I could not get my vessel into harbor at all if I did not keep to the deep channel." So, it may be, you would run aground and suffer shipwreck if your divine Captain did not steer you into the depths of affliction where waves of trouble follow each other in quick succession.

Some plants die if they have too much sunshine. It may be that you are planted where you get but little; you are put there by the loving Husbandman because only in that situation will you bring forth fruit unto perfection. Had any other condition been better for you than the one in which you are, divine love would have put you there. You are placed by God in the most suitable circumstances. Take up your own daily cross; it is the burden best suited for your shoulder and will prove most effective to make you perfect in every good word and work to the glory of God.

THE SONG OF THE BELIEVER

"But no one says, 'Where is God my Maker,
who gives songs in the night?'"
JOB 35:10 NIV

Perhaps there is no music as sweet as that which comes from the lips and heart of a tried believer. It is real then. When Job blessed God, even the devil himself could not insinuate that Job was a hypocrite. When Job prospered, the devil said, "Doth Job serve God for naught?" but when he lost his all and yet said, "Blessed be the name of the Lord," then the good man shone like a star when the clouds are gone. Let us be sure to praise God when things go ill with us. Make certain that you sing then. A holy man, walking one night with a companion, listened to the nightingale, and he said, "That bird in the darkness is praising her Maker. Sing, and let your Lord have a song in the night."

But the other replied, "My voice is hoarse and is not used to singing."

"Then," said the other, "I will sing." And he sang, and the bird seemed to hear him and sang louder still; and he sang on, and other birds joined, and the night seemed sweet with song. But in time the good man says, "My voice fails me, but this bird's throat holds out longer than mine. If only I could even fly away where I could sing on forever."

It is blessed when we can praise God when the sun has gone down, when darkness lowers and trials multiply. Then let us say, "I will sing to my Well-Beloved a song."

Day 35

TASTING GOD'S GOODNESS

O taste and see that the LORD is good.
PSALM 34:8 KJV

Princes would sell their crowns, and peers would renounce their dignities, to have five minutes' fellowship with Christ. I will vouch for that. Why, I have had more joy in my Lord and Master in the space of the ticking of a clock than could be crammed into a lifetime of sensual delights, of the pleasures of taste, of the fascinations of literature. There is a depth, a matchless depth, in Jesus' love. There is a luscious sweetness in the fellowship with Him. You must eat, or you will never know the flavor of it. "O taste and see that the Lord is good!"

Behold how ready He still is to welcome sinners. Trust Him and live. Feed on Him and grow strong. Commune with Him and be happy. May every one of you who shall sit at the table have the nearest approach to Jesus that you ever had! Like two streams that after flowing side by side at length unite, so may Christ and our soul melt into one, until only one life shall flow, so that the life we live in the flesh shall be no more ours but Christ who lives in us.

A FRIEND CLOSER
THAN A BROTHER

"I will never leave you nor forsake you."
HEBREWS 13:5 NKJV

Is it not a wonderful and arresting fact that while others leave us and forsake us that God never does? He says to each of His own redeemed people, "I will never leave you nor forsake you."

How often do people forsake those whom they call their friends when those friends fall into poverty! The tragedies of some of these cruel forsakings! May you never know them! Friends who once were cherished are now forgotten. In fact, the man almost pities himself to think that he should have been so unfortunate to have a friend who has fallen so low, and he has no pity for his friend because he is so much occupied in pitying himself.

In hundreds and thousands and tens of thousands of cases, as soon as the gold has gone, the pretended love has gone; and when the dwelling has been changed from the mansion to the cottage, the friendship that once promised to last forever has suddenly disappeared. But God will never leave us on account of poverty: However low we may fall, there it always stands: "I will never leave you nor forsake you."

Day 37

OUR ADVOCATE

If any man sin, we have an advocate with
the Father, Jesus Christ the righteous.
1 JOHN 2:1 KJV

He who believes in Jesus shall never do anything to fall away
from God's grace. He shall never be so deserted as to give up
his God, for his God will never give him up to the point of
letting him give up his confidence or his hope or his love or
his trust. The Lord, even our God, holds us with His strong
right hand, and we shall not be moved, even if we sin: "If any
man sin, we have an advocate with the Father, Jesus Christ
the righteous."

There are some who would give themselves license to sin,
but in doing so they prove themselves not to be the children
of God. They show that they know nothing of the matter,
for the genuine child of God, when he has a promise that is
unconditional, finds holiness in it. Being moved by gratitude,
he wants no buts and ifs and conditions in order to do right.
He is ruled by love and not by fear, governed by a holy
gratitude that becomes a stronger bond to sacred obedience
than any other bond that could be invented.

GOD'S WORD TO US

*All Scripture is given by inspiration of God,
and is profitable for doctrine, for reproof,
for correction, for instruction in righteousness.*
2 TIMOTHY 3:16 NKJV

The Lord has gone from us, but as He knew what would happen while He was away, He has with blessed forethought provided for our wants. He well knew that we should never be able to preserve the truth purely by tradition. That is a stream that always muddies and defiles everything. So in tender forethought He has given us the consolidated testimony, the unchangeable truth in His own book, for He was moved with compassion.

He knew that no order of men could be trusted to keep hold of sound doctrine from generation to generation; He knew there would be hirelings who dare not be faithful to their conscience lest they should lose their pay, while there would be others who love to tickle men's ears and flatter their arrogance rather than to tell forth plainly and distinctly the whole counsel of God. Therefore He has put it here, so that if you live where there is no preacher of the Gospel, you have the book to go to. He is moved with compassion for you. For where a man cannot go, the book can go, and where in silence no voice is heard, the still clear voice of this blessed book can reach the heart. Because He knew the people would require this sacred teaching and could not have it otherwise, He was moved with compassion toward us all and gave us the blessed book of inspired God-breathed scripture.

Day 39

THE COMPASSION OF CHRIST

But He, being full of compassion,
forgave their iniquity.
PSALM 78:38 NKJV

Though your sin may have ruined you, Christ can enrich you with better riches. He has compassion. "They will pass by me," you say, "and if they see me in the street, they will not speak to me—even Christians will not." Perhaps that may be, but better than other Christians, tenderer by far, is Jesus.

Is there someone with whom one would associate who would be a scandal from which the pure and pious would shrink? The holy, harmless, undefiled One will not disdain even him—for this man receives sinners—He is a friend of sinners. He is never happier than when He is relieving and retrieving the forlorn, the abject, and the outcast. He does not condemn any who confess their sins and seek His mercy. No pride nestles in His dear heart, no sarcastic word rolls off His gracious tongue, no bitter expression falls from His blessed lips. He still receives the guilty.

Pray to Him now; let the silent prayer go up: "My Savior, have pity upon me; be moved with compassion toward me, for if misery be any qualification for mercy, I am a fit object for Your compassion."

Day 40
THE PRESENCE OF GOD

Lo, I am with you always.
MATTHEW 28:20 KJV

The Lord Jesus is in the midst of His Church. Not physically, but still in real truth, Jesus is with us. And a blessed truth it is, for where Jesus is, love becomes inflamed.

Of all the things in the world that can set the heart burning, there is nothing like the presence of Jesus! A glimpse of Him so overcomes us that we are ready to say, "Turn away Your eyes from me for they have overcome me." If we know that Jesus is with us, every power will be developed and every grace will be strengthened, and we shall cast ourselves into the Lord's service with heart and soul and strength; therefore is the presence of Christ to be desired above all things.

His presence will be most realized by those who are most like Him. If you desire to see Christ, you must grow in conformity to Him. Bring yourself, by the power of the Spirit, into union with Christ's desires and motives and plans of action, and you are likely to be favored with His company. Remember His presence may be had. His promise is as true as ever. He delights to be with us. If He does not come, it is because we hinder Him by our indifference. He will reveal Himself to our earnest prayers and graciously suffer Himself to be detained by our entreaties and by our tears, for these are the golden chains which bind Jesus to His people.

Day 41

SEEING JESUS

Yet a little while, and the world
seeth me no more; but ye see me:
because I live, ye shall live also.
JOHN 14:19 KJV

This was, and is, the mark of the true believer, that he sees Jesus. When Jesus was here among men, the world saw Him in a certain sense, but yet in truth it did not see Him at all. The world's eye saw the outside of Christ—the flesh of the man Christ, but the true Christ the ungodly eye could not discern. They could not perceive those wonderful attributes of character, those delightful graces and charms, which made up the true spiritual Christ. They saw but the husk and not the kernel; they saw the quartz of the golden nugget but not the pure gold that quartz contained. They saw but the external man; the real, spiritual Christ they could not see.

But unto as many as God had chosen, Christ manifested Himself as He did not unto the world. There were some to whom He said, "The world seeth Me not, but you see Me." There were some whose eyes were anointed so that they saw in "the man Christ Jesus," the God, the glorious Savior, the King of kings, the Wonderful, the Counselor, the mighty God, the everlasting Father, the Prince of Peace.

Day 42

THE CHRISTIAN'S HOME IN HEAVEN

*"I go to prepare a place for you. And if
I go and prepare a place for you, I will
come again and receive you to Myself."*

JOHN 14:2–3 NKJV

He lives actively—not in some wondrous sleep of quiet and sacred repose. He is as busy now as He was when here. He proposed to Himself, when He went away, a certain work. "I go to prepare a place for you," He said. He is preparing that place for us still.

He intercedes, also, daily for His people. If your faith is strong enough, even now you can see Him distinctly standing before the throne of God, pleading His glorious merits. I think I see Him now as clearly as ever the Jews saw Aaron when he stood with his breastplate on before the mercy seat; for remember, the Jews never did see Aaron at all there, for the curtain was dropped and Aaron was within the veil, and therefore the Jews could only see him in his fancy.

But I say I see Him as clearly as that, for I see my Lord, not by fancy but by faith. There, where the veil is rent, so that He is not hidden from my soul's gaze. I see Him with my name and yours upon His breast, pleading before God.

PERSEVERE!

Because I live, ye shall live also.
JOHN 14:19 KJV

When we once get spiritual life into us, what a thousand enemies there are who try to put it out! Temptation after temptation have I endured until it appeared I must yield my hold on Christ and give up my hope. There has been conflict upon conflict and struggle upon struggle until at last the enemy has gotten his foot upon my neck, and my whole being has trembled; and had it not been for Christ's promise "Because I live, you shall live also," it might been more difficult for me, and I might have despaired and given up all hope and lay down to die.

The assurance, then, that the spiritual life of the Christian must be maintained because Christ lives was the only power to get me the victory. Let it teach us, then, this practical lesson: Whenever our spiritual life is very weak and we want it to grow stronger, let us get to the living Christ for the supply of His strength. When you feel you are ready to die spiritually, go to the Savior for revived life. The text is like a hand that points us to the storehouse. You who are in the desert, there is a secret spring under your feet and you know not where it is; this is the mysterious finger which points you to the spot. Contemplate Christ, believe in Christ, draw yourselves by faith nearer and nearer to the Lord Jesus Christ, and so shall your life receive a divine impetus which it has not known for many a day.

A SINNER'S REPENTANCE

Deliver me from bloodguiltiness, O God,
thou God of my salvation: and my tongue
shall sing aloud of thy righteousness.
PSALM 51:14 KJV

I like that confession and that prayer of David. He does not mince words for he had guiltily caused the blood of Uriah to be shed, and here he admits it with great shame, but with equal honesty and truthfulness. As long as you and I call our sins by pretty names, they will not be forgiven. The Lord knows exactly what your sin is; therefore, do not try to use polite terms for it. Tell Him what it is, so that He knows that you know what it is. "Deliver me from bloodguiltiness, O God, thou God of my salvation."

"But certainly," one may say, "there is no one in the Church who needs to pray that prayer." Well, there is one who often feels that he has the need to pray it; for what will happen if I preach not the Gospel or if I do not preach it with all my heart? It may be that the blood of souls shall be required at my hands. And, my brothers and sisters, if anything in your example should lead others into sin, or if the neglect of any opportunities that are presented to you should lead others to continue in their sin until they perish, could the sin of bloodguiltiness not be possible for you? " 'Deliver me from bloodguiltiness, O God, thou God of my salvation.' And then, O Lord, when I am forgiven of that, 'my tongue shall sing aloud of Your righteousness.' "

THE ORIGIN OF GOD'S LOVE

I trust in God's unfailing love for ever and ever.
PSALM 52:8 NIV

When did Christ's love begin to work for us? It was long before we were born, long before the world was created; far, far back in eternity, our Savior gave the first proof of His love to us.

By His divine foresight, He looked upon human nature as a palace that had been plundered and broken down, and in its ruins He perceived all manner of unclean things. Who was there to undertake the great work of restoring that ruined palace? No one but the Word, who was with God and who was God. "He saw that there was no man and wondered that there was no intercessor: Therefore His own arm brought salvation unto Him, and His righteousness, it sustained Him."

Before the angels began to sing, or the sun and moon and stars threw their first beams across ancient darkness, Christ took up the cause of His people and resolved not only to restore to them all the blessings that He foresaw they would lose but also add to them richer favors than could ever have been theirs except through Him. Even for eternity His delights were with the sons of men; and when I think of Him in that far-distant past of which we can form so slight a conception, becoming "the Head over all things to the Church" which then existed only in the mind of God, my soul cries out in a rapture of delight, "Behold how He loved us!"

Day 46

REJOICE IN THE LOVE OF GOD

Satisfy us in the morning with your unfailing love,
that we may sing for joy and be glad all our days.

PSALM 90:14 NIV

Christ has so completely given Himself to us that all He has is ours. He is the glorious Husband, and His Church is His bride, the Lamb's wife; and there is nothing that He has that is not also hers even now, and that He will not share with her forever. By a marriage bond that cannot be broken, for He "hateth putting away," He has drawn her unto Himself in righteousness and truth, and she shall be one with Him throughout eternity.

He has gone up to His Father's house to take possession of the many mansions there, not for Himself but for His people; and His prayer is "Father, I will that they also, whom Thou hast given Me, be with Me where I am; that they may behold My glory which Thou hast given Me: for Thou lovedst Me before the foundation of the world."

Jesus has an ever-flowing fountain of joy in His heart, but He desires that His joy may be in you if you belong to Him and that your joy may be full; and everything else that He has is yours as much as it is His, so certainly you will again join with me in saying, "Behold how He loved us!"

Day 47

A PROMISE OF HOPE

But if we hope for what we do not
yet have, we wait for it patiently.
ROMANS 8:25 NIV

We are expecting that, one of these days, if the chariot and horses of fire do not stop at our door, our dear Lord and Savior will fulfill His promise to us: "If I go and prepare a place for you, I will come again and receive you unto Myself; that where I am, there you may be also."

To a true believer in Jesus, the thought of departing from this world and going to be "forever with the Lord" has no gloom associated with it. Heaven is our home. We are longing for the great reunion with our beloved Lord, from whom we shall then never again be separated. I cannot attempt to depict the scene when He will introduce us to the principalities and powers in heavenly places and invite us to sit with Him. Surely then the holy angels, who have never sinned, will unite in exclaiming, "Behold how He loved them!"

It is a most blessed thought, to my mind, that we may be up there before the hands of that clock complete another round; and if not that soon, it will not be long before all of us who love the Lord will be with Him where He is, and then the last among us shall know more of His love than the greatest of us can ever know while here below.

Day 48

PROVIDENCE

*Very worthy deeds are done unto
this nation by thy providence.*
ACTS 24:2 KJV

The sea is never still; both day and night it is always moving. In the day, when the sun shines upon it, its waves march up in marshaled order as if about to capture the whole land and drown all the solid earth. Then again they march back, each one as if reluctant to yield its prey. It is always moving: The moon shines upon it, and the stars light it up; still it moves. Or, there is darkness, and nothing is seen; still it moves—by night and day the restless billows chant a boisterous hymn of glory or murmur the solemn dirge of mariners wrecked far out in the depths.

Such is Providence; by night or day Providence is always going on. The farmer sleeps, but his wheat is growing. The mariner on the sea sleeps, but the wind and the waves are carrying on his bark. Providence! You never stop; Your mighty wheels never stay their everlasting circles. As the blue ocean has rolled on impetuously for ages, so shall Providence, until He who first set it in motion shall bid it stop; and then its wheels shall cease, forever fixed by the eternal decree of the mighty God.

Day 49

PERSISTENT PRAYER

And he said, I beseech thee, shew me thy glory.
EXODUS 33:18 KJV

Refer to the thirteenth verse of this chapter, where Moses speaks to God: "Now therefore, I pray thee, if I have found grace in your sight, shew me now your way." Moses asked a lesser favor before he requested the greater. He asked to see God's way before he prayed to see His glory. This is the true manner of prayer.

Do not be content with past answers, but double your request and ask again. Nothing pleases God as much as when a sinner comes again with twice as large a petition: "Lord, You heard me last time, and now I come again." Faith is a mighty grace and always grows upon that which it feeds. When God has heard prayer for one thing, faith comes and asks for two things, and when God has given those two things, faith asks for six.

Faith can scale the walls of heaven. She is a giant grace. She takes mountains by their roots and puts them on other mountains and so climbs to the throne in confidence with large petitions, knowing that she shall not be refused. Most of us are too slow to go to God. If we have been heard once, we go away instead of coming again and again, and each time with a larger prayer. Make your petitions longer and longer. Ask for ten, and if God gives them, then for a thousand, and keep going on until at last you will have enough faith to ask as great a favor as Moses did, "I beseech you, show me your glory."

Day 50
GOD'S GRACE

Where sin abounded, grace did much more abound.
ROMANS 5:20 KJV

The only counterforce against sin is grace. And what is grace? Grace is the free favor of God, the undeserved bounty of the ever-gracious Creator against whom we have sinned, the generous pardon, the infinite, spontaneous lovingkindness of the God who has been provoked and angered by our sin; but who, delighting in mercy and grieving to smite the creatures whom He has made, is always ready to pass by transgression, iniquity, and sin, and to save His people from all the evil consequences of their guilt.

Here is a force that is fully equal to the requirements of the duel with sin; for this grace is divine grace, and thus it is omnipotent, immortal, and immutable. This favor of God never changes, and when once it purposes to bless anyone, bless him it will, and none can revoke the blessing. The gracious purpose of God's free favor to an undeserving man is more than a match for that man's sin, for it brings to bear upon his sin the blood of the incarnate Son of God, and the majestic and mysterious fire of the eternal Spirit who burns up evil and utterly consumes it. With God the Father, God the Son, and God the Holy Spirit united against sin, the everlasting purposes of grace are bound to be accomplished, and sin must be overcome.

Day 51

SINNERS MADE CLEAN

*"I will cleanse them from all their iniquity by which
they have sinned against Me, and I will pardon all
their iniquities by which they have sinned and by
which they have transgressed against Me."*
JEREMIAH 33:8 NKJV

It is very wonderful, but it is certainly true, that there are
many persons in heaven in whom sin once abounded. In the
judgment of their fellowmen, some of them were worse sinners
than others. There was Saul of Tarsus, there was the dying thief,
there was the woman in the city who was a sinner—a sinner
in a very open and terrible sense. These, and many more of
whom we read in the scriptures, were all great sinners, and it
was a great wonder of grace in every instance that they should
be forgiven; but did they make poor Christians when they
were converted? Quite the reverse: They loved much because
they had been forgiven much.

Among the best servants of God are many of those who
were once the best servants of the devil. Sin abounded in them,
but grace much more abounded when it took possession of
their hearts and lives. They were long led captive by the devil
at his will, but they were never such servants to Satan as they
afterward became to the living and true God. They threw all
the fervor of their intense natures into the service of their
Savior and so rose superior to some of their fellow disciples,
who did not fully realize how much they owed to their Lord.

SIN AND GRACE

And when he saw their faith, he said unto
him, Man, thy sins are forgiven thee.
LUKE 5:20 KJV

Sin has brought us very low, but Christ has lifted us higher than we stood before sin cast us down. Sin took away from man his love to God, but Christ has given us a more intense love for God than Adam ever had; for we love God because He has first loved us and given His Son to die for us, and we have, in His greater grace, a good reason for yielding to Him a greater love.

Sin took away obedience from man, but now saints obey to a yet higher degree than they could have done before, for I suppose it would not have been possible for unfallen man to suffer, but now we are capable of suffering for Christ; and many martyrs have gone singing to death for the truth because, while sin made them capable of suffering, Christ's grace has made them capable of obedience to Him in the suffering, and in so doing more prove their allegiance to God than would have been possible if they had never fallen.

Sin has shut us out of Eden; yet let us not weep, for Christ has prepared a better paradise for us in heaven. God has provided for us "a pure river of water of life" and a lovelier garden than Eden ever was; and there we shall forever dwell through the abounding grace of our Lord and Savior Jesus Christ, which has abounded even over our abounding sin.

LISTENING TO THE VOICE OF GOD

"He who is of God hears God's words."
JOHN 8:47 NKJV

Why is it that you are able to confide in God's Word? Surely it is because you know that for God to speak is for Him to do as He has said. By His Word, He made the heavens and the earth, and it is by His Word that the heavens and the earth continue as they are to this day.

God's speaking is very different from man's. Very often, man talks about something that he says he will do, but when he has talked about it, there is an end of the matter as far as he is concerned. Man has spoken, yes, but you can never be sure that with the talking tongue will go the working hand. He who is quick to promise is not always so prompt to perform.

We have many proverbs that remind us that men make light of one another's promises, and well they may; but we must never make light of the promises of God. "He spake, and it was done; he commanded, and it stood fast." So if there is a promise of God to help you in a time of trouble or to preserve you in the hour of temptation or to deliver you out of trial or to give you grace according to your day, that promise is as good as if it had been already performed, since God's Word shall certainly be followed by the fulfillment of it in due season.

GOD HAS SPOKEN

So then faith comes by hearing,
and hearing by the word of God.
ROMANS 10:17 NKJV

Observe that this joy, which faith has, is a joy in the very fact that God has spoken. Though nothing may yet have been done for us, God has spoken, and therefore our heart rejoices. Every divine promise, if it is rightly viewed by faith, will make the heart leap for joy. Suppose you do not need that particular promise just now, rejoice nevertheless, for you will need it eventually. If the promise is not made especially to you, yet it is made to somebody; therefore, rejoice because "God has spoken" and will meet somebody else's need. What if the blessing is too high for you to reach at present? Nevertheless, rejoice that there are mercies stored up for future and more advanced stages of your spiritual growth. And suppose the mercy is one that you long ago enjoyed; still be glad that you did enjoy it in years past, and so rejoice because "God has spoken."

Oh, what hymns of praise there are in the blessed book. The very first pages of Genesis ought to make us rejoice, and we will rejoice because we know how He made the worlds. Read every page, and say, "God has spoken in His holiness; I will rejoice." This shall be the subject of my joy all day long.

Day 55
INFINITE MERCY

I will praise thee, O LORD, among the people:
and I will sing praises unto thee among the nations.
For thy mercy is great above the heavens: and thy
truth reacheth unto the clouds. Be thou exalted, O God,
above the heavens: and thy glory above all the earth.

PSALM 108:3–5 KJV

Haven't some of you found God's mercy to be "great unto the heavens"? It even seemed to reach above the heavens, and as for God's truth, you followed it until you couldn't follow it any further, for it had ascended above the clouds. We could scarcely, I think, ever expect to understand here all the truth that God has pleased to let us hear or read. It reaches "unto the clouds," and there we must leave it for the present.

When God ceases to reveal anything, we may cease to inquire concerning it. I saw, in Florence, a picture of *The Sleeping Savior*. He is represented as sleeping in the manger at Bethlehem, and the artist depicts the angels hovering around Him, with their fingers on their lips as though they would not wake Him from His holy slumber. So when God bids truth sleep, do not try to wake it. There is enough revealed for you to know, and more that you will know in time. Wait for your Lord's appointed time to teach you more of His will.

Day 56
CLOSENESS WITH CHRIST

There I will meet with thee, and I will commune
with thee from above the mercy seat.
EXODUS 25:22 KJV

It should be our earnest aim to keep unbroken our communion with heaven, for it is the most refreshing thing beneath the sun. This world is like an arid desert where there is no water except as we maintain our communion with Christ. As long as I can say that the Lord is mine, all things here below are of small account; but if I once doubt that and if I cease to walk with God, then what is there here below that can content my immortal spirit? Without Christ, this world is to us as thorns without the roses and as bitters without the sweets of life. But You, O Lord, make earth to be a heaven to Your saints even when they lie in dungeons, when Your presence cheers them.

It is most important that you maintain your communion with Christ, for that is the only way to keep yourself clear from corruption. And you who have much to do in the Church must keep up your communion with Christ, for that is the only way of keeping your service from becoming mechanical and of preventing you from doing good works as a mere matter of routine. You too who have much to suffer or even much to enjoy must keep up this holy communion, or else your soul will soon be like a thirsty land where there is no water.

Day 57

GOOD NEWS!

Our conversation is in heaven; from whence also we look for the Saviour, the Lord Jesus Christ: who shall change our vile body, that it may be fashioned like unto his glorious body, according to the working whereby he is able even to subdue all things unto himself.

PHILIPPIANS 3:20–21 KJV

I have good news, and that is there is a house there for you. Our Lord Jesus Christ has made it ready for you. There is a crown there that nobody's head but yours can ever wear. There is a seat in which none but yourself can sit. There is a harp that will be silent until your fingers strike its strings. There is a robe made for you which no one else can wear. And let me also tell you that they are wanting you up there.

"They are so happy," you say, "and so perfect that they certainly do not want me." But they do. What does Paul say in the Epistle to the Hebrews? "They without us should not be made perfect." Nor can they; there cannot be a perfect body until all the members are there. It cannot be a perfect heaven until all the saints are there.

Jesus Christ does not have all the jewels of His crown yet, and He will have a perfect crown. So they are looking for you and waiting and watching for you, and all is ready for your reception. You will go home soon; therefore, live in hope, and having this hope within you, purify yourselves.

Day 58
GOD'S DELIVERANCE

No weapon that is formed against thee shall prosper.
ISAIAH 54:17 KJV

Child of God, will you, for a moment, reflect on the overruling power of God even in the case of the most mighty and wicked of men? They sin grossly, and what they do is done of their own free will; and the responsibility for it lies at their own door. That we never can forget, for the free agency of man is a self-evident truth, but at the same time, God is omnipotent; and He is still working out His wise designs as He did of old, in the whirlwind of human wrath, in the tempest of human sin, and even in the dark mines of human ambition and tyranny, all the while displaying His sovereign will among men.

Why should you, oh believer, be afraid of a man who shall die or the son of a man who is wretched? You are, as a child of God, under divine protection; so who is he who shall harm you while you are a follower of that which is good? Remember the ancient promise: "No weapon that is formed against you shall prosper, and every tongue that shall rise against you in judgment thou shalt condemn. This is the heritage of the servants of the Lord."

HE WILL DIRECT;
WE MUST WALK

---

*The steps of a good man are ordered by
the LORD, and He delights in his way.*
PSALM 37:23 NKJV

He who walks does not need to think of directing his own steps, for there is One who will direct them for him. What if sin persuades us to take the wrong path and if poor judgment makes us err through oversight? There is no need for us to choose our own fate, but we may bow before the Lord and say, "You shall choose our inheritance for us." The choice is difficult for you; do not choose your own way, but leave it to Him who sees the end from the beginning and who is sure to make the wise choice. The burden of life is heavy—do not try to carry it, but "cast your burden upon the Lord, and He shall sustain you. Commit your way unto the Lord; trust also in Him, and He shall bring it to pass." Do not let it be your choice; let it be God's choice.

If only we could but once abandon our own choosing and say to the Lord, "Not as I will, but as You will," how much more happy we could be! We should not be troubled by the thought that we should not direct our own steps, but we should be glad because our very weakness entitles us to cry to the Lord, "Now that I will not direct my own way, what I do not know, teach me."

Day 60
KEEP A LOOSE GRASP

"Lay up for yourselves treasures in
heaven. . . . For where your treasure is,
there your heart will be also."
MATTHEW 6:20–21 NKJV

Avoid all security as to the present. If you have anything that you prize very highly, hold it very loosely for you may easily lose it. Hold everything earthly with a loose hand, but grasp eternal things with a deathlike grip. Grasp Christ in the power of the spirit; grasp God, who is your everlasting portion and your unfailing joy.

Of everything on earth, it is wise for us to say, "This is not mine to keep." It is essential to say this and to realize that it is true, for everything here is temporary. Mind what you are doing, you prosperous people, you who have nice homes, you who are investing your money in the funds. There is nothing permanent for you here. Your home is in heaven, your home is not here, and if you find your treasure here, your heart will be here also; but it must not be so. You must keep all earthly treasures out of your heart; let Christ be your treasure, and let Him have your heart.

Day 61

PETITIONING GOD

Do not be anxious about anything, but in everything by prayer and pleading with thanksgiving let your requests be made known to God.

PHILIPPIANS 4:6 NASB

Pray about everything—I make no exception to this. Pray about waking in the morning, and pray about falling asleep at night. Pray about any great event in your life, but pray equally about what you call the minor events. The simplest thing that is not prayed over may have more evil in it than what appears to be the most oppressive evil when once it has been brought to God in prayer.

I pray that all of you who love the Lord may commit yourselves afresh to Christ. I wish myself to say, "Master, here am I; take me, and do as You will with me. Use me for Your glory in any way that You please. Deprive me of every comfort if then I shall be more able to honor You. Let me surrender my choicest treasures if Your sovereign will shall command so."

Let every child of God make a complete surrender here and now and ask for grace to bear it. Your greatest sorrow will come when you begin to be untrue to your full surrender to the Lord. May you never prove untrue to it!

Day 62
A PERFECT PEACE

Jesus said to the woman,
"Your faith has saved you; go in peace."
LUKE 7:50 NIV

When the many tears from her eyes fell upon His feet, He did not withdraw them. When those feet were wiped with the tresses of her hair, still He did not withdraw them; and when she ventured upon a yet closer familiarity and not only kissed His feet but also did not cease to kiss them, He still did not withdraw them but quietly accepted all that she did. And when the precious ointment was poured in lavish abundance upon those precious feet of His, He did not chastise her; He did not refuse her gifts but tacitly accepted them, although without a word of acknowledgment just then.

It is a very blessed thing for any one of you to be accepted before God, even though no word has come from His lips assuring you that you are. When your tears and cries and secret love and earnest seeking—when your confession of sin, your struggle after faith, and the beginning of your faith—are just accepted by the Lord, although He has not yet said to you, "Your sins are forgiven," it is a very blessed stage for you to have reached; for the Lord does not begin to accept anyone, even by a silence which means consent, and then draw back. He accepted this woman's love and gifts, though, for a time, He gave her no assurance of that acceptance, and that fact must have greatly encouraged her.

Day 63
THE FORGIVENESS OF GOD

He said to her, "Your sins are forgiven."
LUKE 7:48 NKJV

Your sins are forgiven. Oh, how the words must have dropped like dew into her poor soul! How she must have been refreshed by them! She, a sinner—a great sinner, a public sinner, even a professional sinner—hears her Savior say to her, "Your sins are forgiven." The absolution pronounced by the man who calls himself a minister is utterly worthless, but we would give a thousand worlds, if we had them, for absolution from our great High Priest! Yes, He who knew all about the woman's sin, He who had power on earth to forgive sins had said to her, "Your sins are forgiven." Was that enough for her? Would that short sentence set all the bells of her heart ringing as long as ever she lived?

But there was still more to follow, for the Lord spoke to her a second time and said, "Your faith has saved you; go in peace." So she was not only delivered from the guilt of sin, but she was also delivered from the power of sin. Her faith had saved her; she was a saved woman, so she could go in peace.

Bless the Lord Jesus Christ for any favor that He has shown to you, a poor unworthy sinner; and if you have even the faintest ray of light, pray that He will make your path like that of the just, which "shineth more and more unto the perfect day."

GIVING CHEERFULLY

Each of you should give what you have decided
in your heart to give, not reluctantly or under
compulsion, for God loves a cheerful giver.
2 CORINTHIANS 9:7 NIV

That is the most acceptable gift to God which is given rejoicingly. It is well to feel that whatever good your gift may do to the Church or the poor or the sick it is twice as much benefit to you to give it. It is well to give because you love to give: as the flower that pours forth its perfume because it never dreamed of doing otherwise; or like the bird that quivers with song because it is a bird and finds a pleasure in its notes; or like the sun which shines, not by constraint, but because, being a sun, it must shine; or like the waves of the sea which flash back the brilliance of the sun because it is their nature to reflect and not to hoard the light.

Oh, to have such grace in our hearts that we shall joyfully make sacrifices unto our God. The Lord grant that we may have a desire for this; for the bringing of the tithes into the storehouse is the way to the blessing; as the scripture says: "Bring ye all the tithes into the storehouse, that there may be meat in mine house, and prove me now herewith, saith the LORD of hosts, if I will not open you the windows of heaven, and pour you out a blessing, that there shall not be room enough to receive it."

Day 65

STILLNESS OF HEART

"Do not let your hearts be troubled, nor fearful."
JOHN 14:27 NASB

If Christ has saved you, you have the best reason in the world for being the happiest people who ever lived. One man said to another man, who had shared about his salvation, "You should be the happiest man alive."

He answered, "Yes, I am." It was well known that he was very poor. It was said that he did not know where he would get his next meal, but he had eaten the previous meal so he was content to wait for God to provide his next nourishment. He had such simple faith in God that, although he was very poor, he still said he was the happiest man in the world.

Christ has carried your heaviest burdens. He has averted the most terrible disaster that could ever happen to you; the most terrifying calamity you once dreaded can never harm you. You are an heir of God and a joint-heir with Jesus Christ. You will have all you really need in this life, and you will have heaven when this life is over. The Father, the Son, and the Holy Spirit have all united to bless you; and the covenant of peace is signed and sealed and approved, and you will conquer in the end. So, "Let not your heart be troubled; neither let it be afraid."

GOD WILL GRANT RELIEF

God is our refuge and strength,
a very present help in trouble.
PSALM 46:1 KJV

We do not know what we might have been if God's gracious protection had not been like a wall of fire around us, as it still is, for the Lord continues to deliver all those who put their trust in Him. Believe with unquestioning confidence that God is delivering you even now. You know that He *has* delivered you; be just as sure that He *is* delivering you at this moment.

"I am locked in a prison of despair." Yes, but your Lord has a key that can open the door and let you out.

"But I am in great want," another says. But He knows all about it, and He is going to supply all your needs.

Yet another says, "I am sinking in the flood." But He is throwing the life preserver over you.

"I am fainting!" says another. But He is putting smelling salts to your nose to refresh your spirit. God is near, ready to revive and encourage your fainting soul.

Perhaps a person says, "I find faith for the past and the ultimate future quite easy, but I don't have enough faith for the present." We sometimes forget that God is "a very present help in trouble," but it is true. He has delivered us, and He will continue to deliver us.

Day 67

He Has Delivered;
He Will Deliver

He has delivered us from such a deadly peril,
and he will deliver us again. On him we have
set our hope that he will continue to deliver us.

2 Corinthians 1:10 niv

There may be many trials before you, but there is an abundance of mercy ready to meet those trials. Troubles that you do not know yet, as well as repetitions of those you have experienced, you will certainly encounter, but the Lord will give you strength and will continue to deliver you. As the eyes gradually fail and the limbs grow weak and the infirmities of age creep over us, we are likely to be distressed, but our Lord will not forsake us. When severe sickness invades our earthly bodies and our pains multiply and intensify, we wonder how we will endure. As we consider our death, we wonder how we will be able to bear our last hours. Be encouraged: He who has delivered and does deliver will continue to deliver. Even as the trial comes, the Lord will show you a way of escape.

He *has* delivered you; give Him your gratitude. He *is* delivering you; give Him your confidence. He *will* deliver you; give Him your joy, and begin now to praise Him for mercies that He has yet to show you and for grace that you have not yet experienced but that He will grant you in the future.

Day 68

GOD'S UNCHANGING PURPOSE

For the LORD Almighty has purposed,
and who can thwart him? His hand is
stretched out, and who can turn it back?
ISAIAH 14:27 NIV

He is always the same, and everything is always present in His unchanging mind. What was the nature of God when He first determined to deliver me? Was it love? Then it is still love. What was the motive that prompted the Son of God when He came from above and snatched me from the deep waters? It was love, surprising love, and it is surprising love that still moves Him to deliver me. Did I sing about His faithfulness just the other day? That faithfulness is just the same today. Have I adored His wisdom? That wisdom is not depleted.

There is not only the same nature in God as there always was, but there is also the same unchanging purpose. You and I shift and change, and we do so because we make rash promises and flawed plans; but God, who is infinitely wise, always holds to His purpose. Now if it was His original purpose to save us—and it must have been, or He would never have delivered us as He has done—that purpose still stands and shall stand forever. Though earth fades, though heaven and earth shall pass away, as the morning frost dissolves in the beams of the rising sun, the decree of the immutable Jehovah will never be changed.

LIMITLESS GRACE

---

*For of His fullness we have all
received, and grace upon grace.*
JOHN 1:16 NASB

Yesterday God was very gracious to me, tomorrow He will be
very gracious to me, and the same will be true the next day
and the next day and the next day, until there are no more
days and time is swallowed up in eternity. Between here
and heaven, every minute that the Christian lives will be a
minute of grace. From here to the throne of the Highest, you
will have to be continually supplied with new grace from the
Lord who sits on high.

You never live a truly holy, happy, blessed day except
by divine grace. You never think a right thought, never do
a right act except by grace. I like to think that every day I
am a monument of mercy, that every day a fresh display of
sovereign grace is made to me; every day my Father feeds me,
my Savior cleanses me, the Comforter sustains me. Every day
new manifestations of the loving-kindness of the Lord break
forth upon my wondering soul and give me fresh visions of
His miraculous love.

His *miraculous* love! And so it is: miracle-working love,
making the Christian's life to be a series of miracles, at which
angels shall gaze forever in astonished adoration of the amazing
love of God to guilty men. So I suggest that we go forward with
great confidence, for although every day will bring dangers,
every day will also witness divine deliverances.

MEDITATION ON GOD

---

*May the words of my mouth and the
meditation of my heart be pleasing in your
sight, LORD, my Rock and my Redeemer.*
PSALM 19:14 NIV

Meditation is most profitable to the spirit; it is an extremely
healthy and excellent practice. Far from being idle time, it is
a judicious use of time.

Just as a change of posture relieves the weariness of the
body, a change of thoughts will prevent your spirits from
becoming lethargic. Sit down in a silent place in the evening,
open the window, look at the stars that God created, and
try to count them; or if you prefer, pause in the afternoon
and look down on the busy crowd in the streets and count
the people like so many ants upon the anthill of this world;
or if you do not care to look around you, sit down and look
within yourself, count the beats of your heart, and examine
the risings of your chest. At times it is good to think about
heaven; or if you are one who enjoys studying prophecy, open
your Bible to the sacred visions recorded in the book of Daniel
or the book of Revelation. As you enter into these hallowed
intricacies and meditate on these impressive symbols, you
will come away from your study greatly refreshed.

Day 71

GO TO GOD!

Meditate within your heart on your bed, and be still.
PSALM 4:4 NKJV

There should be special times for meditation. I think everyone should set apart a portion of time every day for this exercise. You may tell me that you have so much to do you cannot make the time for it. I generally take lightly the excuses of those who cannot afford time for obvious responsibilities. If you do not have the time, you should make it.

What time do you get up in the morning? Could you manage to get up fifteen minutes earlier? How long do you take for your dinner? Thirty minutes? Then you read something afterward possibly. Could you spend that time in tranquil communion with your own soul? The Christian will always be lacking if he does not have time for spiritual unity with his God. Those men who know God the best are those who meditate most upon Him.

Do you desire to be strong? Do you wish to be mighty? Do you hope to be valiant for the Lord and useful in His cause? Be careful that you follow the occupation of the psalmist David and meditate. This is a happy occupation.

OUR RELATIONSHIP
WITH CHRIST

In Christ all will be made alive.
1 CORINTHIANS 15:22 NASB

Think of your everlasting union with the person of Jehovah Jesus before this planet was sent rolling through space, and how your guilty soul was considered spotless and clean, even before you fell; and after that dire fall, before you were restored, justification was imputed to you in the person of Jesus Christ. Think of your relationship to Him since you have been called by His grace. Think of how He has become your Brother, how His heart has beaten in sympathy with yours, how He has kissed you with the kisses of His love. Think of a time when an angel has stooped from heaven, taken you up on his wings, and carried you to sit in heavenly places where Jesus sits, that you might commune with Him.

Or think of some pensive moments when you have had what Paul wrote about—fellowship with Christ in His sufferings. Think of seasons when the sweat has rolled from your brow, when you have knelt down and felt that you could die with Christ, even as you had risen with Him. Then think of your relationship in Christ that is to be developed in heaven. Picture in your mind that moment when Jesus Christ will salute you as "more than a conqueror" and put a pearly crown upon your head more glittering than stars. And think of that transporting hour when you will take that crown from off your own brow, and climbing the steps of Jesus' throne, you shall put it on His head and crown Him once more Lord of your soul, as well as "Lord of all."

GOD WILL SUSTAIN

The LORD upholdeth all that fall.

PSALM 145:14 KJV

"The Lord upholds all who fall." What a singular expression! How can He hold up those who fall? Yet those who fall, in this sense, are the only persons who stand. It is a remarkable paradox, but it is true. The man who stands on his feet and says, "I am mighty; I am strong enough to stand alone," down he will go; but he who falls into Christ's arms, that man shall not fall. We may well talk then of Christ's upholding power.

Tell it to Christians; tell how He kept you when your feet were going swiftly to hell; how, when fierce temptations did beset you, your Master drove them all away; how, when the enemy was watching, He compassed you with His mighty strength; how, when the arrows fell thickly around you, His mighty arm held the shield before you and so preserved you from them all. Tell how He saved you from death and delivered your feet from falling by making you, first of all, fall down prostrate before Him.

How sweet it is sometimes to talk of God's exalting power after we have been hewed down! How sweet it is to feel God's grace when you have been bowed down! Cannot some of us tell that, when we have been bowed down beneath a load of affliction so that we could not even move, the everlasting arms have been around us and have lifted us up? When Satan has put his foot on our back and we have said, "We shall never be raised up anymore," the Lord has come to our rescue.

Day 74

PROCLAIM WHAT HE HAS DONE FOR YOU

The eyes of all look to you, and you give
them their food at the proper time.
PSALM 145:15 NIV

We should often speak of how God provides for His creatures in providence. Why should we not tell how God has taken us out of poverty and made us rich, or if He has not done that for us, how He has supplied our wants day by day in an almost miraculous manner! Have you not sometimes been brought so low, through painful affliction, that you could not rest? And could you not afterward say, "I was brought low, and He helped me." Yes, "I was brought low, and He helped me out of my distress."

We have been brought into great straits, but the Lord has delivered us out of them all. Do not be ashamed to tell the story. Let the world hear that God provides for His people. Go, speak of your Father. Do as the child does who, when he has a little cake given to him, will take it out, and say, "My father gave me this." Do so with all your mercies: Go and tell all the world that you have a good Father, a gracious Father, a heavenly Provider; and though He gives you a small portion, and you only live from hand to mouth, still tell how graciously He gives it and that you would not change your blessed estate for all the world calls good or great.

Day 75
TALK ABOUT JESUS

"Those who have insight will shine like the glow of the expanse of heaven, and those who lead the many to righteousness, like the stars forever and ever."
DANIEL 12:3 NASB

Oh, think of the crowns that are in heaven! So many souls, so many gems! Have you ever thought what it would be to wear in heaven a starless crown? All the saints will have crowns, but those who win souls will have a star in their crown for every soul. Some of you, my friends, will wear a crown without a star; would you like that? You will be happy, you will be blessed, you will be satisfied, I know, when you will be there; but can you bear the thought of never having brought any to Christ? If you want to win souls, talk about Jesus. There is nothing like talking of Him to lead others to Him.

Souls are often converted through godly conversation. Let the praises of Christ always be on your tongue; let Him live on your lips. Speak of Him always; when you walk by the way, when you sit in your house, when you rise up, and even when you lie down. It may be that you have someone to whom it is possible that you may yet whisper the Gospel of the grace of God.

Sing of Christ alone! Christ alone! Christ alone! Jesus, Jesus only! Make Him the theme of your conversation, for "they shall speak of the glory of Your kingdom, and talk of Your power." God give you grace so to do, for Christ's sake!

THE BEST ANSWER
TO PRAYER

"Call to Me, and I will answer you."
JEREMIAH 33:3 NKJV

We are sure to have our prayers answered if it is right that they should be answered. Sometimes even the Lord's people ask for things that it would not be for God's glory to give or for their profit to receive.

If you should tell your child you would give him anything he asked for, you would not for a moment suppose that you included in the promise any absurd request he might make. Suppose he should ask you for a dose of arsenic, suppose he should request you to kill him—would you fulfill your promise? Certainly not. You would say, "My child, I love you too well to listen to the ravings of your madness. I desire your good too much to grant your absurd request, and I cannot hearken to you." God says the same: " 'Call to Me, and I will answer you,' but I will not always answer you as you wish to be answered. If you ask for a thing that is not fit for you to receive, I will give you something better. I will not give you that very thing; I will hear your prayers, but I will not give you exactly what you ask for. I will grant you something infinitely superior to the thing itself."

THE GLORY OF THE LORD

"And the glory of the LORD will be revealed,
and all people will see it together."
ISAIAH 40:5 NIV

We anticipate the happy day when the whole world shall be converted to Christ, when kings shall bow down before the Prince of Peace and all nations shall call their Redeemer blessed. We know that the world and all that is in it is one day to be burnt up, and afterward we look for new heavens and for a new earth.

We are not discouraged by the length of His delays; we are not disheartened by the long period that He allots to the Church in which to struggle with little success and much defeat. We believe that God will never suffer this world, which has once seen Christ's blood shed upon it, to be always the devil's stronghold. Christ came to deliver this world from the detested sway of the powers of darkness.

What a shout shall that be when men and angels unite to cry, "Hallelujah, hallelujah, for the Lord God Omnipotent reigneth!" What a satisfaction will it be in that day to have had a share in the fight, to have helped to break the arrows of the bow, and to have aided in winning the victory for our Lord! Happy are they who trust themselves with this conquering Lord and who fight side by side with Him, doing their little in His name and by His strength!

Day 78
GOD'S WORKMANSHIP

---

*He who began a good work among you will
complete it by the day of Christ Jesus.*
PHILIPPIANS 1:6 NASB

In the creation of the old world God first gave light, and
afterward He created life—the life that crept, the life that
walked, the life that dived, the life that flew in the midst of
heaven. So has He fashioned in our hearts: He has given us
the life that creeps upon the ground in humiliation for sin,
the life that walks in service, the life that swims in sacred
waters of repentance, the life that flies on the wings of faith
in the midst of heaven; and as God separated the light from
the darkness and the dry land from the sea, so in the new
creature He has separated the old depravity from the new
life. He has given to us a holy and incorruptible life that is
forever separated from and opposed to the old natural death;
and at last, when the old creation was all but finished, God
brought forth man in His own image as the top stone.

A similar work He will do in us as His new creatures.
Having given us light and life and order, He will renew in us
the image of God. Yes, that image is in every man who is in
Christ Jesus. Though it is not yet complete, the outlines, as
it were, are there. The great Sculptor has begun to chisel out
the image of Himself in this rough block of human marble.
You cannot see all the features; the lineaments divine are not
yet apparent. Still, because it is in His design, the Master
sees what we see not; He sees in our unhewn nature His
own perfect likeness as it is to be revealed in the day of the
revealing of our Lord and Savior Jesus Christ.

GOD'S CONTINUED WORK

*By one sacrifice he has made perfect forever
those who are being made holy.*
HEBREWS 10:14 NIV

If God has made a new creature of man, which is the greatest work of grace, will He not do the lesser work of grace—namely, make the new creature grow up unto perfection? If the Lord has turned you to Himself, never be afraid that He will leave you to perish. If He had meant to destroy you, He would not have done this for you. God does not make creatures for annihilation.

Chemists tell us that though many things are resolved into their primary gases by fire, yet there is not a particle less matter on the earth today than there was when it was created. No spiritual life that comes from God is ever annihilated. If you have obtained it, it never shall be taken from you—it shall be in you a well of water springing up unto everlasting life.

If, when you were an enemy, God looked upon you in grace and changed you and made you what you now are, will He not now that you are reconciled continue to preserve and nurture you until He presents you faultless before His presence with exceeding great joy?

MORE THAN CONQUERORS

---

*In all these things we are more than
conquerors through him that loved us.*
ROMANS 8:37 KJV

A joyous man, such as I have now in my mind's eye, is for all intents and purposes a strong man. He is strong in a calm, restful manner. Whatever happens, he is not ruffled or disturbed. He is not afraid of evil tidings; his heart is fixed, trusting in the Lord. The ruffled man is ever weak. He is in a hurry and does things poorly. The man full of joy within is quiet; he bides his time and crouches in the fullness of his strength. Such a man, though he is humble, is firm and steadfast. He is not carried away with every wind or bowed by every breeze; he knows what he knows and holds what he holds, and the golden anchor of his hope enters within the veil and holds him fast. His strength is not pretentious but real. The happiness arising from communion with God breeds in him no boastfulness: He does not talk of what he can do, but he does it; he does not say what he could bear, but he bears all that comes. He does not himself always know what he could do; his weakness is the more apparent to himself because of the strength which the Holy Spirit puts upon him, but when the time comes, his weakness only illustrates the divine might, while the man goes calmly on conquering and to conquer.

THE JOY OF THE LORD

The joy of the LORD is your strength.
NEHEMIAH 8:10 KJV

The man who possesses "the joy of the Lord" finds it his strength, in that it fortifies him against temptation. What is there that he can be tempted with? He has more already than the world can offer him as a reward for treachery. He is already rich; who shall snare him with the wages of unrighteousness? He is already satisfied; who is he who can seduce him with pleasing baits?

"Shall such a man as I flee?" The rejoicing Christian is equally proof against persecution. They may well afford to be laughed at who win at such a rate as he does. "You may scoff," he says, "but I know what true religion is within my soul, and your scoffing will not make me relinquish the pearl of great price." Such a man is, furthermore, made strong to bear affliction; for all the sufferings put upon him are but a few drops of bitterness cast into his cup of bliss, to give a deeper tone to the sweetness which absorbs them.

Such a man becomes strong for service too. What can he not do who is happy in his God? By his God he leaps over a wall or breaks through a troop. He is strong too for any kind of self-sacrifice. To the God who gives him all and remains to him as his perpetual portion, such a man gives up all that he has and does not think it surrender. It is laying up his treasure in his own peculiar treasure house, even in the God of his salvation.

JESUS ONLY

When they had lifted up their eyes,
they saw no one but Jesus only.
MATTHEW 17:8 NKJV

I do desire for my fellow Christians and for myself that more and more the great object of our thoughts, motives, and acts may be "Jesus only." I believe that whenever our religion is most vital it is most full of Christ. Furthermore, when it is most practical, downright, and common sense, it always gets nearest to Jesus.

I can bear witness that whenever I am in deeps of sorrow, nothing will do for me but "Jesus only." I can rest in some degree in the externals of religion, its outward escarpments and bulwarks, when I am in health; but I retreat to the innermost citadel of our holy faith, namely, to the very heart of Christ, when my spirit is assailed by temptation or besieged with sorrow and anguish. What is more, my witness is that whenever I have high spiritual enjoyments—enjoyments right, rare, celestial—they are always connected with Jesus only.

Other religious things may give some kind of joy, and joy that is healthy too, but the most sublime, the most inebriating, the most divine of all joys must be found in Jesus only.

ACCEPTED IN JESUS

Christ accepted you.
ROMANS 15:7 NIV

I will confess to you that over and over I am myself personally driven to do what I trust you may be led to do today. I look back on my life; and while I have much to thank God for, much in which to see His Spirit's hand, yet when I feel my responsibilities and my shortcomings, my heart sinks within me. When I think of my transgressions, better known to myself than to anyone else, and remember too that they are not known even to me as they are to God, I feel all hope swept away and my soul left in utter despair—until I come anew to the cross and think of who it was who died there, and why He died, and what designs of infinite mercy are answered by His death.

It is so sweet to look up to the Crucified One again and say, "I have nothing but You, my Lord, no confidence but You. If You are not accepted as my substitute, I must perish; if God's appointed Savior is not enough, I have no other. But I know You are the Father's well-beloved and I am accepted in You. You are all I want and all I have."

The trial of your faith. . .
1 PETER 1:7 KJV

Faith untried may be true faith, but it is sure to be little faith, and it is likely to remain dwarfish so long as it is without trials. Faith never prospers so well as when all things are against her: Tempests are her trainers, and lightnings are her illuminators. When a calm reigns on the sea, spread the sails as you will, the ship moves not to its harbor; for on a slumbering ocean, the keel sleeps too. Let the winds rush howling forth, and let the waters lift up themselves; though the vessel may rock and her deck may be washed with waves and her mast may creak under the pressure of the full and swelling sail, it is then that she makes headway toward her desired haven. No stars gleam so brightly as those which glisten in the polar sky, no water tastes so sweet as that which springs amid the desert sand, and no faith is so precious as that which lives and triumphs in adversity.

Tried faith brings experience. You could not have believed your own weakness had you not been compelled to pass through the rivers; and you would never have known God's strength had you not been supported amid the waterfloods. Faith increases in solidity, assurance, and intensity, the more it is exercised with tribulation. Faith is precious, and its trial is precious too.

THE EVERLASTING ARMS

Underneath are the everlasting arms.

DEUTERONOMY 33:27 KJV

God—the eternal God—is Himself our support at all times, and especially when we are sinking in deep trouble. There are seasons when the Christian sinks very low in humiliation. Under a deep sense of his great sinfulness, he is humbled before God until he scarcely knows how to pray, because he appears in his own sight so worthless.

Well, child of God, remember that when you are at your worst and lowest, yet "underneath" you "are the everlasting arms." Sin may drag you ever so low, but Christ's great atonement is still under all.

Again the Christian sometimes sinks very deeply in sore trial from without. What then? Still underneath him are "the everlasting arms." He cannot fall so deep in distress and affliction but that the covenant grace of an ever-faithful God will still encircle him. The Christian may be sinking under trouble from within through fierce conflict, but even then he cannot be brought so low as to be beyond the reach of the "everlasting arms"—they are underneath him; and while thus sustained, all Satan's efforts to harm him avail nothing.

This assurance implies a promise of strength for each day, grace for each need, and power for each duty. And further, when death comes, we shall descend into the grave, but we shall go no lower, for the eternal arms prevent our further fall. All through life and at its close, we shall be upheld by the "everlasting arms"—arms that neither flag nor lose their strength, for "the everlasting God fainteth not, neither is weary."

Day 86
JESUS, THE ANOINTED ONE

The Spirit of the Lord GOD is upon me;
because the LORD hath anointed me.
ISAIAH 61:1 KJV

Our Lord was not an amateur Savior who came down from heaven upon an unauthorized mission; but He was chosen, ordained, and anointed of God. He could truly say, "The Spirit of the Lord God is upon Me, because the Lord has anointed Me."

Here is great comfort for all who need a Savior; it is to them no mean consolation that God has Himself authorized Christ to save. There can be no fear of discord between the mediator and the judge, no peril of a nonacceptance of our Savior's work; because God has commissioned Christ to do what He has done, and in saving sinners, He is only executing His Father's own will.

Christ is called "*the* anointed." All His people are anointed, and there were priests after the order of Aaron who were anointed, but He is *the* anointed, "anointed with the oil of gladness above His fellows"; so plenteously anointed that, like the unction upon Aaron's head, the sacred anointing of the Head of the Church distills in copious streams, until we who are like the skirts of His garments are made sweet with the rich perfume.

CHOSEN IN CHRIST

The LORD's portion is his people.
DEUTERONOMY 32:9 KJV

How are they His? By His own sovereign choice. He chose them and set His love upon them. This He did apart from any goodness in them at the time or any goodness which He foresaw in them. He had mercy on whom He would have mercy and ordained a chosen company unto eternal life; thus are they His by His unconstrained election.

They are not only His by choice but by purchase. He has bought and paid for them, not with corruptible things as silver and gold, but with the precious blood of the Lord Jesus Christ. There is no mortgage on His estate; the price was paid in open court, and the Church is the Lord's freehold forever. See the blood mark upon all the chosen, invisible to the human eye but known to Christ. He counts the sheep for whom He laid down His life and remembers well the Church for which He gave Himself.

They are also His by conquest. What a battle He had in us before we would be won! How long He laid siege to our hearts! Do we not remember that glorious hour when He carried our hearts by storm? When He placed His cross against the wall and scaled our ramparts, planting on our strongholds the bloodred flag of His omnipotent mercy? We are the conquered captives of His omnipotent love. Thus chosen, purchased, and subdued, the rights of our divine possessor are inalienable: We rejoice that we never can be our own, and we desire, day by day, to do His will and to show forth His glory.

Day 88

IMMEASURABLE LOVE

"Yes, I have loved you with an everlasting love."
JEREMIAH 31:3 NKJV

Sometimes the Lord Jesus tells His Church His love thoughts. The Holy Spirit is often pleased, in a most gracious manner, to witness with our spirits of the love of Jesus. No voice is heard from the clouds, and no vision is seen in the night, but we have a testimony more sure than either of these. If an angel should fly from heaven and inform the saint personally of the Savior's love to him, the evidence would not be one bit more satisfactory than that which is borne in the heart by the Holy Spirit.

Ask those of the Lord's people who have lived the nearest to the gates of heaven, and they will tell you that they have had seasons when the love of Christ toward them has been a fact so clear and sure that they could no more doubt it than they could question their own existence. You and I have had times of refreshing from the presence of the Lord, and then our faith has mounted to the topmost heights of assurance. We have had confidence to lean our heads upon the bosom of our Lord, and we have no more questioned our Master's affection for us than John did when in that blessed posture; no, nor so much: For the dark question "Lord, is it I who shall betray You?" has been put far from us. He has kissed us with the kisses of His mouth and killed our doubts by the closeness of His embrace. His love has been sweeter than wine to our souls.

Day 89
GOD, OUR REFUGE

"The eternal God is your refuge."
DEUTERONOMY 33:27 NKJV

The word *refuge* may be translated "mansion" or "abiding place," which gives the thought that God is our abode, our home. There is a fullness and sweetness in the metaphor, for dear to our hearts is our home, although it be the humblest cottage or the scantiest garret; and dearer far is our blessed God, in whom we live and move and have our being. It is at home that we feel safe: We shut the world out and dwell in quiet security. He is our shelter and retreat, our abiding refuge.

At home we take our rest; it is there we find repose after the fatigue and toil of the day. And so our hearts find rest in God when, wearied with life's conflict, we turn to Him, and our soul dwells at ease. At home, also, we let our hearts loose; we are not afraid of being misunderstood nor of our words being misconstrued. So when we are with God, we can commune freely with Him, laying open all our hidden desires; for if the "secret of the Lord is with them who fear Him," the secrets of them who fear Him ought to be and must be with their Lord. Home too is the place of our truest and purest happiness: and it is in God that our hearts find their deepest delight.

WALK CLOSE TO CHRIST

So walk in Him.
COLOSSIANS 2:6 NKJV

If we have received Christ Himself in our inmost hearts, our new life will manifest its intimate acquaintance with Him by a walk of faith in Him.

Walking implies action. Our religion is not to be confined to our closet; we must carry out into practical effect that which we believe. If a man walks in Christ, then he so acts as Christ would act; for Christ being in him his hope, his love, his joy, his life, he is the reflex of the image of Jesus—and men say of that man, "He is like his Master; he lives like Jesus Christ."

Walking signifies progress. Proceed from grace to grace, run forward until you reach the uttermost degree of knowledge that a man can attain concerning our Beloved.

Walking implies continuance. There must be a perpetual abiding in Christ. How many Christians think that in the morning and evening they ought to come into the company of Jesus and may then give their hearts to the world all the day. But this is poor living; we should always be with Him, treading in His steps and doing His will.

Walking also implies habit. When we speak of a man's walk and conversation, we mean his habits, the constant tenor of his life. Now if we sometimes enjoy Christ and then forget Him, sometimes call Him ours and again lose our hold, that is not a habit; we do not walk in Him. We must keep to Him, cling to Him, never let Him go but live and have our being in Him.

NOT ETERNALLY
SEPARATED BY SIN

---

*For as high as the heavens are above the earth, so great
is his love for those who fear him; as far as the east is
from the west, so far has he removed our transgressions
from us. As a father has compassion on his children,
so the LORD has compassion on those who fear him.*

PSALM 103:11–13 NIV

Does it not make a man glad to know that though once his
sins had provoked the Lord they are all blotted out, not one
of them remains; though once he was estranged from God
and far away from Him by wicked works, yet he is brought
near by the blood of Christ. The Lord is no longer an angry
judge pursuing us with a drawn sword, but a loving Father
into whose bosom we pour our sorrows and find ease for
every pang of the heart.

Oh, to know that God actually loves us! I cannot preach
upon that theme for it is a subject to muse upon in silence,
a matter to sit by the hour together and meditate upon. The
Infinite to love an insignificant creature, an ephemera of an
hour, a shadow that declines! Is this not a marvel? For God
to pity me, I can understand; for God to condescend to have
mercy upon me, I can comprehend; but for Him to love me,
for the pure to love a sinner, for the infinitely great to love a
reprobate, is matchless, a miracle of miracles! Such thoughts
must comfort the soul.

ABBA, FATHER

The Spirit you received does not make you slaves, so that
you live in fear again; rather, the Spirit you received
brought about your adoption to sonship. And by him
we cry, "Abba, Father." The Spirit himself testifies
with our spirit that we are God's children.

ROMANS 8:15–16 NIV

He cannot be an unhappy man who can cry, "Abba, Father."
The spirit of adoption is always attended by love, joy, and
peace, which are fruits of the Spirit; for we have not received
the spirit of bondage again to fear, but we have received the
spirit of liberty and joy in Christ Jesus.

"My God, my Father." Oh, how sweet the sound. But
all men of God do not enjoy this, you say. Sadly that is true,
but that is their own fault. It is the right and portion of every
believer to live in the assurance that he is reconciled to God,
that God loves him, and that he is God's child, and if he
does not live in that manner, he has himself only to blame.

If there be any starving at God's table, it is because
the guest stints himself, for the feast is superabundant. If,
however, a man comes to live habitually under a sense of
pardon through the sprinkling of the precious blood, and
in a delightful sense of perfect reconciliation with the great
God, he is the possessor of a joy unspeakable and full of glory.

Day 93
OUR FUTURE IS KNOWN BY GOD

Therefore, since we have been justified through faith, we have peace with God through our Lord Jesus Christ, through whom we have gained access by faith into this grace in which we now stand. And we boast in the hope of the glory of God.

ROMANS 5:1–2 NIV

The joy of the Lord in the spirit springs from an assurance that all the future, whatever it may be, is guaranteed by divine goodness; that being children of God, the love of God toward us is not of a mutable character but abides and remains unchangeable. The believer feels an entire satisfaction in leaving himself in the hands of eternal and immutable love. However happy I may be today, if I am in doubt concerning tomorrow, there is a worm at the root of my peace; although the past may now be sweet in retrospect and the present fair in enjoyment, yet if the future be grim with fear, my joy is but shallow.

If my salvation is still a matter of hazard and jeopardy, unmingled joy is not mine and deep peace is still out of my reach. But when I know that He whom I have rested in has power and grace enough to complete that which He has begun in me and for me, when I see the work of Christ to be no halfway redemption but a complete and eternal salvation, when I perceive that the promises are established upon an unchangeable basis and are in Christ Jesus, ratified by oath and sealed by blood, then my soul has perfect contentment.

THE CROWN OF VICTORY

My sheep hear my voice, and I know them, and
they follow me: and I give unto them eternal life;
and they shall never perish, neither shall any man
pluck them out of my hand. My Father, which gave
them me, is greater than all; and no man is able
to pluck them out of my Father's hand.

JOHN 10:27–29 KJV

It is true that looking forward there may be seen long avenues of tribulation, but the glory is at the end of them; battles may be foreseen, and woe to the man who does not expect them, but the eye of faith perceives the crown of victory.

Deep waters are mapped upon our journey; but faith can see Jehovah fording these rivers with us, and she anticipates the day when we shall ascend the banks of the shore and enter into Jehovah's rest.

When we have received these priceless truths into our souls, we are satisfied with favor and full of the goodness of the Lord. I value the Gospel not only for what it has done for me in the past, but for the guarantees which it affords me of eternal salvation. "I give unto them eternal life; and they shall never perish, neither shall any man pluck them out of My hand."

Day 95
FACE-TO-FACE

We will always be with the Lord.
1 THESSALONIANS 4:17 NASB

Even the sweetest visits from Christ, how short they are—and how transitory! One moment our eyes see Him, and we rejoice with joy unspeakable and full of glory, but again a little time and we do not see Him, for our Beloved withdraws Himself from us.

Oh, how sweet the prospect of the time when we shall not behold Him at a distance but see Him face-to-face: when He shall not be as a wayfaring man tarrying but for a night, but shall eternally enfold us in the bosom of His glory.

In heaven there shall be no interruptions from care or sin, no weeping shall dim our eyes, no earthly business shall distract our happy thoughts; we shall have nothing to hinder us from gazing forever on the Sun of Righteousness with unwearied eyes. Oh, if it be so sweet to see Him now and then, how sweet to gaze on that blessed face forever and never have a cloud rolling between, and never have to turn one's eyes away to look on a world of weariness and woe!

Blessed day, when will you dawn? Rise, oh unsetting sun! The joys of sense may leave us as soon as they will, for this shall make glorious amends. If to die is but to enter into uninterrupted communion with Jesus, then death is indeed gain and the black drop is swallowed up in a sea of victory.

GLORY IN TRIBULATIONS

We glory in tribulations also.
ROMANS 5:3 KJV

It is joy, when between the millstones crushed like an olive, to yield nothing but the oil of thankfulness; when bruised beneath the flail of tribulation, still to lose nothing but the chaff, and to yield to God the precious grain of entire submissiveness. Why, this is a little heaven upon earth.

To glory in tribulations also, this is a high degree of moving toward the likeness of our Lord. Perhaps the usual communions which we have with our Beloved, though exceedingly precious, will never equal those which we enjoy when we have to break through thorns and briars to be with Him; when we follow Him into the wilderness, then we feel the love of our union to be doubly sweet. It is a joyous thing when in the midst of mournful circumstances we yet feel that we cannot mourn because the Bridegroom is with us. Blessed is that man who in the most terrible storm is driven—not from his God, but even rides upon the crest of the lofty billows nearer toward heaven. Such happiness is the Christian's lot.

I do not say that every Christian possesses it, but I am sure that every Christian ought to do so. There is a highway to heaven, and all in it are safe; but in the middle of that road there is a special way, an inner path, and all who walk there are happy as well as safe.

DO NOT DESPAIR—PRAY!

"But we will give ourselves continually to prayer."
ACTS 6:4 NKJV

Great God, help us still to pray, and never from the mercy seat may our footsteps be driven by despair. Our blessed Redeemer persevered in prayer even when the cruel iron tore His tender nerves, and blow after blow of the hammer jarred His whole frame with anguish.

This perseverance may be accounted for by the fact that He was so in the habit of prayer that He could not cease from it. Those long nights upon the cold mountainside, those many days that had been spent in solitude, these had formed in Him a habit so powerful that the severest torments could not stay its force. Yet it was more than habit. Our Lord was baptized in the spirit of prayer: He lived in it, it lived in Him; it had come to be an element of His nature. He was like that precious spice, which being bruised does not cease to give forth its perfume but rather yields it all the more abundantly because of the blows of the pestle, its fragrance being no outward and superficial quality but an inward virtue essential to its nature, which the pounding in the mortar did not fetch from it, causing it to reveal its secret soul of sweetness.

So Jesus prays, even as a bundle of myrrh gives forth its smell or as birds sing because they cannot do otherwise. Prayer enwrapped His very soul as with a garment, and His heart went forth in such array. Let this be our example— never, under any circumstances, however severe the trial or depressing the difficulty, let us cease from prayer.

Day 98
AN EXAMPLE OF PRAYER

---

*Jesus said, "Father, forgive them,
for they do not know what they do."*
LUKE 23:34 NKJV

Our Lord was at that moment enduring the first pains of crucifixion; the executioners had just then driven the nails through His hands and feet. He must have been greatly depressed and brought into a condition of extreme weakness by the agony of the night in Gethsemane and by the scourgings and cruel mockings which He had endured all through the morning from Caiaphas, Pilate, Herod, and the Praetorian guards. Yet neither the weakness of the past nor the pain of the present could prevent Him from continuing in prayer.

The Lamb of God was silent to men, but He was not silent to God. Dumb as a sheep before her shearers, He had not a word to say in His own defense to man; but He continued in His heart crying to His Father, and no pain and no weakness could silence His holy supplications.

What an example our Lord presents to us! Let us continue in prayer as long as our heart beats; let no excess of suffering drive us away from the throne of grace but rather let it drive us closer to it.

RESURRECTION POWER

The power of his resurrection. . .
PHILIPPIANS 3:10 KJV

The doctrine of a risen Savior is exceedingly precious. The resurrection is the cornerstone of the entire building of Christianity. It is the keystone of the arch of our salvation. The doctrine is the basis of the experience, but as the flower is lovelier than the root, so is the experience of fellowship with the risen Savior lovelier than the doctrine itself.

I would have you believe that Christ rose from the dead so as to sing of it and derive all the consolation that is possible for you to extract from this well-ascertained and well-witnessed fact; but I beseech you, rest not contented even there. Though you cannot, like the disciples, see Him visibly, yet I bid you aspire to see Christ Jesus by the eye of faith; and though, like Mary Magdalene, you may not "touch" Him, yet may you be privileged to converse with Him and to know that He is risen, you yourselves being risen in Him to newness of life.

To know a crucified Savior as having crucified all my sins is a high degree of knowledge; but to know a risen Savior as having justified me and to realize that He has bestowed upon me new life, having given me to be a new creature through His own newness of life, this is a noble style of experience: Short of it, none ought to rest satisfied. May you both "know Him and the power of His resurrection." Why should souls who are quickened with Jesus wear the grave clothes of worldliness and unbelief? Rise, for the Lord is risen.

Day 100
GAZING UPON JESUS

Behold the man!
JOHN 19:5 KJV

If there be one place where our Lord Jesus most fully becomes the joy and comfort of His people, it is where He plunged deepest into the depths of woe. Come, behold the man in the garden of Gethsemane; behold His heart so brimming with love that He cannot hold it in. Behold the bloody sweat as it distills from every pore of His body and falls upon the ground. Behold the man as they drive the nails into His hands and feet. Look up and see the sorrowful image of your suffering Lord. Mark Him as the ruby drops stand on the thorn crown. Behold the man when all His bones are out of joint, and He is poured out like water and brought into the dust of death. God has forsaken Him, and hell encompasses Him. Behold and see, was there ever sorrow like the sorrow done unto Him?

Gaze upon Him, for if there is no consolation in a crucified Christ, there is no joy in earth or heaven. If in the ransom price of His blood there is not hope, the right hand of God shall know no pleasures forevermore. We have only to sit longer at the cross to be less troubled with our doubts and woes. We have but to see His sorrows, and our sorrows we shall be ashamed to mention. We have but to gaze into His wounds and heal our own. If we would live correctly, it must be by the contemplation of His death; if we would rise to dignity, it must be by considering His humiliation and His sorrow.

CRUCIFIED WITH CHRIST

I am crucified with Christ.
GALATIANS 2:20 KJV

The Lord Jesus Christ acted in what He did as a great public representative person, and His dying upon the cross was the virtual dying of all His people. Then all His saints rendered unto justice what was due and made a reparation to divine vengeance for all their sins.

The apostle of the Gentiles delighted to think that as one of Christ's chosen people he died upon the cross in Christ. He did more than believe this doctrinally; he accepted it confidently, resting his hope upon it. He believed that by virtue of Christ's death, he had satisfied divine justice and found reconciliation with God. Beloved, what a blessed thing it is when the soul can, as it were, stretch itself upon the cross of Christ and feel "I am dead. The law has slain me, and I am therefore free from its power; because in my Surety I have borne the curse, and in the person of my Substitute, the whole that the law could do by way of condemnation has been executed upon me, for I am crucified with Christ."

The Christian's life is a matchless riddle. No human can comprehend it; even the believer himself cannot understand it. Dead, yet alive! Crucified with Christ, and yet at the same time risen with Christ in newness of life! Union with the suffering, bleeding Savior, and death to the world and sin, are soul-cheering things. Oh, for more enjoyment of them!

CHRIST AS KING

---

*To the King eternal, immortal, invisible, the only
God, be honor and glory for ever and ever.*
1 TIMOTHY 1:17 NIV

If we should always regard prayer as an entrance into the
courts of the royalty of heaven, if we are to behave ourselves as
courtiers should in the presence of an illustrious majesty, then
we are not at a loss to know the right spirit in which to pray.

If in prayer we come to a throne, it is clear that our
spirit should, in the first place, be one of lowly reverence. It
is expected that the subject in approaching the king should
pay him homage and honor. The pride that will not own the
king, the treason that rebels against the sovereign will—if it
be wise—avoid any near approach to the throne. Let pride
bite the curb at a distance, let treason lurk in corners, for only
lowly reverence may come before the king himself when he
sits clothed in his robes of majesty.

In our case, the King before whom we come is the
highest of all monarchs, the King of kings, the Lord of lords.
Emperors are but the shadows of His imperial power. They
call themselves kings by divine right, but what divine right
have they? Common sense laughs their pretensions to scorn.
The Lord alone has divine right, and to Him only does the
kingdom belong. He is the blessed and only potentate. They
are but nominal kings, to be set up and put down at the will
of men or the decree of providence, but He is Lord alone,
the Prince of the kings of the earth.

Day 103

CHRIST ON HIS THRONE

You will fill me with joy in your presence.
PSALM 16:11 NIV

A throne is to be approached with devout joyfulness. If I find myself favored by divine grace to stand among those favored ones who frequent His courts, shall I not feel glad? I might have been in His prison, but I am before His throne. I might have been driven from His presence forever, but I am permitted to come near to Him, even into His royal palace, into His secret chamber of gracious audience; shall I not then be thankful? Shall not my thankfulness ascend into joy, and shall I not feel that I am honored, that I am made the recipient of great favors when I am permitted to pray?

Why then is your countenance sad when you stand before the throne of grace? If you were before the throne of justice to be condemned for your iniquities, your hands might well be on your sides; but now you are favored to come before the King in His silken robes of love, let your face shine with sacred delight. If your sorrows are heavy, tell them to Him, for He can ease them; if your sins are multiplied, confess them, for He can forgive them.

Oh, you courtiers in the halls of such a monarch, be you exceedingly glad and mingle praises with your prayers.

GOD'S WILL

Therefore submit to God.
JAMES 4:7 NKJV

A throne should be approached with complete submission. We do not pray to God to instruct Him as to what He ought to do, neither for a moment must we presume to dictate the line of the divine procedure. We are permitted to say unto God, "Thus and thus would we have it," but we must furthermore add, "But seeing that we are ignorant and may be mistaken—seeing that we are still in the flesh and therefore may be actuated by carnal motives—not as we will, but as You will."

Who shall dictate to the throne? No loyal child of God will for a moment imagine that he is to occupy the place of the King, but he bows before Him who has a right to be Lord of all; and though he utters his desire earnestly, vehemently, importunately, and pleads and pleads again, yet it is evermore with this needful reservation: "Your will be done, my Lord, and if I ask anything that is not in accordance with it, my inmost will is that You would be good enough to deny Your servant. I will take it as a true answer if You refuse me, if I ask that which seems not good in Your sight."

If we constantly remembered this, we should be less inclined to push certain suits before the throne, for we should feel "I am here in seeking my own ease, my own comfort, my own advantage, and perhaps I may be asking for that which would dishonor God; therefore will I speak with the deepest submission to the divine decrees."

CONFIDENCE IN THE PRESENCE OF THE KING

Let us then approach God's throne of grace with
confidence, so that we may receive mercy and
find grace to help us in our time of need.
HEBREWS 4:16 NIV

The right spirit in which to approach the throne of grace is that of unwavering confidence. Who shall doubt the King? Who dares impugn the imperial Word? It was well said that if integrity were banished from the hearts of all mankind, it ought still to dwell in the hearts of kings. Shame on a king if he can lie.

The lowest beggar in the streets is dishonored by a broken promise, but what shall we say of a king if his word cannot be depended upon? Oh, shame upon us, if we are unbelieving before the throne of the King of heaven and earth. With our God before us in all His glory, sitting on the throne of grace, will our hearts dare to say we mistrust Him? Shall we imagine either that He cannot or will not keep His promise?

Banished be such blasphemous thoughts; and if they must come, let them come upon us when we are somewhere in the outskirts of His dominions, if such a place there be, but not in prayer when we are in His immediate presence and behold Him in all the glory of His throne of grace. There, surely, is the place for the child to trust his Father, for the loyal subject to trust his monarch; and, therefore, far from it be all wavering or suspicion. Unwavering faith should be predominant before the mercy seat.

THE PRIVILEGE OF PRAYER

Come, let us worship and bow down:
let us kneel before the LORD our maker.
PSALM 95:6 KJV

Prayer is no trifling matter. It is an eminent and elevated act. It is a high and wondrous privilege.

Under the old Persian Empire, a few of the nobility were permitted at any time to come in to the king, and this was thought to be the highest privilege possessed by mortals. You and I, the people of God, have a permit, a passport to come before the throne of heaven at any time we desire, and we are encouraged to come there with great boldness; but still let us not forget that it is no mean thing to be a courtier in the courts of heaven and earth, to worship Him who made us and sustains us in being.

Truly when we attempt to pray, we may hear the voice saying out of the excellent glory: "Bow the knee." From all the spirits who behold the face of our Father who is in heaven, even now I hear a voice saying, "Oh, come let us worship and bow down, let us kneel before the Lord our Maker; for He is our God, and we are the people of His pasture and the sheep of His hand. Oh, worship the Lord in the beauty of holiness; fear before Him all the earth."

THE THRONE OF GRACE

---

*"Hear from heaven their prayer and
their plea, and uphold their cause."*
1 KINGS 8:45 NIV

If in prayer I come before a throne of grace, then the faults of my prayer will be overlooked. The groanings of your spirit are such that you think there is nothing in them. What a blotted, blurred, smeared prayer it is. Never mind; you are not come to the throne of justice, otherwise when God perceived the fault in the prayer, He would spurn it—your gaspings and stammerings are before a throne of grace.

When any one of us has presented his best prayer before God, if he saw it as God sees it, he would lament over it; for there is enough sin in the best prayer that was ever prayed to secure its being cast away from God. But our King does not maintain a stately etiquette in His court like that which has been observed by princes, where a little mistake or a flaw would secure the petitioner's being dismissed with disgrace. No, the faulty cries of His children are not criticized. Our Lord Jesus Christ takes care to alter and amend every prayer before He presents it, and He makes the prayer perfect and prevalent with His own merits. God looks upon the prayer, as presented through Christ, and forgives all its own inherent faultiness.

How this ought to encourage any of us who feel ourselves to be feeble, wandering, and unskillful in prayer. If you feel as if somehow or other you have grown rusty in the act of supplication, never give up, but come still, come more often, for it is a throne of grace to which you come.

Day 108

UNWORTHY MAN MADE WORTHY

To him who is able to. . .present you before
his glorious presence without fault. . .
JUDE 1:24 NIV

Inasmuch as it is a throne of grace, the faults of the petitioner himself shall not prevent the success of his prayer. Oh, what faults there are in us! To come before a throne, how unfit we are—we who are all defiled with sin within and without! Dare any of you think of praying were it not that God's throne is a throne of grace? An absolute God, infinitely holy and just, could not in consistency with His divine nature answer any prayer from such a sinner as I am, were it not that He has arranged a plan by which my prayer comes up no longer to a throne of absolute justice but to a throne which is also the mercy seat, the propitiation, the place where God meets sinners through Jesus Christ.

I could not say to you, "Pray," not even to you saints, unless it were a throne of grace. A throne of grace is a place fitted for you: Go to your knees; by simple faith go to your Savior, for He, He it is who is the throne of grace. It is in Him that God is able to dispense grace to the most guilty of mankind. Blessed be God; the faults of the prayer shall not shut out our petitions from the God who delights in broken and contrite hearts.

INTERPRETED PLEADINGS

---

*The Spirit himself intercedes for
us through wordless groans.*
ROMANS 8:26 NIV

If it is a throne of grace, then the desires of the pleader will
be interpreted. If I cannot find words in which to utter my
desires, God in His grace will read my desires without the
words. He takes the meaning of His saints, the meaning
of their groans. A throne that was not gracious would not
trouble itself to make out our petitions; but God, the infinitely
gracious One, will dive into the soul of our desires, and He
will read there what we cannot speak with the tongue.

Have you never seen the parent, when his child is trying
to say something to him and he knows very well what it
is the little one has to say, help him with the words and
utter the syllables for him? And so the ever-blessed Spirit,
from the throne of grace, will teach us words and write in
our hearts the desires themselves. He will put the desires
and the expression of those desires into your spirit by His
grace, He will direct your desires to the things which you
ought to seek for, He will suggest to you His promises that
you may be able to plead them; He will, in fact, be Alpha
and Omega to your prayer, just as He is to your salvation,
for as salvation is from first to last of grace, so the sinner's
approach to the throne of grace is of grace from first to last.

What comfort this is. Will we not with the greater
boldness draw near to this throne?

Day 110

NEEDS SUPPLIED

---

*My God will supply all your needs according
to His riches in glory in Christ Jesus.*
PHILIPPIANS 4:19 NASB

If it is a throne of grace, then all the wants of those who
come to it will be supplied. The King from off such a throne
will not say, "You must bring to Me gifts; you must offer to
Me sacrifices." It is not a throne for receiving tribute; it is a
throne for dispensing gifts.

Come then you who are poor as poverty itself, come you
who have no merits and are destitute of virtues, come you
who are reduced to a beggarly bankruptcy by Adam's fall and
by your own transgressions; this is not the throne of majesty
which supports itself by the taxation of its subjects, but a
throne which glorifies itself by streaming forth like a fountain
with floods of good things. Come now, and receive the wine
and milk which are freely given; yes, come buy wine and milk
without money and without price. All the petitioner's wants
shall be supplied, because it is a throne of grace.

Day 111
GOD KNOWS YOUR PAIN

You, O Lord, are a God full of compassion, and gracious,
longsuffering and abundant in mercy and truth.
PSALM 86:15 NKJV

All the petitioner's miseries shall be compassionated. Suppose I come to the throne of grace with the burden of my sins; there is One on the throne who felt the burden of sin in ages long gone by and has not forgotten its weight. Suppose I come loaded with sorrow; there is One there who knows all the sorrows to which humanity can be subjected. Am I depressed and distressed? Do I fear that God Himself has forsaken me? There is One upon the throne who said, "My God, My God, why have You forsaken Me?" It is a throne from which grace delights to look upon the miseries of mankind with tender eye, to consider them and to relieve them.

Come then you who are not only poor but wretched, whose miseries make you long for death and yet dread it. You captive ones, come in your chains; you slaves, come with the irons upon your souls; you who sit in darkness, come forth all blindfolded as you are. The throne of grace will look on you, if you cannot look on it, and will give to you, though you have nothing to give in return, and will deliver you, though you cannot raise a finger to deliver yourself.

Day 112
BE BOLD!

In him and through faith in him we may
approach God with freedom and confidence.
EPHESIANS 3:12 NIV

To me it is a most delightful reflection that if I come to the throne of God in prayer, I may feel a thousand defects, but yet there is hope. I usually feel more dissatisfied with my prayers than with anything else I do. We sometimes hear of persons commended for preaching well, but if any shall be enabled to pray well, there will be an equal gift and a higher grace in it.

But suppose in our prayers there should be defects of knowledge: It is a throne of grace, and our Father knows that we have need of these things. Suppose there should be defects of faith: He sees our little faith and still does not reject it, small as it is. He does not in every case measure out His gifts by the degree of our faith, but by the sincerity and trueness of faith. And if there should be grave defects in our spirit even, and failures in the fervency or in the humility of the prayer, still, though these should not be there and are much to be deplored, grace overlooks all this, forgives all this, and still its merciful hand is stretched out to enrich us according to our needs.

Surely this ought to induce many to pray who have not prayed and should make us who have been long accustomed to use the consecrated art of prayer to draw near with greater boldness than ever to the throne of grace.

GOD IS LOVE

God is love.

1 JOHN 4:8 KJV

It is written "God is love," which is an alias for grace. Oh, come and bow before it; come and adore the infinite mercy and grace of God. Doubt not, halt not, hesitate not. Grace is reigning, grace is God, God is love.

Oh, that you seeing grace is thus enthroned would come and receive it. I say then that grace is enthroned by conquest, by right, and by power; and, I will add, it is enthroned in glory, for God glorifies His grace. It is one of His objects now to make His grace illustrious. He delights to pardon penitents, and so to show His pardoning grace; He delights to look upon wanderers and restore them, to show His reclaiming grace; He delights to look upon the brokenhearted and comfort them, that He may show His consoling grace. There is a grace to be had of various kinds, or rather the same grace acting different ways, and God delights to make His grace glorious. There is a rainbow around the throne like unto an emerald, the emerald of His compassion and love.

Oh, happy souls who can believe this, and believing it can come at once and glorify grace by becoming instances of its power.

THE COVENANT

Ask, and it shall be given you; seek, and ye shall find;
knock, and it shall be opened unto you.

MATTHEW 7:7 KJV

On the throne of grace, God is again bound to us by His promises. The covenant contains in it many gracious promises, exceeding great and precious. "Ask, and it shall be given you; seek, and you shall find; knock, and it shall be opened unto you."

Until God had said that word or a word to that effect, it was at His own option to hear prayer or not, but it is not so now; for now if it be true prayer offered through Jesus Christ, His truth binds Him to hear it. A man may be perfectly free, but the moment he makes a promise, he is not free to break it; and the everlasting God wants not to break His promise. He delights to fulfill it. He has declared that all His promises are "yea and amen" in Christ Jesus; but for our consolation when we survey God under the high and terrible aspect of a sovereign, we have this to reflect on: That He is under covenant bonds of promise to be faithful to the souls who seek Him. His throne must be a throne of grace to His people.

THE BLOOD OF CHRIST

In Him we have redemption through His blood, the forgiveness of sins, according to the riches of His grace.
EPHESIANS 1:7 NKJV

Every covenant promise has been endorsed and sealed with blood, and far be it from the everlasting God to pour scorn upon the blood of His dear Son. The signature is the handwriting of God Himself, and the seal is the blood of the Only Begotten. The covenant is ratified with blood, the blood of His own dear Son.

It is not possible that we can plead in vain with God when we plead the blood-sealed covenant, ordered in all things and sure. Heaven and earth shall pass away, but the power of the blood of Jesus with God can never fail. It speaks when we are silent, and it prevails when we are defeated. Better things than that of Abel does it ask for, and its cry is heard. Let us come boldly, for we hear the promise in our hearts. When we feel alarmed because of the sovereignty of God, let us cheerfully sing—

> *The Gospel bears my spirit up,*
> *A faithful and unchanging God*
> *Lays the foundation for my hope*
> *In oaths, and promises, and blood.*

Day 116
ALTOGETHER LOVELY

Yea, he is altogether lovely.
SONG OF SOLOMON 5:16 KJV

Altogether lovely. The words are evidently uttered by one who is under the influence of overwhelming emotion. The words are rather a veil to the heart than a glass through which we see its emotions. The sentence labors to express the inexpressible; it pants to utter the unutterable. The person writing these words evidently feels a great deal more than any language can possibly convey to us. It is the utterance of a soul that is altogether overcome with admiration, and therefore feels that in attempting to describe the Well-Beloved, it has undertaken a task beyond its power. Lost in adoring wonder, the gracious mind desists from description and cries with rapture, "Yea, He is altogether lovely."

It has often been thus with true saints; they have felt the love of Jesus to be overpowering and inebriating. Believers are not always cool and calm in their thoughts toward their Lord: There are seasons with them when they pass into a state of rapture, their hearts burn within them, they are in ecstasy, they mount up with wings as eagles, they feel what they could not tell, they experience what they could not express though the tongues of men and of angels were perfectly at their command.

Day 117

A GLIMPSE OF CHRIST

---

*But we all, with unveiled face, beholding as in a
mirror the glory of the Lord, are being transformed
into the same image from glory to glory.*

2 CORINTHIANS 3:18 NKJV

Every soul who sees Jesus by faith is saved thereby. If I look
to Christ with a bleared eye that is ever so weak and clouded
with tears, and if I only catch a glimpse of Him through
clouds and mists, yet the sight saves me. But who will remain
content with such a poor gleam of His glory as that? Who
wishes to see only "through a glass darkly"?

No, let my eyes be cleansed until I can see my Lord as
He is and can sing of those beauties which are the light and
crown of heaven itself. If you do but touch the hem of Jesus'
garment, you shall be made whole; but will this always satisfy
you? Will you not desire to get beyond the hem and beyond
the garment, to Himself and to His heart, and there forever
take up your residence? Who desires to be forever a babe in
grace, with a half-awakened dreamy twilight consciousness
by the Redeemer?

Be diligent in the school of the cross, for there is enduring
wisdom. Study your Savior much. The science of Christ
crucified is the most excellent of sciences, and to know Him
and the power of His resurrection is to know that which is
best worth knowing. Ignorance of Jesus deprives many saints
of those divine raptures which carry others out of themselves;
therefore let us be among those children of Zion who are
taught of the Lord.

---

*"You shall love the LORD your
God with all your heart."*
DEUTERONOMY 6:5 NASB

Altogether lovely. Note that these words have a world of meaning in them, but chiefly they tell us this: That Jesus is to the true saint the only lovely One in the world. "He is altogether lovely"; then there is no loveliness anywhere else. Is not Jesus worthy of all the admiration and love of all intelligent beings?

But may we not love our friends and kinsfolk? Yes, but in Him and in subservience to Him; so, and so only, is it safe to love them. Did not our Lord Himself say, "If any man love father or mother more than Me, he is not worthy of Me"? Yes, and in another place He put it more strongly still, for He said, "Except a man hate father and mother," or love them not at all in comparison with Him, "he is not worthy of Me."

Except these are put on a lower stage than Jesus is, we cannot be His disciples. Christ must be monarch; our dear ones may sit at His footstool, and we may love them for His sake, but He alone must fill the throne of our hearts. I may see excellences in my Christian brethren, but I must not forget that there would be none in them if they were not derived from Him, that their loveliness is only a part of His loveliness, for He fashioned it in them by His own Spirit. I am to give Him all my love, for "He is altogether lovely."

THE PARADISE OF PERFECTION

---

*Whatsoever things are true, whatsoever things
are honest, whatsoever things are just, whatsoever
things are pure, whatsoever things are lovely, whatsoever
things are of good report; if there be any virtue, and if
there be any praise, think on these things.*

PHILIPPIANS 4:8 KJV

In Jesus loveliness of all kinds is to be found. If there be anything that is worthy of the love of an immortal spirit, it is to be seen in abundance in the Lord Jesus. "Whatsoever things are true, whatsoever things are honest, whatsoever things are just, whatsoever things are pure, whatsoever things are lovely, whatsoever things are of good report; if there be any virtue and if there be any praise," all can be found without measure in Christ Jesus.

As all the rivers meet in the sea, so all beauties unite in the Redeemer. Take the character of any gracious man, and you shall find a measure of loveliness, but it has its bounds and its mixtures. Peter has many virtues, but he has not a few failings. John too excels, but in certain points he is deficient; but herein our Lord transcends all His saints, for all human virtues, all divine are harmoniously blended in Him. He is not this flower or that, but He is the paradise of perfection. He is not a star here or a constellation there; He is the whole heaven of stars; no, He is the heaven of heavens; He is all that is fair and lovely condensed in one.

LOVED IN SHAME AND GLORY

Your face is lovely.
SONG OF SOLOMON 2:14 NIV

When the text says that Jesus "is altogether lovely," it declares that He is lovely in all views of Him. You shall contemplate Him from all points and only find new confirmation of the statement that "He is altogether lovely."

As the everlasting God before the world was made, angels loved Him and adored: as the babe at Bethlehem or as the man at Bethany; as walking the sea or as nailed to the cross; in His grave, dead and buried, or on His throne triumphant; rising as forerunner or descending a second time to judge the world in righteousness; in His shame, despised and spit upon, or in His glory, adored and beloved; with the thorns about His brow and the nails piercing His hands, or with the keys of death and hell swinging at His sash. View Him as you will and where you will and when you will; "He is altogether lovely."

Under all aspects, and in all offices and in all relations, at all times and all seasons, under all circumstances and conditions, anywhere, everywhere, "He is altogether lovely."

Day 121
SEEK ONLY CHRIST

Earnestly I seek you.
PSALM 63:1 NIV

We want to feel that no gift is too great for Christ, though we give Him all we have and consecrate to Him all our time and ability, and sacrifice our very lives to Him. No suffering is too great to bear for the sake of the Crucified, and it is a great joy to be reproached for Christ's sake. Then I charge you think nothing hard to which He calls you, nothing sharp that He bids you endure. As the knight of the olden time consecrated himself to the Crusade and wore the red cross on his arm, so we too would face all foes for Jesus' sake.

This day God's Christ is still unknown to millions, and the precious blood cleanses not the nations. How long will you have it so? Shall we refuse our gifts, withhold our witness, and suffer the Lord to be dishonored? Oh, for a flash of the celestial fire! Oh, when shall the Spirit's energy visit us again! When shall men put down their selfishness and seek only Christ? When shall they leave their strifes about trifles to rally around His cross! When shall we end the glorification of ourselves and begin to make Him glorious, even to the world's end?

God help us in this matter and kindle in our hearts the old consuming, heart-inflaming fire, which shall make men see that Jesus is all in all to us.

IMITATE CHRIST

Be imitators of God.
EPHESIANS 5:1 NASB

The Lord Jesus "is altogether lovely." Then if I want to be lovely, I must be like Him, and the model for me as a Christian is Christ. Copy Jesus: "He is altogether lovely."

We want to have Christ's zeal, but we must balance it with His prudence and discretion. We must seek to have Christ's love for God, and we must feel His love for men, His forgiveness of injury, His gentleness of speech, His incorruptible truthfulness, His meekness and lowliness, His utter unselfishness, His entire consecration to His Father's business. Oh, that we had all this! For depend on it—whatever other pattern we select, we have made a mistake; we are not following the true classic model of the Christian artist. Our master model is the "altogether lovely" One. How sweet it is to think of our Lord in the double aspect as our example and our Savior!

The laver which stood in the temple was made of brass: In this the priests washed their feet whenever they offered sacrifices, so does Christ purify us from sin; but the tradition is that this laver was made of very bright brass and acted as a mirror, so that as often as the priests came to it, they could see their own spots in it. Oh, when I come to my Lord Jesus, not only do I get rid of my sins, but also I see my spots in the light of His perfect character; and I am humbled and taught to follow after holiness.

Day 123
HE FIRST LOVED US

We love him, because he first loved us.

1 JOHN 4:19 KJV

God's love is evidently prior to ours: "He first loved us." It is also clear enough from the text that God's love is the cause of ours, for "We love Him, because He first loved us." Therefore going back before all time, when we find God loving us with an everlasting love, we gather that the reason of His choice is not because we loved Him, but because He willed to love us.

His reasons are known to Himself, but they are not to be found in any inherent goodness in us or which was foreseen to be in us. We were chosen simply because He will have mercy on whom He will have mercy. He loved us because He would love us. The gift of His dear Son was too great a sacrifice on God's part to have been drawn from Him by any goodness in the creature. It was not possible for the highest piety to have deserved so vast a gain as the gift of the Only Begotten; it was not possible for anything in man to have merited the incarnation and the passion of the Redeemer. Our redemption, like our election, springs from the spontaneous self-originating love of God. And our regeneration, in which we are made actual partakers of the divine blessings in Jesus Christ, was not of us nor by us.

We owe our new birth entirely to His potent love, which dealt with us by effectually turning us from death to life, from darkness to light, and from the alienation of our mind and the enmity of our spirit into that delightful path of love.

Day 124
BORN OF GOD

Born, not of blood, nor of the will of the flesh,
nor of the will of man, but of God.
JOHN 1:13 NKJV

As believers on Christ's name, we "were born, not of blood, nor of the will of the flesh, nor of the will of man, but of God." The sum and substance of the text is that God's uncaused love, springing up within Himself, has been the sole means of bringing us into the condition of loving Him. Our love for Him is like a trickling rill speeding its way to the ocean because it first came from the ocean. All the rivers run into the sea, but their floods first arose from it: The clouds that were exhaled from the mighty main distilled in showers and filled the brooks. Here was their first cause and prime origin, and as if they recognized the obligation, they pay tribute in return to the parent source.

The ocean love of God, so broad that even the wing of imagination could not traverse it, sends forth its treasures of the rain of grace, which drop upon our hearts, which are as the pastures of the wilderness; they make our hearts to overflow, and in streams of gratitude the life imparted flows back again to God. All good things are of You, Great God: Your goodness creates our good; Your infinite love for us draws forth our love for You.

Day 125

INDISPENSABLE LOVE

---

*Every one that loveth is born
of God, and knoweth God.*

1 JOHN 4:7 KJV

There are some graces which in their vigor are not absolutely essential to the bare existence of spiritual life, though very important for its healthy growth; but love for God must be in the heart, or else there is no grace there whatever. If any man does not love God, He is not a renewed man.

Love for God is a mark that is always set upon Christ's sheep and never set upon any others. "Every one that loveth is born of God, and knoweth God." I have no right, therefore, to believe that I am a regenerated person unless my heart truly and sincerely loves God. If I have been regenerated, I may not be perfect, but this one thing I can say, "Lord, You know all things. You know that I love You."

When by believing we receive the privilege to become the sons of God, we receive also the nature of sons, and with filial love we cry, "Abba, Father." There is no exception to this rule: If a man loves not God, neither is he born of God. Show me a fire without heat, then show me regeneration that does not produce love to God; for as the sun must give forth its light, so must a soul that has been created anew by divine grace display its nature by sincere affection toward God. You are not born again unless you love God. How indispensable then is love to God.

HOLY PEACE

Being justified by faith, we have peace with
God through our Lord Jesus Christ.
ROMANS 5:1 KJV

Love for God is a chief means of that holy peace which is an essential mark of a Christian. "Being justified by faith, we have peace with God through Jesus Christ our Lord." But where there is no love, there is no such peace, for fear distresses the soul; thus love is the indispensable companion of faith, and when they come together, peace is the result. Where there is fervent love for God, there is set up a holy familiarity with God, and from this flow satisfaction, delight, and rest. Love must cooperate with faith and cast out fear, so that the soul may have boldness before God.

Oh Christian, you cannot have the nature of God implanted within you by regeneration; it cannot reveal itself in love to the brotherhood, it cannot blossom with the fair flowers of peace and joy except your affection be set upon God. Let Him then be your exceeding joy. Delight yourself also in the Lord. Oh, love the Lord, you His saints!

Day 127
LOVE AND OBEY

This is love: that we walk in
obedience to his commands.
2 JOHN 1:6 NIV

Love is the spring of true obedience. "This is the love of God, that we keep His commandments." Now a man who is not obedient to God's commandments is evidently not a true believer; for although good works do not save us, yet, being saved, believers are sure to produce good works. Though the fruit is not the root of the tree, yet a well-rooted tree will, in its season, bring forth its fruits. So, though the keeping of the commandments does not make me a child of God, yet, being a child of God, I shall be obedient to my heavenly Father.

But this I cannot be unless I love God. A mere external obedience, a decent formal recognition of the laws of God, is not obedience in God's sight. He abhors the sacrifice where the heart is not found. I must obey because I love, or else I have not in spirit and in truth obeyed at all. See then, that to produce the indispensable fruits of saving faith, there must be love for God; for without it, they would be unreal and indeed impossible.

Day 128
GOD LOVES YOU

---

*"For God so loved the world that he gave his
one and only Son, that whoever believes in
him shall not perish but have eternal life."*
JOHN 3:16 NIV

It is certain, beloved brethren, that faith in the heart always precedes love. We first believe the love of God for us before we love God in return. And, oh, what an encouraging truth this is. I, a sinner, do not believe that God loves me because I feel I love Him; but I first believe that He loves me, sinner as I am, and then having believed that gracious fact, I come to love my Benefactor in return.

Perhaps some of you seekers are saying to yourselves, "Oh, that we could love God, for then we could hope for mercy." That is not the first step. Your first step is to believe that God loves you, and when that truth is fully fixed in your soul by the Spirit, a fervent love for God will spontaneously issue from your soul, even as flowers willingly pour forth their fragrance under the influence of the dew and the sun. Every man who ever was saved had to come to God not as a lover of God but as a sinner, and to believe in God's love for him as a sinner.

LOVE FOR THE UNLOVELY

*When we were yet without strength,
in due time Christ died for the ungodly.*
ROMANS 5:6 KJV

You think that God loves men because they are godly, but listen to this: "God commendeth His love toward us, in that while we were yet sinners, Christ died for us." "He came not to call the righteous but sinners to repentance." "When we were yet without strength, in due time Christ died for the ungodly."

Think of His "great love wherewith He loved us, even when we were dead in trespasses and sins." God has love in His heart toward those who have nothing in them to love. He loves you, poor soul, who feel that you are most unlovable; loves you who mourn over a stony heart, which will not warm or melt with love for Him. Thus says the Lord: "I have blotted out, as a thick cloud, your transgressions and, as a cloud, your sins; return unto Me, for I have redeemed you."

Oh, that God's gracious voice might so call some of His poor wandering ones that they may come and believe His love for them, and then cast themselves at His feet to be His servants forever.

Day 130

THE GREATNESS OF GOD'S LOVE

But God, being rich in mercy, because of
His great love with which He loved us. . .
made us alive together with Christ.
EPHESIANS 2:4–5 NASB

Brethren, rest assured that in proportion as we are fully persuaded of God's love for us, we shall be affected with love for Him. Do not let the devil tempt you to believe that God does not love you because your love is feeble; for if he can in any way weaken your belief in God's love for you, he cuts off or diminishes the flow of the streams which feed the sacred grace of love for God. If I lament that I do not love God as I ought, that is a holy regret; but if I therefore conclude that God's love for me is less because of this, I deny the light because my eye is dim, and I deprive myself also of the power to increase in love.

Let me rather think more and more of the greatness of God's love for me, as I see more and more my unworthiness of it; the more a sinner I am, let me the more fully see how great must be that love which embraces such a sinner as I am; and then as I receive a deeper sense of the divine mercy, I shall feel the more bound to gratitude and constrained to affection. Oh, for a great wave of love to carry us right out into the ocean of love.

COMPASSED ABOUT WITH LOVE

We know and rely on the love God has for
us. God is love. Whoever lives in love
lives in God, and God in them.
1 JOHN 4:16 NIV

Day by day the deeds of God's love for you may be seen in
the gift of food and raiment, in the mercies of this life, and
especially in the covenant blessings which God gives you; the
peace which He sheds abroad in your hearts, the communion
which He offers you with Himself and His blessed Son, and
the answers to prayer which He grants you. Note well these
things, and if you consider them carefully and weigh their
value, you will be accumulating the fuel on which love feeds
its consecrated flame.

In proportion as you see in every good gift a new token of
your Father's love, in that proportion will you make progress
in the sweet school of love. Oh, it is heavenly living to taste
God's love in every morsel of bread we eat; it is blessed living
to know that we breathe an atmosphere purified and made
fragrant with divine love, that love protects us while we sleep,
and that love opens the eyelids of the morning to smile upon
us when we wake. Even when we are sick, it is love that
chastens us; when we are impoverished, love relieves us of a
burden, love gives and love takes, love cheers and love smites.
We are compassed about with love—above, beneath, around,
within, without. If we could but recognize this, we should
become as flames of fire, ardent and fervent toward our God.

Day 132

COME TO JESUS

Behold, we come unto thee;
for thou art the LORD our God.
JEREMIAH 3:22 KJV

Does He not declare that He is God and changes not, and therefore you are not consumed? Rekindled are the flames of love in the backslider's bosom when he feels all this to be true; he cries, "Behold, we come unto You for You are the Lord our God."

Come just as you are, bad as you are, hardened, cold, dead as you feel yourselves to be; come even so, and believe in the boundless love of God in Christ Jesus. Then shall come the deep repentance; then shall come the brokenness of heart; then shall come the holy jealousy, the sacred hatred of sin, and the refining of the soul from all her dross; then, indeed, all good things shall come to restore your soul and lead you in the paths of righteousness.

Do not look for these first; that would be looking for the effects before the cause. The great cause of love in the restored backslider must be the love of God for him, to whom he clings with a faith that dares not let go its hold.

Day 133
GOD'S LOVE; OUR DESIRE

"I have loved you with an everlasting love."
JEREMIAH 31:3 NIV

If you know that God has loved you, then you will feel grateful; every doubt will diminish your gratitude, but every grain of faith will increase it. Then as we advance in grace, love for God in our soul will excite desire after Him. Those we love, we long to be with: We count the hours that separate us; no place is so happy as that in which we enjoy their company. Thus, love for God produces a desire to be with Him, a desire to be like Him, a longing to be with Him, eternally in heaven, and this breaks us away from worldliness; this keeps us from idolatry, and therefore has a most blessedly sanctifying effect upon us, producing that elevated character which is now so rare, but which wherever it exists is powerful for the good of the Church and for the glory of God.

Would to God we had a band of men full of faith and of the Holy Spirit, strong in the Lord and in the power of His might. It may help those who aspire to mount high in grace, if they keep in mind that every step they climb they must use the ladder that Jacob saw. The love of God for us is the only way to climb to the love of God.

Day 134

GOD'S LOVE FOR THE UNDESERVING

"I have loved you," says the LORD.
MALACHI 1:2 NASB

God loves me—not merely bears with me, thinks of me, feeds me, but loves me. Who is it that loves you? God, the Maker of heaven and earth, the Almighty, All in all, does He love me? Even He? If all men and all angels and all the living creatures who are before the throne loved me, it would be nothing to this—the Infinite loves me! And who is it that He loves? Me. He loves me, an insignificant nobody, full of sin—who deserved to be in hell, who loves Him so little in return—God loves me. And how did He love me? He loved me so that He gave up His only begotten Son for me, to be nailed to the tree, and made to bleed and die. And because He loved me and forgave me, I am on the way to heaven, and I shall see His face and sing His praises. He loved me before I was born; before a star began to shine, He loved me, and He has never ceased to do so all these years. When I have sinned, He has loved me; when I have forgotten Him, He has loved me; and He will love me when my knees tremble and my hair is gray. He will bear and carry His servant; and He will love me forever and ever.

ALIKE, YET DIFFERENT

---

*The birds make their nests: as for the stork, the fir
trees are her house. The high hills are a refuge for
the wild goats; and the rocks for the conies.*
PSALM 104:17–18 KJV

God has not made two creatures precisely alike. You shall
gather leaves from a tree, and you shall not find two veined
in precisely the same way. In Christian experience it is the
same. Wherever there is living Christian experience, it is
different from everybody else's experience in some respect.
In a family, each child may be like his father, and yet each
child shall be different from each other child; and among
the children of God, though they all have the likeness of
Christ in a measure, yet they are not all exactly like the other.

Are you emptied of self, and do you look to Christ
alone? If no other soul has trod the same path as you have,
you are on a right path; and though your experience may
have eccentricities in it that differs from all others, it is
right it should be so. God has not made the wild goat like
the coney, nor has He made the stork like any other bird,
but He has made each to fit the place it is to occupy; and
He makes your experience to be suitable to bring out some
point of His glory, which could not be brought out otherwise.
Some are full of rejoicing, others are often depressed, a few
keep the happy medium, many soar aloft and then dive into
the deeps again; let these varied experiences, as they are all
equally clear phases of the same divine loving-kindness, be
accepted, and let them be rejoiced in.

Day 136
GOD'S PROVISION

I long to. . .take refuge in the shelter of your wings.
PSALM 61:4 NIV

Birds fly to the trees, and the stork to the fir, the wild goat to the high hills, and the coney to the rocks. There is a shelter for every one of these creatures, great and small. Think a moment then: If God has made each creature happy and given a place of refuge to each creature, then depend on it, He has not left man's soul without a shelter. And here is an important truth, for every man is certainly in danger, and every thinking man knows it.

My God, do You shield and shelter the coney in the rock, and is there no rock for me to shelter in? Assuredly You have not made man and left him without a refuge; when You give to the rabbit the cleft in which he may hide himself, there must be a shelter for man.

This must certainly be true because you and I, if we have observed our inner life, must have felt conscious that nothing here below can fill an immortal soul. Have you not felt yearnings after the Infinite—hungerings which bread cannot satisfy, thirstings which a river could not quench? Well then, if you have such longings as these, surely there must be a provision to meet them. With my thirstings, my longings, my mysterious instincts, there is a God somewhere; there is a heaven somewhere, there is an atonement somewhere, there is a fullness somewhere to meet my emptiness. Man wants a shelter; there must be a shelter.

A REFUGE FROM FEAR

For God has not given us a spirit of fear,
but of power and of love and of a sound mind.
2 TIMOTHY 1:7 NKJV

Beloved, there is a shelter for man from the sense of past guilt. It is because we are guilty that we are fearful: We have broken our Maker's law, and therefore we are afraid. But our Maker came from heaven to earth; Jesus, the Christ of God, came here and was made man and bore our sins that we might never bear His Father's righteous wrath, and whoever believes in Jesus shall find perfect rest in those dear wounds of His.

Since Christ suffered for me, my guilt is gone, my punishment was endured by my Substitute; therefore I hear the voice that says, "Comfort ye, comfort you My people! Say unto them that their warfare is accomplished, for they have received at the Lord's hand double for all their sins." And as for future fears, he who believes in Jesus finds a refuge from them in the Fatherhood of God. He who trusts Christ says: "Now I have no fear about the present nor about the future. Let catastrophe follow catastrophe, let the world crash and all the universe go to ruin; beneath the wings of the Eternal God, I must be safe. All things must work together for my good, for I love God and have been called according to His purpose." What a blessed shelter this is!

I WILL PRAISE YOU
MORE AND MORE

But I will hope continually, and will
yet praise thee more and more.
PSALM 71:14 KJV

When sin conquered the realm of manhood, it slew all the minstrels except those of the race of Hope. For humanity, amid all its sorrows and sins, hope sings on.

To believers in Jesus, there remains a royal race of bards, for we have a hope of glory, a lively hope, a hope eternal and divine. Because our hope abides, our praise continues: "I will hope continually and will yet praise thee." Because our hopes grow brighter and are every day nearer and nearer to their fulfillment, therefore the volume of our praise increases. "I will hope continually and yet praise you *more and more*."

A dying hope would bring forth declining songs; as the expectations grew more dim, so would the music become more faint. But a hope immortal and eternal, flaming forth each day with more intense brightness, brings forth a song of praise which, as it shall always continue to arise, so shall it always gather new force.

Day 139
ETERNAL HOPE

*Because your love is better than life, my lips will
glorify you. I will praise you as long as I live,
and in your name I will lift up my hands. I will
be fully satisfied as with the richest of foods;
with singing lips my mouth will praise you.*
PSALM 63:3–5 NIV

It is humbling to remember that we may very well praise God
more than we have done, for *we have praised Him very little
as yet.* What we have done, as believers, in glorifying God is
far, far short of His due.

Think, my dear brother or sister, what the Lord has done
for you. Some years ago you were in your sin and death and
ruin; He called you by His grace. You were under the burden
and curse of sin; He delivered you. Did you not expect in the
first joy of pardon to have done more for Him, to have loved
Him more, to have served Him better? Let us therefore be
shamed into a firm resolve and say with resolute spirit: "By
the good help of infinite grace, I, at any rate, having been so
great a laggard, will quicken my pace; I will yet praise You
more and more."

Day 140

GENUINE WORSHIP

Ascribe to the LORD the glory due his name;
bring an offering and come before him. Worship
the LORD in the splendor of his holiness.
1 CHRONICLES 16:29 NIV

The happiest moments I have ever spent have been occupied with the worship of God. I have never been so near heaven as when adoring before the eternal throne. I think every Christian will bear like witness.

Among all the joys of earth, and I shall not depreciate them, there is no joy comparable to that of praise. The innocent mirth of the fireside, the chaste delights of household love, even these are not to be mentioned side by side with the joy of worship, the rapture of drawing near to the Most High. The purest and most exhilarating joy is the delight of glorifying God, and so anticipating the time when we shall enjoy Him forever.

If God's praise has been no wilderness to you, return to it with zest and ardor, and say: "I will yet praise You more and more." If any suppose that you grow weary with the service of the Lord, tell them that His praise is such freedom, such recreation, such felicity that you desire never to cease from it. As for me, if men call God's service slavery, I desire to be such a bondslave forever and gladly be branded with my Master's name indelibly.

Day 141

A HEART OF GRATITUDE

Enter into his gates with thanksgiving,
and into his courts with praise: be thankful
unto him, and bless his name.

PSALM 100:4 KJV

We ought surely to praise God more today than any other previous day, because we have received more mercies. Even of temporal favors we have been large partakers. Begin with these, and then rise higher. Some of you may well be reminded of the great temporal mercies that have been lavished upon you. How highly God has favored some of you!

Look back to what you were, and give the Lord His due. You were unknown and insignificant, and now His mercy has placed you in prominence and esteem. Will you not praise the Lord more and more for this? Surely you should do so and must do so. Perhaps divine providence has not dealt with you exactly in that way, but with equal goodness and wisdom has revealed itself to you in another form. You have continued in the same sphere in which you commenced life, but you have been enabled to pursue your work, have been preserved in health and strength, have been supplied with food and raiment and what is best, have been blessed with a contented heart and a gleaming eye. My dear friend, are you not thankful? Will you not praise your heavenly Father more and more?

INCREASE YOUR PRAISE

Great is the LORD,
and greatly to be praised.
1 CHRONICLES 16:25 KJV

Every Christian as he grows in grace should have a loftier idea of God. Our highest conception of God falls infinitely short of His glory, but an advanced Christian enjoys a far clearer view of what God is than he had at the first.

Now the greatness of God is ever a claim for praise. "Great is the Lord, and"—what follows?—"greatly to be praised." If then God is greater to me than He was, let my praise be greater. If I think of Him now more tenderly as my Father—if I have a clearer view of Him in the terror of His justice—if I have a clearer view of the splendors of His wisdom by which He devised the atonement—if I have larger thoughts of His eternal, immutable love—let every advance in knowledge constrain me to say: " 'I will yet praise You more and more.' I heard of You by the hearing of the ear, but now my eyes see You: Therefore while I abhor myself in dust and ashes, my praise shall rise yet more loftily; up to Your throne shall my song ascend."

Day 143
ALMOST HOME

*For we know that if our earthly house of this
tabernacle were dissolved, we have a building of God,
an house not made with hands, eternal in the heavens.*

2 CORINTHIANS 5:1 KJV

Heaven is indeed the only home of our souls, and we shall
never feel that we have come to our rest until we have reached
its mansions. One reason why we shall be able to rest in heaven
is because we shall there be able perpetually to achieve the
object of our creation. Am I nearer heaven? Then I will be
doing more of the work that I shall do in heaven. I shall soon
use the harp: Let me be carefully tuning it; let me rehearse the
hymns which I shall sing before the throne, for if the words
in heaven shall be sweeter and more rich than any that poets
can put together here, yet the essential song of heaven shall
be the same as that which we present to Jehovah here below.

My aged brethren, I congratulate you, for you are almost
home; be yet more full of praise than ever. Quicken your
footsteps as the glory land shines more brightly. You are close
to the gate of pearl; sing on, dear brother, though infirmities
increase, and let the song grow sweeter and louder until it
melts into the infinite harmonies.

Day 144
TIME WITH GOD

I will sing to the LORD all my life; I will sing praise to my God as long as I live. May my meditation be pleasing to him, as I rejoice in the LORD.
PSALM 104:33–34 NIV

If we would praise God more and more, let us improve our private devotions. God is much praised by really devout prayer and adoration. Preachings are not fruits: They are sowings. True song is fruit. I mean this, that the green blade of the wheat may be the sermon, but the wheat ear is the hymn you sing, the prayer in which you unite. The true result of life is praise to God.

"The chief end of man," says the catechism, and I cannot put it better, "is to glorify God and enjoy Him forever"; and when we glorify God in our private devotions, we are answering the true end of our being. If we desire to praise God more, we must ask for grace that our private devotions may rise to a higher standard. I am more and more persuaded from my own experience that in proportion to the strength of our private life with God will be the force of our character and the power of our work for God among men. Let us look well to this.

PRAISING MORE OR PRAISING LESS?

Let everything that has breath praise the LORD.
PSALM 150:6 NIV

Are you praising God more and more? If you are not, I am afraid of one thing, and that is that you are probably praising Him less and less. It is a certain truth that if we do not go forward in the Christian life, we go backward. You cannot stand still; there is a drift one way or the other. Now he who praises God less than he did, and goes on to praise Him less tomorrow and less the next day, and so on—what will he get to? And what is he? Evidently he is one of those who draw back unto perdition, and there are no persons upon whom a more dreadful sentence is pronounced.

May you grow in grace, for life is proven by growth. May you march like pilgrims toward heaven, singing all the way. The lark may serve us as a final picture and an example of what we all should be. We should be mounting: Our prayer should be "Nearer, my God, to Thee." We should be mounting: Our motto might well be "Higher! Higher! Higher!" As we mount, we should sing, and our song should grow louder, clearer, more full of heaven. Upward, brother, I sing as you soar. Upward, sing until you are dissolved in glory.

THE PRAYER OF JABEZ

Oh that thou wouldest bless me indeed!
1 CHRONICLES 4:10 KJV

More honorable than his brothers was the child whom his mother bore with sorrow. As for this Jabez, whose aim was so well pointed, his fame so far sounded, his name so lastingly embalmed—he was a man of prayer. The honor he enjoyed would not have been worth having if it had not been vigorously contested and equitably won. His devotion was the key to his promotion. Those are the best honors that come from God, the award of grace with the acknowledgment of service.

The best honor is that which a man gains in communion with the Most High. Jabez, we are told, was more honorable than his brothers, and his prayer is recorded as if to intimate that he was also more prayerful than his brothers. We are told of what petitions his prayer consisted. All through it was very significant and instructive.

"Oh, that You would bless me indeed!" I commend it as a prayer for yourselves, dear brothers and sisters, one which will be available at all seasons, a prayer to begin Christian life with, a prayer to end it with, a prayer which would never be unseasonable in your joys or in your sorrows.

BLESSING AFTER TEARS

Those who sow in tears shall reap in joy.
He who continually goes forth weeping. . .
shall doubtless come again with rejoicing.
PSALM 126:5–6 NKJV

To a great extent we find that we must sow in tears before we can reap in joy. Many of our works for Christ have cost us tears. Difficulties and disappointments have wrung our soul with anguish. Yet those projects that have cost us more than ordinary sorrow have often turned out to be the most honorable of our undertakings. You may expect a blessing in serving God if you are enabled to persevere under many discouragements.

There are many bounties given to us mercifully by God for which we are bound to be very grateful; but we must not set too much store by them. We may accept them with gratitude, but we must not make them our idols. When we have them, we have great need to cry, "Oh, that You would bless me indeed, and make these inferior blessings real blessings"; and if we have them not, we should with greater vehemence cry, "Oh, that we may be rich in faith, and if not blessed with these external favors, may we be blessed spiritually, and then we shall be blessed indeed."

Day 148

BLESSINGS INDEED

"Blessing I will bless you."
GENESIS 22:17 NKJV

The blessings of God's grace are blessings indeed, which we ought to earnestly seek after. By these marks shall you know them. Blessings indeed are such blessings as come from the pierced hand, blessings that come from Calvary's bloody tree, streaming from the Savior's wounded side—your pardon, your acceptance, your spiritual life: The bread that is meat indeed, the blood that is drink indeed—your oneness to Christ and all that comes of it—these are blessings indeed. Anything that He does, accept it; do not be dubious of it, but pray that He may continue His blessed operations in your soul. Whatever leads you to God is in like manner a blessing indeed. Anything that draws you nearer to Him is a blessing indeed. What if it be a cross that raises you? Yet if it raises you to God, it shall be a blessing indeed. And anything which helps me to glorify God is a blessing indeed.

See whether the blessings are blessings indeed, and do not be satisfied unless you know that they are of God, tokens of His grace and pledges of His saving purpose.

DRAW CLOSER TO JESUS

"We will come to you, for you are the Lord our God."
JEREMIAH 3:22 NIV

"Come." A simple word, but very full of meaning. To *come* is to leave one thing and to advance to another. Come then you laboring and heavy laden, leave your legal labors, leave your self-reliant efforts, leave your sins, leave your presumptions, leave all in which you until now have trusted, and come to Jesus; that is, think of, advance toward, rely upon the Savior.

Let your contemplations think of Him who bore the load of human sin upon the cross of Calvary, where He was made sin for us. Let your minds consider Him who from His cross, hurled the enormous mass of His people's transgressions into a bottomless grave, where it was buried forever. Think of Jesus, the divinely appointed substitute and sacrifice for guilty man. Then seeing that He is God's own Son, let faith follow your contemplation; rely upon Him, trust in Him as having suffered in your stead, look to Him for the payment of the debt which is due from you to the wrath of God.

This is to come to Jesus. Repentance and faith make up this "Come"—the repentance which leaves that place where you now stand, the faith which comes into reliance upon Jesus.

THE GIFT OF REST

*"Come to Me, all who are weary and
burdened, and I will give you rest."*
MATTHEW 11:28 NASB

"I will give you rest." "I will *give*." It is a rest that is a gift,
not a rest found in our experience by degrees, but given at
once. We come to Jesus; we put out the empty hand of faith,
and rest is given us at once most freely. We possess it at
once, and it is ours forever. It is a *present* rest, rest now—
not rest after death, not rest after a time of probation and
growth and advancement—but it is rest given when we come
to Jesus, given there and then. And it is *perfect* rest too, for
it is not said nor is it implied that the rest is incomplete.
We do not read, "I will give you partial rest," but "rest," as
if there were no other form of it. It is perfect and complete
in itself. In the blood and righteousness of Jesus, our peace
is perfect.

Have you come to Jesus, and has He given you perfect
and present rest? If so, I know your eye will catch joyously
those two little words, "*And I*"; and I would implore you
lovingly remember the promiser who speaks. Jesus promises
and Jesus performs.

A PETITION TO GOD FOR HIS CLOSENESS

Forsake me not, O LORD.
PSALM 38:21 KJV

Frequently we pray that God would not forsake us in the hour of trial and temptation, but we often forget that we have need to use this prayer at all times. There is no moment of our life, however holy, in which we can do without His constant upholding. Whether in light or in darkness, in communion or in temptation, we alike need the prayer "Forsake me not, O Lord."

We cannot do without continued aid from above; let it then be your prayer today, "Forsake me not. Father, forsake not Your child, lest he fall by the hand of the enemy. Shepherd, forsake not Your lamb, lest he wander from the safety of the fold. Great Husbandman, forsake not Your plant, lest it wither and die. 'Forsake me not, O Lord,' now—and forsake me not at any moment of my life. Forsake me not in my joys, lest they absorb my heart. Forsake me not in my sorrows, lest I murmur against You. Forsake me not in the day of my repentance, lest I lose the hope of pardon and fall into despair; and forsake me not in the day of my strongest faith, lest faith degenerate into presumption. Forsake me not, for without You I am weak, but with You I am strong. Forsake me not, for my path is dangerous and full of snares, and I cannot do without Your guidance. 'Be not far from me, O Lord, for trouble is near, for there is none to help. Leave me not, neither forsake me, O God of my salvation!'"

Day 152
JOY IN PERSECUTION

*If any man will come after me, let him deny himself,
and take up his cross daily, and follow me.*
LUKE 9:23 KJV

You must be willing to bear Christ's burden. Now the burden
of Christ is His cross, which every Christian must take up.
Expect to be reproached, expect to meet with some degree
of the scandal of the cross, for the offense of it never ceases.
Persecution and reproach are a blessed burden; when your soul
loves Jesus, it is a joyful thing to suffer for Him, and therefore
never, by any cowardly retirement or refusal to profess your
faith, evade your share of this honorable load.

Woe unto those who say, "I will never be a martyr." No
rest is sweeter than the martyr's rest. Woe unto those who
say, "We will go to heaven by night along a secret road and
so avoid the shame of the cross." The rest of the Christian
is found not in cowardice but in courage; it lies not in
providing for ease but in the brave endurance of suffering
for the truth. The restful spirit counts the reproach of Christ
to be greater riches than all treasures; he falls in love with
the cross and counts the burden light, and so finds rest in
service and rest in suffering.

REST FOR GOD'S PEOPLE

There remaineth therefore a rest to the people of God.
For he that is entered into his rest, he also hath ceased
from his own works, as God did from his. Let us
labour therefore to enter into that rest.
HEBREWS 4:9–11 KJV

It is very evident that the rest which we are to find is a rest which grows entirely out of our spirits being conformed to the Spirit of Christ. "Learn of Me, and you shall find rest." It is then a spiritual rest altogether independent of circumstances. It is a vain idea of ours to suppose that if our circumstances were altered we should be more at rest.

My brother, if you cannot rest in poverty, neither would you in riches; if you cannot rest in the midst of persecution, neither would you in the midst of honor. It is the Spirit within that gives the rest; that rest has little to do with anything without. The Spirit is the spring of rest; as for the outward surroundings, they are of small account. Let your mind be like the mind of Christ, and you shall find rest unto your souls: a deep rest, a growing rest, a rest found out more and more, an abiding rest, not only which you have found, but which you shall go on to find.

Day 154

THE BLOOD INTERCEDES
FOR OUR MERCY

For we have become partakers of Christ if we hold the
beginning of our confidence steadfast to the end.
HEBREWS 3:14 NKJV

We are made partakers of Christ, beloved, when first of all by faith in Him we procure a share in His merits. Sinful and sad, covered with transgressions and conscious of our shame, we come to the fountain filled with His blood; we washed in it and were made white as snow. In that hour we became partakers of Christ.

Christ is the substitute for sin. He suffered the penalty due from the unjust for whom He died to the violated law of God. When we believe in Him, we become partakers of those sufferings, or rather of the blessed fruit of them. The fact of His having borne what we ought to have borne becomes available to us. We present that memorial at the altar of God, the throne of the heavenly grace, in prayers and professions and in spiritual worship. The blood pleads our cause.

The blood of Jesus, which speaks better things than that of Abel, intercedes for mercy, not for vengeance. By its rich virtue, its real value, its vital merit, it puts our sins forever to death and lays our fears forever to rest. Oh, how blessed to be a partaker of Christ, the sin-atoning sacrifice—to stand before God as a sinner who deserves nothing but damnation in himself, and yet knows by precious faith, that "Covered is my unrighteousness. From condemnation I am free."

PARTAKERS OF CHRIST

That we may be partakers of His holiness.
HEBREWS 12:10 NKJV

Partakers of Christ! Yes, and therefore with Him partakers in destiny. When He shall come, His holy ones shall come with Him. That He has risen from the dead is the earnest of their resurrection. At the day of His appearing, they shall rise and participate in the fruition of His mediatorial work. Then, in the judging of the world, in the destruction of all His spiritual foes, in the great marriage day when the bride shall have made herself ready and He shall drink of the new wine in the kingdom of His Father, and in all else that is to come, too glorious to be described except by symbols like those of the Apocalypse; His people shall participate with Him, for this honor have all His saints.

All right and all might, all that can extol or delight, all that forever and ever shall contribute to the glory of Christ shall be shared by all the faithful, for we are partakers not only with Him but *of* Him—*of* Christ—therefore of all the surroundings of glory and honor that shall belong to Him.

Rejoice evermore. Pray without ceasing.
In every thing give thanks.
1 THESSALONIANS 5:16–18 KJV

"Pray without ceasing." Observe what it follows. It comes immediately after the precept "Rejoice evermore," as if that command had somewhat staggered the reader and made him ask, "How can I always rejoice?" and therefore the apostle appended as answer, "Always pray." The more praying, the more rejoicing. Prayer gives a channel to the pent-up sorrows of the soul; they flow away, and in their stead streams of sacred delight pour into the heart. At the same time the more rejoicing, the more praying; when the heart is in a quiet condition and full of joy in the Lord, then also will it be sure to draw near to the Lord in worship. Holy joy and prayer act and react upon each other.

Observe, however, what immediately follows the text: "In every thing give thanks." When joy and prayer are married, their firstborn child is gratitude. When we joy in God for what we have and believingly pray to Him for more, then our souls thank Him both in the enjoyment of what we have and in the prospect of what is yet to come. Those three texts are three companion pictures, representing the life of a true Christian. These three precepts are an ornament of grace to every believer's neck; wear them, every one of you, for glory and for beauty: "Rejoice evermore"; "Pray without ceasing"; "In every thing give thanks."

Day 157
PRAY CONTINUALLY

Men always ought to pray and not lose heart.
LUKE 18:1 NKJV

"Pray without ceasing." That precept at one stroke overthrows the idea of particular times when prayer is more acceptable or more proper than at others. If I am to pray without ceasing, then every second must be suitable for prayer, and there is not one unholy moment in the hour nor one unaccepted hour in the day nor one unhallowed day in the year. The Lord has not appointed a certain week for prayer, but all weeks should be weeks of prayer: Neither has He said that one hour of the day is more acceptable than another. All time is equally legitimate for supplication, equally holy, equally accepted with God, or else we should not have been told to pray without ceasing.

It is good to have your times of prayer; it is good to set apart seasons for special supplication—we have no doubt of that—but we must never allow this to beget the superstition that there is a certain holy hour for prayer in the morning, a specially acceptable hour for prayer in the evening, and a sacred time for prayer at certain seasons of the year. Wherever we seek the Lord with true hearts, He is found of us; whenever we cry to Him, He hears us. Every place is hallowed ground to a hallowed heart, and every day is a holy day to a holy man. From January to December, the calendar has not one date in which prayer is forbidden. All the days are red-letter days; whether holy days or weekdays, they are all accepted times for prayer.

PRAY AT ANY TIME

*Evening, and morning, and at noon, will I pray,
and cry aloud: and he shall hear my voice.*
PSALM 55:17 KJV

"Pray without ceasing." Our Lord Jesus Christ in these words assures you that you may pray without ceasing. There is no time when we may not pray. You have permission given to come to the mercy seat when you will, for the veil of the most holy place is torn from the top to the bottom, and our access to the mercy seat is undisputed and indisputable.

Kings hold their receptions upon certain appointed days, and then their courtiers are admitted; but the King of kings holds a constant reception. The dead of night is not too late for God; the breaking of the morning, when the first gray light is seen, is not too early for the Most High; at midday He is not too busy; and when the evening gathers, He is not weary with His children's prayers. "Pray without ceasing" is a most sweet and precious permit to the believer to pour out his heart at all times before the Lord.

The doors of the temple of divine love shall not be shut. Nothing can set a barrier between a praying soul and its God. The road of angels and of prayers is ever open. Let us but send out the dove of prayer, and we may be certain that she will return to us with an olive branch of peace in her mouth. The Lord continually regards the pleadings of His servants and waits to be gracious to them.

PERSECUTION WILL
LEAD TO GLORY

Everyone who wants to live a godly life
in Christ Jesus will be persecuted.
2 TIMOTHY 3:12 NIV

It is by no means pleasant to be opposed in doing right by those who ought to help us in it. It is very painful to flesh and blood to go contrary to those we love. What is more, those who hate Christians have a way of reviling so that they are sure to make us wince. They watch our weak points, and with very wonderful skill, they turn their discoveries to account. If one thing is more provoking than another, they will be sure to say it, and say it when we are least able to bear it. It may be they are very polite people, and if so, your refined persecutors have a very dainty way of cutting to the bone and yet smiling all the while. They can say a malicious thing so delicately that you can neither resent it nor endure it. They are perfect masters of it and know how to make the iron enter into the soul.

Do not be astonished, therefore, if you are sorely vexed, neither be amazed as though some strange thing happened to you. The martyrs did not suffer sham pains; the racks on which they were stretched were not beds of ease, nor were their prisons rooms of comfort. Their pains were agonies; their martyrdoms were torments. If you had sham griefs, you might expect counterfeit joys; let the reality of your tribulation assure you of the reality of the coming glory.

CHEERFUL THROUGH PERSECUTION

We are. . .persecuted, but not forsaken.
2 CORINTHIANS 4:8–9 KJV

Persecution will try your love to Jesus. If you really love Him, you will cheerfully stand in the humiliation of reproach with Him, and when enemies have rubbish to hurl, you will say, "Throw it upon me rather than upon Him; if there is a harsh thing to be said, say it about me rather than against my Lord."

It will try your love, I say, and so it will all your graces in their turn; and this is good for you. These virtues will not increase in strength unless they are brought into action, and if they are not tested, who is to know of what sort they are? Your valiant soldier in quiet barracks at home could fight, no doubt, but how do you know until he has passed through a battle? He who has charged up to the cannon's mouth, he who is adorned with a saber cut across his brow and bears many wounds beside which he gained in the service of his king, he is brave beyond question. Good gold must expect to be tried in the fire, and these oppositions are sent on purpose that our faith and our love and all our graces should be proved genuine by enduring the test.

THE OIL OF GLADNESS

You love righteousness and hate wickedness;
therefore God, Your God, has anointed You with
the oil of gladness more than Your companions.

PSALM 45:7 NKJV

You cannot conceive the gladness of Christ. If you have ever brought one soul to Christ, you have had a drop of it; but His gladness lies not only in receiving them, but also in actually being the author of salvation to every one of them. The Savior looks upon the redeemed with an unspeakable delight, thinks of what they used to be, thinks of what they would have been but for His interposition, thinks of what they now are, thinks of what He means to make them in that great day when they shall rise from the dead; and as His heart is full of love for them, He joys in their joy and exults in their exultation.

I speak with humblest fear lest in any word I should speak amiss, for He is God as well as man; but this is certain, that there is a joy of our Lord into which He will give His faithful ones to enter, a joy which He has won by passing through the shame and grief by which He has redeemed mankind. The oil of gladness is abundantly poured on that head which once was crowned with thorns.

Day 162
THE JOY OF JESUS

Make a joyful noise unto the LORD, all ye lands.
Serve the LORD with gladness: come before
his presence with singing.
PSALM 100:1–2 KJV

His birth set the skies ringing with heavenly music and made the hearts of expectant saints to leap for joy. In later days, a touch of the hem of His garment made a woman's heart glad when she felt the issue of her blood stanched, and a word from His lips made the tongue of the mute to sing. For Him to lay His hand upon the sick was to raise them from their beds of sickness and deliver them from pain and disease. His touch was gladness then, and a spiritual touch is the same now.

Today to preach of Him is gladness, to sing of Him is gladness, to trust Him is gladness, to work for Him is gladness, to have communion with Him is gladness. To come to His table and there to feast with Him is gladness; to see His image in the eyes of His saints is gladness; to see that image only as yet begun to form in the heart of a young convert is gladness. Everything about Him is gladness.

AN EVERLASTING COVENANT

Yet he hath made with me an everlasting covenant.
2 SAMUEL 23:5 KJV

This covenant is divine in its origin. "He has made with me an everlasting covenant." Oh, that great word: *He!* God, the everlasting Father, has positively made a covenant with you; yes, that God who spoke the world into existence by a word. He, stooping from His majesty, takes hold of your hand and makes a covenant with you. Can we really understand it? "He has made with me a covenant." A king has not made a covenant with me—that would be something—but the Prince of the kings of the earth, Shaddai, the Lord All-Sufficient, the Jehovah of ages, the everlasting Elohim, "He has made with me an everlasting covenant."

But notice, it is particular in its application. "Yet has He made with *me* an everlasting covenant." Here lies the sweetness of it to each believer. It is nothing for me that He made peace for the world; I want to know whether He made peace for *me!* It is little that He has made a covenant; I want to know whether He has made a covenant with me. Blessed is the assurance that He has made a covenant with me! If God the Holy Spirit gives me assurance of this, then His salvation is mine, His heart is mine, He Himself is mine—He is my God.

This covenant is everlasting in its duration. An everlasting covenant means a covenant which had no beginning, and which shall never, never end. How sweet amidst all the uncertainties of life to know that "the foundation of the Lord standeth sure."

Day 164
WE SHALL SEE GOD

*I know that my redeemer liveth, and that he
shall stand at the latter day upon the earth:
and though after my skin worms destroy this
body, yet in my flesh shall I see God.*
JOB 19:25–26 KJV

Beloved, if these distant glimpses are so precious, what must
it be to see Him face-to-face? I have tried to conceive it,
and even in attempting the conception, my spirit seems to
swoon at the prospect of such supreme delight. Only to hear
the music of His footfall on the other side of the partition
wall raises longings in my heart too strong, too eager to be
long endured.

What, death, are you all that divides me from seeing my
Lord? I would gladly die a million deaths to see Him as He
is and to be like Him. What, a slumber in the grave for this
poor body! Is that all I have to dread? Then let it slumber.

Oh, what will it be to see Him? To see Him who loved
us so, to mark the wounds with which He purchased our
redemption, to behold His glory, to listen to His voice, and
to hear Him say, "Well done, good and faithful servant."
To lie in His bosom forever, truly eye has not seen nor ear
heard the like of this bliss. More than the bride longs for the
marriage day, do we expect the bridal feast of heaven; but
of all the dainties on that royal table, there will not be one
that will be equal to Himself, for to see Him will be all the
heaven we desire.

GOD'S WILL UPHOLDS US THROUGH TRIALS

I am crucified with Christ: nevertheless I live;
yet not I, but Christ liveth in me.
GALATIANS 2:20 KJV

We should receive chastisement with meek submission, presenting ourselves to God that He may do with us still as He has dealt with us—not wishing to move to the right hand or to the left: asking Him if it may be His will to remove the load, to heal the pain, to deliver us from the bereavement, and the like, but still always leaving ample margin for full resignation of spirit. The gold is not to rebel against the goldsmith, but should at once yield to be placed in the crucible and thrust into the fire. The wheat as it lies upon the threshing floor is not to have a will of its own, but to be willing to endure the strokes of the flail that the chaff may be separated from the precious corn.

We are not far off being purged from dross and cleansed from chaff when we are perfectly willing to undergo any process which the divine wisdom may appoint us. Self and sin are married and will never be divorced, and until our selfhood is crushed, the seed of sin will still have abundant vitality in it; but when it is "not I" but "Christ who liveth in me," then have we come near to that mark to which God has called us and to which, by His Spirit, He is leading us.

Day 166
THE WILL OF GOD

"Then they will seek My face; in their
affliction they will earnestly seek Me."
HOSEA 5:15 NKJV

We should accept chastisement cheerfully. It is a hard lesson, but a lesson that the Comforter is able to teach us—to be glad that God should have His way. Do you know what it is sometimes to be very pleased to do what you do not like to do? I mean you would not have liked to do it, but you find that it pleases someone you love, and straightaway the irksome task becomes a pleasure. Have you not felt sometimes, when one whom you very much esteem is sick and ill, that you would be glad enough to bear the pain, at least for a day or two, that you might give the suffering one a little rest? Would you not find a pleasure in being an invalid for a while to let your beloved one enjoy a season of health?

Let the same motive, in a higher degree, sway your spirit! Try to feel, "If it pleases God, it pleases me. If, Lord, it is *Your* will, it shall be *my* will. Let the lashes of the scourge be multiplied, if then You will be the more honored and I shall be permitted to bring You some degree of glory." The cross becomes sweet when our health is so sweetened by the Spirit that our will runs parallel with the will of God. We should learn to say, in the language of Elihu, "I have borne, I do bear, I accept it all."

FORGIVENESS OF SINS

"Everyone who believes in him receives
forgiveness of sins through his name."
ACTS 10:43 NIV

All our transgressions are swept away at once, carried off as by a flood, and so completely removed from us that no guilty trace of them remains. They are all gone! Oh believers, think of this, for it is no little thing. Sins against a holy God, sins against His loving Son, sins against the Gospel as well as against the law, sins against man as well as against God, sins of the body as well as sins of the mind, sins as numerous as the sands on the seashore and as great as the sea itself: All, all are removed from us as far as the east is from the west.

All this evil was rolled into one great mass and laid upon Jesus, and having borne it all, He has made an end of it forever. When the Lord forgave us, He forgave us the whole debt. He did not take the bill and say, "I strike out this item and that," but the pen went through it all: PAID. It was a receipt in full of all demands; Jesus took the handwriting that was against us and nailed it to His cross, to show before the entire universe that its power to condemn us had ceased forever. We have in Him a full forgiveness.

Day 168
OUR SINS ARE FORGOTTEN

Their sins and iniquities will I remember no more.
HEBREWS 10:17 KJV

There is such a truth, reality, and emphasis in the pardon of God as you can never find in the pardon of man; for though a man should forgive all you have done against him, if you have treated him very badly, yet it is more than you could expect that he should also *forget* it, but the Lord says, "Their sins and iniquities will I remember no more forever."

If a man has sinned against you, although you have forgiven him, you are not likely to trust him again. But see how the Lord deals with His people. The Lord lets bygones be bygones so completely that He trusts pardoned souls with His secrets, for "the secret of the Lord is with them who fear Him"; and He entrusts some of us with His choicest treasures.

Let us rejoice in that grand promise which comes to us by the mouth of Jeremiah of old, "In those days, and in that time, saith the Lord, the iniquity of Israel shall be sought for, and there shall be none; and the sins of Judah, and they shall not be found: for I will pardon them whom I reserve." Here is annihilation—the only annihilation I know of—the absolute annihilation of sin through the pardon that the Lord gives to His people. Let us sing it as though it were a choice hymn: "The iniquity of Israel shall be sought for, and there shall be none."

FORGIVING OTHERS

Be kind. . .forgiving one another,
even as God in Christ forgave you.
EPHESIANS 4:32 NKJV

Observe how the apostle puts it. Does he say, "forgiving another"? No, that is not the text, if you look at it. It is "forgiving *one another*." One another! Ah, then that means that if you have to forgive today, it is very likely that you will yourself need to be forgiven tomorrow, for it is "forgiving *one another*."

It is a mutual operation, a cooperative service. You forgive me, and I forgive you, and we forgive them, and they forgive us, and so a circle of unlimited forbearance and love goes around the world. There is something wrong about me that needs to be forgiven by my brother, but there is also something wrong about my brother that needs to be forgiven by me, and this is what the apostle means—that we are all mutually to be exercising the sacred art and mystery of forgiving one another. If we always did this, we should not endure those who have a special faculty for spying out faults.

You may know very well what a man is by what he says of others. It is a gauge of character that very seldom will deceive you, to judge other men by their own judgment of their fellows. Their speech betrays their heart. Show me your tongue. He who speaks with an ill tongue about his neighbor has an ill heart; rest assured of that. We shall have a great deal to forgive in other people, but there will be a great deal more to be forgiven in ourselves.

VENGEANCE IS
RESERVED FOR GOD

Vengeance is mine; I will repay, saith the Lord.
ROMANS 12:19 KJV

Never in any way, directly or indirectly, avenge yourselves. For any fault that is ever done to you, the Master says to you, "Resist not evil." In all things bend, bow, yield, submit.

Brother, the most splendid vengeance you can ever have is to do good to those who do evil to you and to speak well of those who speak ill of you. They will be ashamed to look at you; they will never hurt you again if they see that you cannot be provoked except it be to greater love and larger kindness. This ought to be the mark of Christians; not "I will have the law reprimand you" or "I will avenge myself," but "I will bear and forbear even to the end."

"Vengeance is Mine. I will repay, saith the Lord." Do not take that into your hand which God says belongs to Him, but as He for Christ's sake has forgiven you, so also forgive all those who do you wrong. "How long am I to do that?" one asks. "I would not mind doing it three or four times." There was one of old who would go the length of six or seven, but Jesus Christ said "unto seventy times seven." That is a very considerable number. You may count whether you have yet reached that amount, and if you have, you will now be glad to begin again, still forgiving, even as God for Christ's sake has forgiven you.

MEDITATION ON SCRIPTURE

"Have you not read?. . .
If you had known what this means. . ."
MATTHEW 12:3, 7 NKJV

If you are to understand what you read, you will need to meditate upon it. Some passages of scripture lie clear before us—blessed shallows in which the lambs may wade—but there are deeps in which our mind might rather drown itself than swim with pleasure, if it came there without caution. There are texts of scripture which are made and constructed on purpose to make us think. Many of the veils which are cast over scripture are not meant to hide the meaning from the diligent but to compel the mind to be active, for often the diligence of the heart in seeking to know the divine mind does the heart more good than the knowledge itself.

Meditation and careful thought exercise us and strengthen for the reception of the yet more lofty truths. We must meditate. The Word of God is always most precious to the man who most lives upon it. With God's Word it is well for us to be like squirrels, living in it and living on it. Let us exercise our minds by leaping from bough to bough of it, find our rest and food in it, and make it our all in all. We shall be the people who get the profit out of it if we make it to be our food, our medicine, our treasury, our armory, our rest, our delight. May the Holy Spirit lead us to do this and make the Word so precious to our souls.

Day 172

A PRAYER TO UNDERSTAND THE BIBLE

The meditation of my heart shall be of understanding.
PSALM 49:3 KJV

It is a grand thing to be driven to think; it is a grander thing to be driven to pray through having been made to think. Am I not addressing some of you who do not read the Word of God, and am I not speaking to many more who do read it but do not read it with the strong resolve that they will understand it? I know it must be so. Do you wish to begin to be true readers? Will you from this time forth labor to understand? Then you must get to your knees. You must cry to God for direction.

Who understands a book best? The author of it. So, beloved, the Holy Spirit is with us, and when we take His book and begin to read and want to know what it means, we must ask the Holy Spirit to reveal the meaning. He will not work a miracle, but He will elevate our minds; and He will suggest to us thoughts that will lead us on by their natural relation, the one to the other, until at last we come to the core of His divine instruction. Seek then very earnestly the guidance of the Holy Spirit, for if the very soul of reading be the understanding of what we read, then we must in prayer call upon the Holy Spirit to unlock the secret mysteries of the inspired Word.

STUDY OF GOD'S WORD WILL PRODUCE GROWTH

---

*Study to shew thyself approved unto God, a
workman that needeth not to be ashamed,
rightly dividing the word of truth.*

2 TIMOTHY 2:15 KJV

The diligent reading of the Word of God with the strong resolve to get at its meaning often produces spiritual life. We are begotten by the Word of God: It is the instrumental means of regeneration. Therefore love your Bibles. Keep close to your Bibles.

You seeking sinners, you who are seeking the Lord, your first business is to believe in the Lord Jesus Christ; but while you are yet in darkness and in gloom, oh, love your Bibles and search them! Take them to bed with you, and when you wake up in the morning, if it is too early to go downstairs and disturb the house, get half an hour of reading upstairs. Say, "Lord, guide me to that text which shall bless me. Help me to understand how I, a poor sinner, can be reconciled to You." Oh, cling to scripture. Scripture is not Christ, but it is the silken clue that will lead you to Him. Follow its leadings faithfully.

When you have received regeneration and a new life, keep on reading because it will comfort you. You will see more of what the Lord has done for you. You will learn that you are redeemed, adopted, saved, sanctified. Half the errors in the world spring from people not reading their Bibles.

Day 174
GOD'S WORD,
OUR COMFORT

*When you received the word of God. . .you accepted it
not as a human word, but as it actually is, the word of
God, which is indeed at work in you who believe.*

1 Thessalonians 2:13 niv

Read the Word, and it will be much for your comfort. It will
be for your nourishment too. It is your food as well as your
life. Search it, and you will grow strong in the Lord and in
the power of His might.

Oh, you will get a thousand helps out of that wondrous
book if you read it; for understanding the words more, you
will prize it more, and as you get older, the book will grow
with your growth and turn out to be an older person's manual
of devotion just as it was previously a child's sweet storybook.
Yes, it will always be a new book—just as new a Bible as when
it was printed and nobody had ever seen a word of it; and yet
it will be much more precious for all the memories which
cluster around it. As we turn over its pages, how sweetly do we
recollect passages in our history that will never be forgotten
for all eternity but will stand forever intertwined with gracious
promises. Beloved, we should ask the Lord to teach us to read
His book of life which He has opened before us here below,
so that we may read our titles clear in that other book of love
which we have not seen as yet, but which will be opened at
the last great day.

A CRY FOR MERCY

God be merciful to me a sinner.
LUKE 18:13 KJV

Let us praise His name because you and I are still spared to pray and permitted to pray. What if we are greatly afflicted, yet it is of the Lord's mercy that we are not consumed. If we had received our deserts, we should not now have been on praying ground and pleading terms with Him. But let it be for our comfort and to God's praise that still we may stand with bowed head and cry each one, "God, be merciful to me, a sinner." Still may we cry like sinking Peter, "Lord, save me, or I perish." Like David, we may be unable to go up to the temple, but we can still go to our God in prayer.

Therefore let us give thanks to God that He has nowhere said to us, "Seek My face in vain." If we find a desire to pray trembling within our soul, and if though almost extinct we feel some hope in the promise of our gracious God, if our heart still groans after holiness and after God, though she has lost her power to pray with joyful confidence as once she did, yet let us be thankful that we can pray even if it be but a little. In the will and power to pray, there lies the capacity for infinite blessedness: He who has the key of prayer can open heaven; yes, he has access to the heart of God. Therefore bless God for prayer.

THANKSGIVING AND REQUESTS

Let your requests be made known to God.
PHILIPPIANS 4:6 NKJV

Beloved, beyond the fact of prayer and our power to exercise it, there is a further ground of thanksgiving that we have already received great mercy at God's hands. We are not coming to God to ask favors and receive them for the first time in our lives. Why, blessed be His name if He never granted me another favor; I have enough for which to thank Him as long as I have any being. And this, furthermore, is to be recollected: That whatever great things we are about to ask, we cannot possibly be seeking for blessings one-half so great as those which we have already received if we are indeed His children.

If you are a Christian, you have life in Christ. Are you about to ask for food and clothing? Life is more than these. You have already obtained Christ Jesus to be yours, and He who spared Him not will not deny you anything. Let us perpetually thank our Benefactor for what we have while we make requests for something more. Shall not the abundant utterances of the memory of His great goodness run over into our requests, until our petitions are baptized in gratitude. While we come before God in one aspect empty-handed to receive of His goodness, on the other hand we should never appear before Him empty, but come with the fat of our sacrifices, offering praise and glorifying God.

HELP IN TROUBLE

Give us help from trouble.
PSALM 60:11 KJV

When we come before God in the hour of trouble, remembering His great goodness to us in the past and therefore thanking Him, we should have faith enough to believe that the present trouble about which we are praying is sent in love. You will win with God in prayer if you can look at your trials in this light: "Lord, I have this thorn in the flesh. I beg You, deliver me from it, but for now I bless You for it; for although I do not understand, I am persuaded there is love within it. Therefore, while I ask You to remove it, as it seems evil to me, yet it may to Your better knowledge be for my good. I bless You for it, and I am content to endure it as long as You see fit."

Is that not a sweet way of praying? "Lord, I am in want: Be pleased to supply me; but meanwhile, if You do not, I believe it is better for me to be in need, and so I praise You for my necessity while I ask You to supply it. I glory in my infirmity even while I ask You to overcome it. I triumph before You in my affliction and bless You for it even while I ask You to help me in it and to rescue me out of it."

Day 178
ASK GOD

I urge, then, first of all, that petitions, prayers,
intercession and thanksgiving be made for all people.
1 TIMOTHY 2:1 NIV

Whenever we are on our knees in prayer, it becomes us to bless God that our prayer has been answered so many times before. "Here Your poor petitioner bends before You to ask again, but as I ask, I thank You for having heard me so many times before. I know that You always hear me, therefore do I continue to cry to You. My thanksgivings urge me to make fresh petitions, encouraging me in the full confidence that You will not send me away empty."

Why, many of the mercies that you possess today and rejoice in are answers to prayer. They are dear to you because, like Samuel whom his mother so named because he was "asked of God," they came to you as answers to your supplications. When mercies come in answer to prayer, they have a double delight about them, not only because they are good in themselves but also because they are certificates of our favor with the Lord. Well then as God has heard us so often and we have the proofs of His hearing, should we ever pray with murmuring and complaining? Should we not rather feel an intense delight when we approach the throne of grace, a rapture awakened by sunny memories of the past?

Day 179
A THANKFUL SPIRIT

Through Him then, let's continually offer
up a sacrifice of praise to God, that is,
the fruit of lips praising His name.
HEBREWS 13:15 NASB

I believe that when a man begins to pray with thanksgiving, he is upon the eve of receiving the blessing. God's time to bless you has come when you begin to praise Him as well as pray to Him. God has His set time to favor us, and He will not grant us our desire until the due season has arrived. But the time has come when you begin to bless the Lord.

Our thanksgiving will show that the reason for our waiting is now exhausted; that the waiting has answered its purpose, and we may now come to a joyful end. Sometimes we are not in a fit state to receive a blessing, but when we reach the condition of thankfulness, then is the time when it is safe for God to indulge us. If you will but desire God to be glorified and aim at glorifying Him yourself, then the joys of true godliness will come to you in answer to prayer. The time for the blessing is when you begin to praise God for it. For, brethren, you may be sure that when you offer thanksgiving on the ground that God has answered your prayer, you really have prevailed with God.

WORK AS FOR THE LORD

Therefore, whether you eat or drink,
or whatever you do, do all to the glory of God.
1 CORINTHIANS 10:31 NKJV

Do we perhaps limit our estimate of serving God? You say, "I cannot serve God," when you cannot teach in the school or preach in the pulpit, when you are unable to sit on a committee or speak on a platform, as if these were the only forms of service to be taken into account. Do you not think that a mother nursing her baby is serving God? Do you not think that men and women going about their daily labor with patient diligence, fulfilling the duties of domestic life are serving God? If you think correctly, you will understand that they are.

The servant sweeping the room, the mistress preparing the meal, the workman driving a nail, the merchant completing his ledger ought to do all in the service of God. Though it is very desirable that we should each have some definitely religious work before us, yet it is much better that we should hallow our common skill and make our ordinary work chime with the melodies of a soul attuned for heaven. Let true religion be our life, and then our life will be true religion. Let the stream of your common life as it flows on be holy and courageous; you will find that you shall not be neglected or overlooked who simply sit at Jesus' feet and listen to His words when you can do no more. This is service done for Him which He can appreciate; complain who may.

Day 181
FAITH

Take up the shield of faith, with which you can
extinguish all the flaming arrows of the evil one.
EPHESIANS 6:16 NIV

Faith is that blessed grace which is most pleasing to God, and thus it is the most displeasing to the devil. By faith God is greatly glorified, and consequently by faith Satan is greatly annoyed. He rages at faith because he sees his own defeat and the victory of grace.

It is by our faith that we are saved, justified, and brought near to God, and therefore it is no marvel that it is attacked. It is by believing in Christ that we are delivered from the reigning power of sin and receive power to become the sons of God. Faith is as vital to salvation as the heart is vital to the body; for this reason the javelins of the enemy are mainly aimed at this essential grace. Faith is the standard-bearer, and the object of the enemy is to strike him down that the battle may be gained. All the powers of darkness which are opposed to right and truth are sure to fight against our faith, and manifold temptations will march in their legions against our confidence in God.

It is by our faith that we live; we began to live by it and continue to live by it. Faith is your jewel, your joy, your glory; and the thieves who haunt the pilgrim's way are all scheming to tear it from you. Hold fast; this your choice treasure.

Day 182

COMPLY WITH GOD'S WILL

And he who searches our hearts knows the mind of the Spirit, because the Spirit intercedes for the saints in accordance with the will of God.

ROMANS 8:27 NIV

Our Father's will will certainly be done, for the Lord "doeth according to His will in the army of heaven, and among the inhabitants of the earth." Let us adoringly consent that it shall be so, desiring no alteration in that.

That "will" may cost us dearly, yet let it never cross our wills: Let our minds be wholly subjugated to the mind of God. That "will" may bring us bereavement, sickness, and loss; but let us learn to say, "It is the Lord; let Him do what seems good."

We should not only yield to the divine will, but also acquiesce in it so as to rejoice in the tribulation which it ordains. This is a high attainment, but we set ourselves to reach it. He who taught us this prayer used it Himself in the most unrestricted sense. When the bloody sweat stood on His face, and all the fear and trembling of a man in anguish were upon Him, He did not dispute the decree of the Father but bowed His head and cried, "Nevertheless, not as I will, but as You will." When we are called to suffer bereavements personally, or when as a holy brotherhood we see our best men taken away, let us know that it is well and say most sincerely, "The will of the Lord be done."

Day 183
THE TWINKLING
OF AN EYE

We shall not all sleep, but we shall all be changed, in a
moment, in the twinkling of an eye, at the last trump.
1 CORINTHIANS 15:51–52 KJV

Between earth and heaven there is but a thin partition.
Heaven is much nearer than we think. I question if "the
land that is very far off" is a true name for heaven. Was it
not an extended kingdom on earth that was intended by the
prophet rather than the celestial home? Heaven is by no
means the far country, for it is the Father's house. Are we
not taught to say, "Our Father which art in heaven"? Where
the Father is, the true Spirit of adoption counts itself near.

Our Lord would have us mingle heaven with earth by
naming it twice in this short prayer. See how He makes
us familiar with heaven by mentioning it next to our usual
food, making the next petition to be "Give us this day our
daily bread." This does not look as if it should be thought
of as a remote region. Heaven is, at any rate, so near that
in a moment we can speak with Him who is King of the
place and He will answer to our call. Yes, before the clock
ticks again, you and I may be there. Can that be a far-off
country that we can reach so soon?

We are within hearing of the shining ones; we are nearly
home. A little while and we shall see our Lord. Perhaps
another day's march will bring us within the city gate. And
what if another fifty years of life on earth should remain,
what is it but the twinkling of an eye?

Day 184

GOD'S WILL
DONE IN HEAVEN

"Your will be done on earth as it is in heaven."
MATTHEW 6:10 NKJV

Mark the words "be done," for they touch a vital point of the text. God's will is "done" in heaven. How very practical! On earth His will is often forgotten and His rule ignored. In the Church of the present age, there is a desire to be doing something for God, but few inquire what He wills them to do.

I am afraid that Christ's will on earth is very much more discussed than done. I have heard of people spending days in disputing a precept that their dispute was breaking. In heaven they have no disputes, but they do the will of God without discord. We are best employed when we are actually doing something for this fallen world and for the glory of our Lord.

"Your will be done": We must come to actual works of faith and labors of love. Too often we are satisfied with having approved of that will or with having spoken of it in words of commendation. But we must not stay in thought, resolve, or word; the prayer is practical and businesslike: "Your will be 'done' on earth as it is in heaven." Up yonder there is no playing with sacred things: They do His commandments, heeding the voice of His Word. If only God's will were not merely preached and sung below, but actually "done" as it is in heaven.

FREE FAVOR

"I will. . .make You a covenant of the people."
ISAIAH 49:8 NASB

Jesus Christ is Himself the sum and substance of the covenant. Can you estimate what you have in Christ? "In Him dwelleth all the fullness of the Godhead bodily." Consider that word "God" and its infinity, and then meditate on "perfect man" and all His beauty; for all that Christ as God and man ever had or can have is yours—out of pure free favor, passed over to you to be yours forever. Our blessed Jesus, as God, is omniscient, omnipresent, omnipotent. Will it not console you to know that all these great and glorious attributes are altogether yours?

Is He powerful? That power is yours to support and strengthen you, to overcome your enemies, and to preserve you even to the end. Has He love? Well, there is not a drop of love in His heart that is not yours; you may dive into the immense ocean of His love, and you may say of it all, "It is mine." Does He have justice? It may seem a stern attribute, but even that is yours, for He will by His justice see to it that all that is promised to you in the covenant of grace shall be most certainly secured to you.

And all that He has as perfect man is yours. As a perfect man, the Father's delight was upon Him. He stood accepted by the Most High. God's acceptance of Christ is your acceptance; for the love that the Father set on a perfect Christ, He sets on you now. All that Christ did is yours.

---

*Grow in grace, and in the knowledge
of our Lord and Saviour Jesus Christ.*
2 PETER 3:18 KJV

"Grow in grace"—not in one grace only but in all grace. Grow in the starting place of grace: faith. Believe the promises more firmly than you have before. Let faith increase in fullness, constancy, simplicity. Grow also in love. Ask that your love may become extended, more intense, more practical, influencing every thought, word, and deed. Grow likewise in humility. Seek to lie very low and know more of your own nothingness. As you grow downward in humility, seek also to grow upward—having nearer approaches to God in prayer and more intimate fellowship with Jesus.

To know Him is "life eternal," and to advance in the knowledge of Him is to increase in happiness. Whoever has sipped this wine will thirst for more, for although Christ satisfies, yet it is such a satisfaction, that the appetite is not satisfied but whetted. If you know the love of Jesus, so will you pant after deeper draughts of His love. If you do not desire to know Him better, then you love Him not, for love always cries, "Nearer, nearer." Seek to know more of Him in His divine nature, in His human relationship, in His finished work, in His death, in His resurrection, in His present glorious intercession, and in His future royal advent. Remain by the cross and search the mystery of His wounds. An increase of love for Jesus, and a more perfect apprehension of His love for us, is one of the best tests of growth in grace.

CASTING OUR
CARES ON JESUS

Casting all your care upon him; for he careth for you.
1 PETER 5:7 KJV

It is a happy way of soothing sorrow when we feel "He cares for me." Come, cast your burden upon your Lord. You are staggering beneath a weight that your Father would not feel. What seems to you a crushing burden would be to Him but as dust.

Oh child of suffering, be patient; God has not passed you over in His providence. He who is the feeder of sparrows will also furnish you with what you need. Do not sit down in despair; hope on, hope ever. There is One who cares for you. His eye is fixed on you, His heart beats with pity for your woe, and His hand omnipotent will bring you the needed help. He, if you are one of His family, will bind up your wounds and heal your broken heart.

Do not doubt His grace because of your tribulation, but believe that He loves you as much in seasons of trouble as in times of happiness. What a serene and quiet life might you lead if you would leave providing to the God of providence! If God cares for you, why should you care too? Can you trust Him for your soul and not for your body? He has never refused to bear your burdens; He has never fainted under their weight.

Come then, soul! Cease fretting, and leave all your concerns in the hand of a gracious God.

Day 188

SWEET FELLOWSHIP WITH JESUS

Your love is better than wine.
SONG OF SOLOMON 1:2 NKJV

Nothing gives the believer as much joy as fellowship with Christ. Where can such sweetness be found as we have tasted in communion with our Beloved?

In our esteem, the joys of earth are little better than husks for swine compared with Jesus, the heavenly manna. We would rather have one mouthful of Christ's love and a sip of His fellowship than a whole world full of carnal delights. What is the chaff to the wheat? What is the sparkling paste to the true diamond? What is a dream to the glorious reality? What is time's mirth compared to our Lord Jesus in His most despised estate?

If you know anything of the inner life, you will confess that our highest, purest, and most enduring joys must be the fruit of the tree of life that is in the midst of the paradise of God. No spring yields such sweet water as that well of God which was dug with the soldier's spear. All earthly bliss is of the earth, but the comforts of Christ's presence are like Himself, heavenly. We can review our communion with Jesus and find no regrets of emptiness within.

The joy of the Lord is solid and enduring. Vanity has not looked upon it, but discretion and prudence testify that it abides the test of years, and is in time and in eternity worthy to be called "the only true delight." For nourishment, consolation, exhilaration, and refreshment, no wine can rival the love of Jesus.

Day 189
GOD IS MINE

"I will be their God."
JEREMIAH 31:33 NIV

Are you not complete when God is yours? Do you want anything but God? Is not His all-sufficiency enough to satisfy you if all else should fail? But you want more than quiet satisfaction; you desire rapturous delight. Come, soul, here is music fit for heaven in this your portion, for God is the Maker of heaven. Not all the music blown from sweet instruments or drawn from living strings can yield such melody as this sweet promise "I will be their God." Here is a deep sea of bliss, a shoreless ocean of delight; come, bathe your spirit in it; swim, and you will find no shore; dive throughout eternity, and you will find no bottom.

"I will be their God." If this does not make your eyes sparkle and your heart beat high with bliss, then assuredly your soul is not in a healthy state. But you want more than present delights—you crave something concerning which you may exercise hope; and what more can you hope for than the fulfillment of this great promise "I will be their God"? This is the masterpiece of all the promises; its enjoyment makes a heaven below and will make a heaven above. Dwell in the light of your Lord, and let your soul be always ravished with His love. Live up to your privileges, and rejoice with unspeakable joy.

BEHOLDING GOD

In my flesh shall I see God.
JOB 19:26 KJV

Mark the subject of Job's devout anticipation: "I shall see God." He does not say, "I shall see the saints"—though doubtless that will be untold delight—but "I shall see God." It is not "I shall see the pearly gates, I shall behold the walls of jasper, I shall gaze upon the crowns of gold," but "I shall see God." This is the sum and substance of heaven; this is the joyful hope of all believers. They love to behold Him in communion and in prayer; but there in heaven they shall have unclouded vision and therefore seeing "Him as He is" shall be made completely like Him.

Likeness to God—what more can we wish for? And a sight of God—what can we desire better? Christ shall be the object of our eternal vision; we shall never want any joy beyond that of seeing Him. It is but one source of delight, but that source is infinite. All His attributes shall be subjects for contemplation, and as He is infinite in each aspect, there is no fear of exhaustion. His works, His gifts, His love to us, and His glory in all His purposes and in all His actions, these shall make a theme that will be ever new.

Take realizing views of heaven's bliss; think what it will be to you. "Your eyes shall see the King in His beauty." All earthly brightness fades and darkens as we gaze upon it, but here is a brightness that can never dim, a glory that can never fade: "I shall see God."

Beginning to sink he cried out,
saying, "Lord, save me!"
MATTHEW 14:30 NKJV

Sinking times are praying times with the Lord's servants. Peter neglected prayer at the start of his venturous journey; but when he began to sink, his danger made him a beggar, and his cry, though late, was not too late. In our hours of bodily pain and mental anguish, we find ourselves naturally driven to prayer. The tried believer hastens to the mercy seat for safety; heaven's great harbor of refuge is prayer.

Short prayers are long enough. There were only three words in the petition that Peter gasped, but they were sufficient for his purpose. Not length but strength is desirable. A sense of need is a mighty teacher of brevity. All that is real prayer in many a long address might have been uttered in a petition as short as that of Peter.

Our boundaries are the Lord's opportunities. Immediately a keen sense of danger forces an anxious cry. The ear of Jesus hears, and with Him ear and heart go together and the hand does not long linger. At the last moment, we appeal to our Master, but His swift hand makes up for our delays by instant and effectual action. Are we nearly engulfed by the boisterous waters of affliction? Let us then lift up our souls unto our Savior, and we may rest assured that He will not suffer us to perish. When we can do nothing, Jesus can do all things; let us enlist His powerful aid upon our side, and all will be well.

GOD'S PROMISES

"Do as You have said."
2 SAMUEL 7:25 NKJV

God's promises were never meant to be thrown aside as wastepaper; He intended that they should be used. Nothing pleases our Lord better than to see His promises put in circulation; He loves to see His children bring them up to Him and say, "Lord, do as You have said." We glorify God when we plead His promises. Faith lays hold upon the promise of pardon, and it does not delay, saying, "This is a precious promise; I wonder if it be true?" but it goes straight to the throne with it and pleads, "Lord, here is the promise—do as You have said."

Our Lord replies, "Let it be done even as you will." When a Christian grasps a promise, if he does not take it to God, he dishonors Him; but when he hastens to the throne of grace and cries, "Lord, I have nothing to recommend me but this: You have said it," then his desire will be granted. Our heavenly Banker delights to cash His own notes.

Never let the promise rust. Draw the word of promise out of its cover, and use it with holy violence. Do not think that God will be troubled by your importunately reminding Him of His promises. He loves to hear the loud outcries of needy souls. It is His delight to bestow favors. He is more ready to hear than you are to ask. It is God's nature to keep His promises; therefore go at once to the throne with "Do as You have said."

NO TASK IS TOO
SMALL FOR GOD

"I will help you," declares the LORD.
ISAIAH 41:14 NASB

The Lord says to each one of us: "I will help you. It is but a small thing for Me, your God, to help you. Consider what I have done already. I bought you with My blood. I have died for you; and if I have done the greater, will I not do the less? Help you! It is the least thing I will ever do for you; I have done more and will do more. Before the world began, I chose you. I made the covenant for you. I laid aside My glory and became a man for you; I gave up My life for you; and if I did all this, I will surely help you now. In helping you, I am giving you what I have bought for you already. If you had need of a thousand times as much help, I would give it you; you require little compared with what I am ready to give. Help you? Do not fear! I will help you."

Oh my soul, is not this enough? Do you need more strength than the omnipotence of the united Trinity? Do you want more wisdom than exists in the Father, more love than displays itself in the Son, or more power than is manifest in the influences of the Spirit? Bring your empty pitcher! Surely this well will fill it. Gather up your wants and bring them here—your emptiness, your woes, your needs. Behold, this river of God is full for your supply; what can you desire beside? The eternal God is your helper!

Day 194

WEARY NO MORE

There remains therefore a rest for the people of God.
HEBREWS 4:9 NKJV

How different will be the state of the believer in heaven from what it is here! Here he toils and suffers weariness, but in the land of the immortal, fatigue is never known. Anxious to serve his Master, he finds his strength unequal to his zeal: His constant cry is "Help me to serve You, O my God."

Christian, the hot day of weariness does not last forever; the sun is nearing the horizon, and it shall rise again with a brighter day than you have ever seen upon a land where they serve God day and night, and yet rest from their labors. Here, rest is but partial; there, it is perfect. Here, the Christian is always unsettled; he feels that he has not yet attained. There, all are at rest; they have attained the summit of the mountain; they have ascended to the bosom of their God.

Ah, toil-worn laborer, only think when you shall rest forever! Can you conceive it? It is a rest eternal; a rest that "remains." Here, my best joys bear "mortal" on their brow, my fair flowers fade, my sweetest birds fall before death's arrows, my most pleasant days are shadowed into nights, and the floods of my bliss subside into ebbs of sorrow; but there, everything is immortal, the harp abides unrusted, the crown unwithered, the eye undimmed, the voice unfaltering, the heart unwavering, and the immortal being is wholly absorbed in infinite delight. Happy day! When mortality shall be swallowed up of life, and the eternal Sabbath shall begin.

Day 195
OUR CHOSEN CHRIST

I have exalted one chosen out of the people.
PSALM 89:19 KJV

Why was Christ chosen out of the people? Speak, my heart, for heart thoughts are best. Was it not that He might be able to be our Brother in the blessed tie of kindred blood? Oh, what relationship there is between Christ and the believer! The believer can say, "I have a Brother in heaven; I may be poor, but I have a Brother who is rich and is a King. He loves me; He is my Brother."

Believer, wear this blessed thought like a necklace of diamonds around the neck of your memory; put it as a golden ring on the finger of recollection, and use it as the King's own seal, stamping the petitions of your faith with confidence of success. He is a Brother born for adversity; treat Him as such.

Christ was also chosen out of the people that He might know our wants and sympathize with us. "He was tempted in all points like as we are, yet without sin." In all our sorrows we have His sympathy. Temptation, pain, disappointment, weakness, weariness, poverty—He knows them all, for He has felt all. Remember this, Christian, and let it comfort you. However difficult and painful your road, it is marked by the footsteps of your Savior; and even when you reach the dark valley of the shadow of death, you will find His footprints there. Wherever we go, He has been our forerunner; each burden we have to carry has once been laid on the shoulders of Immanuel.

Day 196

A REMINDER OF GOD'S LOVE

We will remember your love more than wine.
SONG OF SOLOMON 1:4 NKJV

Jesus will not let His people forget His love. If all the love they have enjoyed should be forgotten, He will visit them with fresh love. "Do you forget My cross?" He says. "I will cause you to remember it; for at My table I will manifest Myself anew to you. Do you forget what I did for you in the council chamber of eternity? I will remind you of it, for you shall need a counselor and shall find Me ready at your call."

Jesus says to us, "Remember Me," and our response is, "We will remember Your love." We will remember Your love and its matchless history. It is as ancient as the glory that You had with the Father before the world was. We remember, Jesus, Your eternal love. We remember the love that suggested the sacrifice of Yourself, the love which, until the fullness of time, mused over that sacrifice and longed for the hour when in the volume of the book it was written of You, "Lo, I come." We remember Your love, O Jesus, as it was manifest to us in Your holy life, from the manger of Bethlehem to the garden of Gethsemane. We track You from the cradle to the grave—for every word and deed of Yours was love—and we rejoice in Your love which death did not exhaust, Your love which shone resplendent in Your resurrection. We remember that burning fire of love that will never let You hold Your peace until Your chosen ones are all safely housed.

DELIVERANCE FROM DANGER

---

*Surely He shall deliver you
from the snare of the fowler.*
PSALM 91:3 NKJV

God delivers His people from the snare of the fowler in two senses. First, He delivers them from the snare—does not let them enter it—and secondly, if they should be caught in it, He delivers them out of it.

"He shall deliver you from the snare." How? Trouble is often the means whereby God delivers us. God knows that our backsliding will soon end in our destruction, and He in mercy sends the rod. We say, "Lord, why is this?" not knowing that our trouble has been the means of delivering us from far greater evil. Many have been saved from ruin by their sorrows and their crosses. At other times, God keeps His people from the snare of the fowler by giving them great spiritual strength, so that when they are tempted to do evil, they say, "How can I do this great wickedness and sin against God?" But what a blessed thing it is that if the believer shall, in an evil hour, fall into the net; God will bring him out of it!

Backslider, be cast down, but do not despair. Although you have been wandering, hear what your Redeemer says: "Return, backsliding children; I will have mercy upon you." You shall yet be brought out of all evil into which you have fallen, and though you shall never cease to repent of your ways, yet He who loves you will not cast you away; He will receive you and give you joy and gladness.

OBEDIENCE TO OUR HEAVENLY FATHER

"Your heavenly Father. . ."
MATTHEW 6:26 NIV

God's people are doubly His children: They are His offspring by creation, and they are His sons by adoption in Christ. Thus they are privileged to call Him, "Our Father which art in heaven." Father! Oh, what a precious word.

The obedience which God's children yield to Him must be loving obedience. Do not go about the service of God as slaves to a taskmaster's labor, but follow His commands because it is your Father's way. Yield your bodies as instruments of righteousness, because righteousness is your Father's will; and His will should be the will of His child.

Father! Here is a kingly attribute so sweetly veiled in love that the King's crown is forgotten in the King's face, and His scepter becomes not a rod of iron but a silver scepter of mercy—the scepter indeed seems to be forgotten in the tender hand of Him who wields it.

Father! Here is honor and love. How great is a father's love to his children! That which friendship cannot do and mere benevolence will not attempt, a father's heart and hand must do for his sons. They are his offspring, he must bless them; they are his children; he must show himself strong in their defense. If an earthly father watches over his children with unceasing love and care, how much more does our heavenly Father?

Abba, Father! There is heaven in the depth of that word—Father! There is all I can ask, all my necessities can demand, all my wishes can desire. I have all in all throughout all eternity when I can say, "Father."

OUR MARVELOUS GOD

All they that heard it wondered at those things.
LUKE 2:18 KJV

We must not cease to wonder at the great marvels of our God. It would be very difficult to draw a line between holy wonder and real worship; for when the soul is overwhelmed with the majesty of God's glory, though it may not express itself in song or even utter its voice with bowed head in humble prayer, yet it silently adores.

Our incarnate God is to be worshipped as "the Wonderful." That God should consider His fallen creature, man, and should Himself undertake to be man's Redeemer and to pay his ransom price is indeed marvelous! But to each believer, redemption is most marvelous as he views it in relation to himself. It is a miracle of grace indeed that Jesus should forsake the thrones and royalties above to suffer shamefully below for you. Let your soul lose itself in wonder, for wonder is in this way a very practical emotion. Holy wonder will lead you to grateful worship and heartfelt thanksgiving. It will cause within you godly watchfulness; you will be afraid to sin against such a love as this.

You will be moved at the same time to glorious hope. If Jesus has done such marvelous things on your behalf, you will feel that heaven itself is not too great for your expectation. Who can be astonished at anything when he has once been astonished at the manger and the cross? What is there wonderful left after one has seen the Savior?

STRENGTHEN, O GOD

Strengthen, O God, that which
thou hast wrought for us.
PSALM 68:28 KJV

It is our wisdom as well as our necessity to beseech God continually to strengthen "that which He has wrought in us." It is because of their neglect in this that many Christians may blame themselves for those trials and afflictions that arise from unbelief.

We often forget that the Author of our faith must be the Preserver of it also. The lamp burning in the temple was never allowed to go out, but it had to be daily replenished with fresh oil; in like manner, our faith can only live by being sustained with the oil of grace, and we can only obtain this from God Himself. He who built the world upholds it, or it would fall in one tremendous crash; He who made us Christians must maintain us by His Spirit, or our ruin will be speedy and final. Let us then go to our Lord for the grace and strength we need. Do you think He will fail to protect and sustain? Only let your faith take hold of His strength, and all the powers of darkness, led on by the master fiend of hell, cannot cast a cloud or shadow over your joy and peace.

Why faint when you may be strong? Why suffer defeat when you may conquer? Take your wavering faith and drooping graces to Him who can revive and replenish them, and earnestly pray, "Strengthen, O God, that which thou hast wrought for us."

MY LORD, MY ALL

"The LORD is my portion," says my soul.
LAMENTATIONS 3:24 NKJV

It is not "The Lord is partly my portion" nor "The Lord is in my portion," but He Himself makes up the sum total of my soul's inheritance. Within the circumference of that circle lies all that we possess or desire. "The Lord is my portion." Not His grace merely, nor His love, nor His covenant, but Jehovah Himself. He has chosen us for His portion, and we have chosen Him for ours. The Lord must first choose our inheritance for us, or else we shall never choose it for ourselves.

The Lord is our all-sufficient portion. God fills Himself, and if God is all-sufficient in Himself, He must be all-sufficient for us. It is not easy to satisfy man's desires. When he dreams that he is satisfied, he again wakes to the perception that there is more beyond, and without delay his heart cries, "Give." But all that we can wish for is to be found in our divine portion so that we ask, "Whom have I in heaven but You? And there is none upon earth that I desire beside You."

Well may we "delight ourselves in the Lord" who makes us to drink of the river of His pleasures. Our faith stretches her wings and mounts like an eagle into the heaven of divine love as to her proper dwelling place. Let us rejoice in the Lord always; let us show to the world that we are a happy and a blessed people, and thus induce them to exclaim, "We will go with you, for we have heard that God is with you."

THE UNSEEN PRIZE

The things which are not seen. . .
2 CORINTHIANS 4:18 KJV

In our Christian pilgrimage, it is well, for the most part, to be looking forward. Forward lies the crown, and onward is the goal. Whether it be for hope, for joy, for consolation, or for the inspiring of our love, the future must, after all, be the grand object of the eye of faith.

Looking into the future, we see sin cast out, the body of sin and death destroyed, the soul made perfect and fit to be a partaker of the inheritance of the saints in light. Looking further yet, the believer's enlightened eye can see death's river passed, the gloomy stream forded, and the hills of light attained on which stands the celestial city; he sees himself enter within the pearly gates, hailed as more than conqueror, crowned by the hand of Christ, embraced in the arms of Jesus, glorified with Him, and made to sit together with Him on His throne, even as He has overcome and has sat down with the Father on His throne.

The thought of this future may well relieve the darkness of the past and the gloom of the present. The joys of heaven will surely compensate for the sorrows of earth. Hush, my fears! This world is but a narrow span, and you shall soon have passed it. Hush, hush, my doubts! Death is but a narrow stream, and you shall soon have forded it. Time, how short—eternity, how long! Death, how brief—immortality, how endless! The road is so, so short! I shall soon be there.

Day 203
OUR INHERITANCE

In whom also we have obtained an inheritance.
EPHESIANS 1:11 KJV

When Jesus gave Himself for us, He gave us all the rights and privileges which went with Himself; so that now, although as eternal God, He has essential rights to which no creature may venture to pretend, yet as Jesus, the Mediator, the federal Head of the covenant of grace, He has no heritage apart from us. All the glorious consequences of His obedience unto death are the joint riches of all who are in Him and on whose behalf He accomplished the divine will. See, He enters into glory, but not for Himself alone.

Consider this, believer: You have no right to heaven in yourself—your right lies in Christ. If you are pardoned, it is through His blood; if you are justified, it is through His righteousness; if you are sanctified, it is because He is made of God unto your sanctification; if you shall be kept from falling, it will be because you are preserved in Christ Jesus; and if you are perfected at the last, it will be because you are complete in Him. Thus Jesus is magnified—for all is in Him and by Him; thus the inheritance is made certain to us—for it is obtained in Him; thus each blessing is the sweeter, and even heaven itself the brighter, because it is Jesus our Beloved "in whom" we have obtained all.

Reach the bottom of Christ's sea of joy, and then hope to understand the bliss that God has prepared for them who love Him.

PERFECT IN JESUS

"The LORD Our Righteousness. . ."
JEREMIAH 23:6 NASB

It will always give a Christian the greatest calm, quiet, ease, and peace to think of the perfect righteousness of Christ.

How often are the saints of God downcast and sad! I do not think they would be if they could always see their perfection in Christ. There are some who are always talking about corruption and the depravity of the heart and the innate evil of the soul. This is quite true, but why not go a little further and remember that we are "perfect in Christ Jesus."

It is no wonder that those who are dwelling upon their own corruption should wear such downcast looks; but surely if we call to mind that "Christ is made unto us righteousness," we shall be of good cheer. Though distresses afflict me, though Satan assault me, though there may be many things to be experienced before I get to heaven, those are done for me in the covenant of divine grace; there is nothing wanting in my Lord.

Christ has done it all. On the cross He said, "It is finished!" and if it is finished, then I am complete in Him and can rejoice with joy unspeakable and full of glory. You will not find on this side of heaven a holier people than those who receive into their hearts the doctrine of Christ's righteousness.

SING TO THE LORD

They will sing of the ways of the LORD.
PSALM 138:5 NASB

The time when Christians begin to sing in the ways of the Lord is when they first lose their burden at the foot of the cross. Not even the songs of the angels seem so sweet as the first song of rapture that gushes from the inmost soul of the forgiven child of God.

Believer, do you recollect the day when your fetters fell off? Do you remember the place where Jesus met you and said, "I have loved you with an everlasting love. I have blotted out as a cloud your transgressions, and as a thick cloud your sins; they shall not be mentioned against you anymore forever"? Oh! What a sweet season is that when Jesus takes away the pain of sin.

But it is not only at the commencement of the Christian life that believers have reason for song; as long as they live, they discover cause to sing in the ways of the Lord, and their experience of His constant loving-kindness leads them to say, "I will bless the Lord at all times: His praise shall continually be in my mouth." See to it, brother, that you magnify the Lord this day.

NOTHING CAN SEPARATE US FROM GOD

For I am persuaded, that neither death, nor life,
nor angels, nor principalities, nor powers, nor things
present, nor things to come, nor height, nor depth,
nor any other creature, shall be able to separate us from
the love of God, which is in Christ Jesus our Lord.
ROMANS 8:38–39 KJV

Look back through all your experiences and think of the way the Lord has led you in the wilderness, and how He has fed and clothed you every day, how He has put up with all your murmurings, how He has opened the rock to supply you and fed you with manna that came down from heaven. Think of how His grace has been sufficient for you in all your troubles, how His blood has been a pardon to you in all your sins, how His rod and His staff have comforted you. When you have looked back upon the love of the Lord, then let faith survey His love in the future, for remember that Christ's covenant and blood have something more in them than the past.

He who has loved you and pardoned you shall never cease to love and pardon. He is Alpha, and He shall be Omega, also: He is first, and He shall be last. Therefore when you pass through the valley of the shadow of death, you need fear no evil for He is with you. Death cannot separate you from His love. When you shall come into the mysteries of eternity, you need not tremble. Surely as we meditate on "the love of the Lord," our hearts burn within us and we long to love Him more.

THE NAME ABOVE
ALL NAMES

"You are to give him the name Jesus."
MATTHEW 1:21 NIV

When a person is dear, everything connected with him becomes dear for his sake. Thus so precious is the person of the Lord Jesus in the estimation of all true believers, that everything about Him they consider to be inestimable beyond all price. Certain it is that there is not a spot where that hallowed foot has trodden—there is not a word which those blessed lips have uttered nor a thought which His loving Word has revealed—which is not to us precious beyond all price. And this is true of the names of Christ—they are all sweet in the believer's ear.

Whether He be called the Husband of the Church, her Bridegroom, her Friend; whether He be styled the Lamb slain from the foundation of the world, the King, the Prophet, or the Priest, every title of our Master—Shiloh, Emmanuel, Wonderful, the Mighty Counselor—every name is like the honeycomb dripping with honey, and luscious are the drops that distill from it. But if there be one name sweeter than another in the believer's ear, it is the name of Jesus. Jesus! It is the name that moves the harps of heaven to melody. Jesus! The life of all our joys. If there be one name more charming, more precious than another, it is this name.

Day 208
MIRROR IMAGE OF JESUS

---

*They marveled. And they realized
that they had been with Jesus.*
ACTS 4:13 NKJV

A Christian should be a striking likeness of Jesus Christ. If we were what we profess to be and what we should be, we should be pictures of Christ—yes, such striking likenesses of Him that the world would not have to hold us up and say, "He seems somewhat of a likeness"; but they would, when they once beheld us, exclaim, "He has been with Jesus, he has been taught of Him, he is like Him, he has caught the very idea of the Holy Man of Nazareth, and he demonstrates it in his life and everyday actions."

A Christian should be like Christ in his boldness. Be like Jesus, valiant for your God. Imitate Him in your loving spirit; think kindly, speak kindly, and do kindly, that men may say of you, "He has been with Jesus." Imitate Jesus in His holiness. Was He zealous for His Master? So should you be; ever go about doing good. Was He self-denying, never looking to His own interest? Be the same. Was He devout? Be fervent in your prayers. Had He deference to His Father's will? So submit yourselves to Him. Was He patient? So learn to endure. And best of all, as the highest portraiture of Jesus, try to forgive your enemies as He did. Forgive as you hope to be forgiven. Heap coals of fire on the head of your foe by your kindness to him.

In all ways and by all means, so live that all may say of you, "He has been with Jesus."

OUR COMFORTER

He shall give you another Comforter,
that he may abide with you for ever.
JOHN 14:16 KJV

The great Father revealed Himself to believers of old and was known to Abraham, Isaac, and Jacob as the God Almighty. Then Jesus came, and the ever-blessed Son was the delight of His people's eyes. At the time of the Redeemer's ascension, the Holy Spirit became the head of the present dispensation, and His power was gloriously manifested on and after Pentecost. He remains at this hour the present Immanuel— God with us—dwelling in and with His people, guiding and ruling in their midst. Is His presence recognized as it should be?

We cannot control His working; He is most sovereign in all His operations, but are we sufficiently anxious to obtain His help or sufficiently watchful lest we provoke Him to withdraw His aid? Without Him we can do nothing, but by His almighty energy the most extraordinary results can be produced: Everything depends upon His manifesting or concealing His power. Do we always look up to Him with the respectful dependence that is fitting? Do we not too often run before His call and act independently of His aid? Let us humble ourselves for past neglects.

The Holy Spirit is no temporary gift; He abides with the saints. We have but to seek Him properly, and He will be found of us. He is jealous, but He is pitiful; if He leaves in anger, He returns in mercy. Condescending and tender, He does not weary of us but awaits to be gracious still.

Day 210
GLORY TO GOD!

To him be glory both now and forever!
2 PETER 3:18 NIV

Heaven will be full of the ceaseless praises of Jesus. Never shall His praises cease. That which was bought with blood deserves to last while immortality endures. O Jesus! You shall be praised forever. As long as immortal spirits live—as long as the Father's throne endures—forever unto You shall be glory.

Believer, you are anticipating the time when you shall join the saints above in ascribing all glory to Jesus; but are you glorifying Him now? The apostle's words are "To Him be glory both now and forever." Will you not this day make it your prayer? "Lord, help me to glorify You. I am poor, help me to glorify You by contentment; I am sick, help me to give You honor by patience; I have talents, help me to extol You by spending them for You; I have time, Lord, help me to redeem it that I may serve You; I have a heart to feel, Lord, let that heart feel no love but Yours and glow with no flame but affection for You; I have a head to think, Lord, help me to think of You and for You; You have put me in this world for something, Lord, show me what that is and help me to work out my life purpose. I cannot do much, but I am all Yours; take me and enable me to glorify You now, in all that I say, in all that I do, and with all that I have."

GROWING IN GRACE

"Show me why You contend with me."
JOB 10:2 NKJV

There are some of your graces that would never be discovered if it were not for your trials. Do you not know that your faith never looks so grand in summer as it does in winter? Love is too often like a glowworm, showing little light except in the midst of darkness. Hope is like a star—not to be seen in the sunshine of prosperity and only to be discovered in the night of adversity. Afflictions are often the black foils in which God sets the jewels of His children's graces to make them shine better.

A little while ago, you were on your knees saying, "Lord, I fear I have no faith: Let me know that I have faith." Was not this really, though perhaps unconsciously, praying for trials? For how can you know that you have faith until your faith is exercised? God often sends us trials so that our graces may be discovered and that we may be assured of their existence. Besides, it is not merely discovery; growth in grace is the result of sanctified trials. God often takes away our comforts and our privileges in order to make us better Christians. May this not account for the troubles that you are passing through? Is not the Lord bringing out your graces and making them grow?

THE GOD OF
ALL COMFORT

God, that comforteth those that are cast down...
2 CORINTHIANS 7:6 KJV

Who comforts like Him? Go to some poor, melancholy, distressed child of God; tell him sweet promises and whisper in his ear words of comfort. Comfort him as you may, it will be only a note or two of mournful resignation that you will get from him; you will bring forth no psalms of praise, no hallelujahs, no joyful sonnets. But let God come to His child, let Him lift up his countenance, and the mourner's eyes glisten with hope.

You could not have cheered him, but the Lord has done it: "He is the God of all comfort." It is marvelous how one sweet word of God will make whole songs for Christians. One word of God is like a piece of gold, and the Christian is the gold beater and can hammer that promise out for whole weeks.

So, Christian, you need not sit down in despair. Go to the Comforter, and ask Him to give you consolation. You are a poor, dry well. You have heard it said that when a pump is dry, you must pour water down it first, and then you will get water; and so, Christian, when you are dry, go to God, ask Him to shed abroad His joy in your heart, and then your joy shall be full. Do not go to earthly acquaintances, for you will find them Job's comforters after all; but go first and foremost to your "God who comforteth those who are cast down," and you will soon say, "In the multitude of my thoughts within me, Your comforts delight my soul."

GOD, SLOW TO ANGER

The LORD is slow to anger and great in power.
NAHUM 1:3 NKJV

Jehovah "is slow to anger." God takes no pleasure in the sinner's death. God's rod of mercy is ever in His hands outstretched; His sword of justice is in its scabbard, held down by that pierced hand of love that bled for the sins of men. "The Lord is slow to anger" because He is great in power. He is truly great in power who has power over himself. When God's power restrains Himself, then it is power indeed: The power that binds omnipotence is omnipotence surpassed.

God marks His enemies, and yet He bestirs not Himself but holds in His anger. If He were less divine than He is, He would long before this have sent forth the whole of His thunders and emptied the arsenal of heaven. He would long ago have blasted the earth with the wondrous fires of its lower regions, and man would have been utterly destroyed; but the greatness of His power brings us mercy.

Dear reader, what is your state? Can you by humble faith look to Jesus and say, "My substitute, You are my rock, my trust"? Then, beloved, be not afraid of God's power; for now that you are forgiven and accepted, now that by faith you have fled to Christ for refuge, the power of God need no more terrify you than the shield and sword of the warrior need terrify those whom He loves. Rather rejoice that He who is "great in power" is your Father and Friend.

CONSTANT COMPANIONSHIP

"I will never leave you nor forsake you."
HEBREWS 13:5 NKJV

No promise is of private interpretation. Whatever God has said to any one saint, He has said to all. When He opens a well for one, it is that all may drink. Whether He gave the Word to Abraham or to Moses matters not; He has given it to you as one of the covenanted seed.

There is not a high blessing too lofty for you nor a wide mercy too extensive for you. Lift up your eyes now to the north and to the south, to the east and to the west, for all this is yours; the land is all your own. There is not a brook of living water of which you may not drink. If the land flows with milk and honey, eat the honey and drink the milk, for both are yours.

Be bold to believe, for He has said, "I will never leave you nor forsake you." In this promise, God gives to His people everything. "I will never leave you." Then no attribute of God can cease to be engaged for us. Is He mighty? He will show Himself strong on behalf of those who trust Him. Is He love? Then with loving-kindness will He have mercy on us. Whatever attributes may compose the character of Deity, every one of them to its fullest extent shall be engaged on our side.

DWELL IN SAFETY

If. . .you make the Most High your dwelling,
no harm will overtake you.
PSALM 91:9–10 NIV

The Israelites in the wilderness were continually exposed to change. Whenever the pillar halted its motion, the tents were pitched; but tomorrow, before the morning sun had risen, the trumpet sounded, the ark was in motion, and the fiery, cloudy pillar was leading the way through the narrow defiles of the mountain, up the hillside, or along the arid waste of the wilderness. Yet they had an abiding home in their God, His cloudy pillar, and its flame by night. They must go onward from place to place, continually changing, never having time to settle and to say, "Now we are secure; in this place we shall dwell."

"Yet," says Moses, "though we are always changing, Lord, You have been our dwelling place throughout all generations." The Christian knows no change with regard to God. He may be rich today and poor tomorrow, he may be sickly today and well tomorrow, he may be in happiness today, tomorrow he may be distressed—but there is no change with regard to his relationship to God. If He loved me yesterday, He loves me today. My unmoving mansion of rest is my blessed Lord. Let prospects be ruined, let hopes be blasted, let joy be withered, let mildews destroy everything; I have lost nothing of what I have in God. He is "my strong habitation where unto I can continually resort." I am a pilgrim in the world but at home in my God. In the earth I wander, but in God I dwell in a quiet habitation.

Day 216
PRECIOUS JESUS

He is precious.
1 PETER 2:7 KJV

Peter tells us that Jesus is precious; but he did not and could not tell us how precious, nor could any of us compute the value of God's unspeakable gift. Words cannot set forth the preciousness of the Lord Jesus to His people nor fully tell how essential He is to their satisfaction and happiness.

Believer, have you not found in the midst of plenty a sore famine if your Lord has been absent? The sun was shining, but Christ had hidden Himself; and all the world was black to you—or it was night, and since the Bright and Morning Star was gone, no other star could yield you so much as a ray of light. What a howling wilderness is this world without our Lord! If once He hid Himself from us, withered are the flowers of our garden, our pleasant fruits decay, the birds suspend their songs, and a tempest overturns our hopes. All earth's candles cannot make daylight if the Sun of Righteousness is eclipsed. He is the soul of our soul, the light of our light, the life of our life.

Dear reader, what would you do in the world without Him, when you wake up and look forward to the day's battle? What would you do at night, when you come home jaded and weary, if there were no door of fellowship between you and Christ? Blessed be His name, He will not suffer us to try our lot without Him for Jesus never forsakes His own. Yet let the thought of what life would be without Him enhance His preciousness.

COMFORT IN AFFLICTION

I have chosen thee in the furnace of affliction.
ISAIAH 48:10 KJV

Let affliction come—God has chosen me. Poverty, you may enter my door, but God is in the house already; and He has chosen me. Sickness, you may intrude, but I have a balsam ready—God has chosen me. Whatever befalls me in this vale of tears, I know that He has "chosen" me.

If, believer, you require still greater comfort, remember that you have the Son of Man with you in the furnace. In that silent chamber of yours, there sits by your side One whom you have not seen but whom you love; and often when you know it not, He makes all your bed in your affliction and smooths your pillow for you. You are in poverty, but in that lonely house of yours, the Lord of life and glory is a frequent visitor. He loves to come into these desolate places that He may visit you. Your Friend sticks closely to you. You cannot see Him, but you may feel the pressure of His hands. Do you not hear His voice? Even in the valley of the shadow of death, He says, "Fear not, I am with you; be not dismayed for I am your God."

Fear not, Christian; Jesus is with you. In all your fiery trials, His presence is both your comfort and safety. He will never leave one whom He has chosen for His own. "Fear not for I am with you" is His sure word of promise to His chosen ones in the "furnace of affliction."

GRACE WITHOUT LIMIT

"My grace is sufficient for you."
2 CORINTHIANS 12:9 NKJV

If none of God's saints were poor and tried, we should not know half so well the consolations of divine grace. When we find the wanderer who does not have a place to lay his head, who yet can say, "Still will I trust in the Lord"; when we see the pauper starving on bread and water, who still glories in Jesus; when we see the bereaved widow overwhelmed in affliction, and yet having faith in Christ, oh, what honor it reflects on the Gospel.

God's grace is illustrated and magnified in the poverty and trials of believers. Saints bear up under every discouragement, believing that all things work together for their good and that out of apparent evils a real blessing shall ultimately spring—that their God will either work a deliverance for them speedily or most assuredly support them in the trouble, as long as He is pleased to keep them in it. This patience of the saints proves the power of divine grace.

He who would glorify his God must set his account upon meeting with many trials. No man can be illustrious before the Lord unless his conflicts are many. If then yours is a much-tried path, rejoice in it because you will better show forth the all-sufficient grace of God. As for His failing you, never dream of it—hate the thought. The God who has been sufficient until now should be trusted to the end.

Day 219
MY SALVATION

Say unto my soul, I am thy salvation.
PSALM 35:3 KJV

David had his doubts; for why should he pray, "Say unto my soul, I am your salvation," if he did not sometimes have doubts and fears? I am not the only saint who has to complain of weakness of faith. If David doubted, I need not conclude that I am no Christian because I have doubts. The text reminds me that David was not content while he had doubts and fears; but he went at once to the mercy seat to pray for assurance, for he valued it as much fine gold. I too must labor after an abiding sense of my acceptance in the Beloved.

David knew where to obtain full assurance. He went to God in prayer. I must be alone with God if I would have a clear sense of Jesus' love. Let my prayers cease, and my eye of faith will grow dim. Much in prayer, much in heaven; slow in prayer, slow in progress.

David would not be satisfied unless his assurance had a divine source. Nothing short of a divine testimony in the soul will ever content the true Christian. Moreover, David could not rest unless his assurance had a vivid personality about it.

"Lord, if You should say this to all the saints, it were nothing unless You should say it to me. I have sinned, I deserve not Your smile, I scarcely dare to ask it; but oh, say to my soul, even to my soul, 'I am your salvation.' Let me have a present, personal, infallible, indisputable sense that I am Yours and that You are mine."

ABIDING IN CHRIST

Abide in me.
JOHN 15:4 KJV

Communion with Christ is a certain cure for every ill. Live near to Jesus, Christian, and it is a matter of secondary importance whether you live on the mountain of honor or in the valley of humiliation. Living near to Jesus, you are covered with the wings of God and underneath you are the everlasting arms.

Let nothing keep you from that hallowed intercourse, which is the choice privilege of a soul wedded to the Well-Beloved. Seek always to retain His company, for only in His presence do you have comfort or safety. Jesus should not be unto us a friend who calls upon us now and then, but one with whom we walk evermore.

You have a difficult road before you: See that you do not go without your guide. You had to pass through the fiery furnace; do not enter it unless, like Shadrach, Meshach, and Abednego, you have the Son of God to be your companion. You have to storm the Jericho of your own corruptions: Do not attempt the warfare until, like Joshua, you have seen the Captain of the Lord's host with His sword drawn in His hand. In every case, in every condition, you will need Jesus, but most of all when the iron gates of death open to you.

Keep close to your soul's Husband, lean your head upon His bosom, and you shall be found of Him at the last, without spot or wrinkle or any such thing. Seeing you have lived with Him and lived in Him here, you shall abide with Him forever.

Day 221
SOUGHT OUT

Thou shalt be called, Sought out.
ISAIAH 62:12 KJV

The surpassing grace of God is seen very clearly in that we were not only sought, but also sought out. Men seek for a thing that is lost upon the floor of the house, but in such a case there is only seeking, not seeking out. The loss is more perplexing and the search more persevering when a thing is sought out.

Glory be to unconquerable grace, we were sought out! No gloom could hide us, no filthiness could conceal us; we were found and brought home. Glory be to infinite love, God the Holy Spirit restored us! The lives of some of God's people, if they could be written, would fill us with holy astonishment. Strange and marvelous are the ways which God used in their case to find His own.

Blessed be His name, He never relinquishes the search until the chosen are sought out effectually. They are not a people sought today and cast away tomorrow. Almightiness and wisdom combined will make no failures; they shall be called "Sought out"! That any should be sought out is matchless grace, but that we should be sought out is grace beyond degree! We can find no reason for it but God's own sovereign love and can only lift up our heart in wonder and praise the Lord that this night we wear the name of "Sought out."

Day 222
NEIGHBORLY LOVE

"You shall love your neighbor."
MATTHEW 5:43 NASB

"Love your neighbor." Perhaps he rolls in riches and you are poor. God has given him these gifts; covet not his wealth, and think no evil thoughts concerning him. Be content with your own lot if you cannot improve it, but do not look upon your neighbor and wish that he were as yourself. Love him, and then you will not envy him.

Perhaps you are rich and near you reside the poor. Do not resist calling them neighbor. You are bound to love them. The world calls them your inferiors. In what are they inferior? They are far more your equals than your inferiors. You are by no means better than they. They are men, and what are you more than that? Take heed that you love your neighbor even though he is in rags or sunken in the depths of poverty.

But perhaps you say, "I cannot love my neighbors, because for all I do, they return ingratitude and contempt." So much the more room for the heroism of love. He who dares the most shall win the most; and if rough be your path of love, tread it boldly, still loving your neighbors through thick and thin. Heap coals of fire on their heads, and if they be hard to please, seek not to please them but to please your Master; and remember if they spurn your love, your Master has not spurned it; and your deed is as acceptable to Him as if it had been acceptable to them. Love your neighbor, for in so doing, you are following the footsteps of Christ.

BEWARE OF BOASTING

*Let the one who thinks he stands
watch out that he does not fall.*

1 CORINTHIANS 10:12 NASB

It is a curious fact that there is such a thing as being proud of grace. He who boasts of grace has little grace to boast of. Take heed that you glory not in your graces, but let all your glorying and confidence be in Christ and His strength, for only so can you be kept from falling.

Be much more in prayer. Spend longer time in holy adoration. Read the scriptures more earnestly and constantly. Watch your lives more carefully. Live nearer to God. Take the best examples for your pattern. Let your conversation be redolent of heaven. Let your hearts be perfumed with affection for men's souls. So live that men may take knowledge of you that you have been with Jesus and have learned of Him; and when that happy day shall come, when He whom you love shall say, "Come up higher," may it be your happiness to hear Him say, "You have fought a good fight, you have finished your course, and therefore there is laid up for you a crown of righteousness which does not fade away."

On, Christian, with care and caution! On, with holy fear and trembling! On, with faith and confidence in Jesus alone, and let your constant petition be, "Uphold me according to Your Word." He is able, and He alone, "to keep you from falling, and to present you faultless before the presence of His glory with exceeding joy."

THE GRACE OF CHRIST

Be strong in the grace that is in Christ Jesus.
2 TIMOTHY 2:1 NIV

Christ has grace without measure in Himself, but He has not retained it for Himself. As the reservoir empties itself into the pipes, so has Christ emptied out His grace for His people. He stands like the fountain, always flowing, but only running in order to supply the empty pitchers and the thirsty lips which draw near to it. Like a tree, He bears sweet fruit, not to hang on boughs but to be gathered by those who need. Grace, whether its work be to pardon, to cleanse, to preserve, to strengthen, to enlighten, to quicken, or to restore, is ever to be had from Him freely and without price; nor is there one form of the work of grace which He has not bestowed upon His people.

As the blood of the body, though flowing from the heart, belongs equally to every member, so the influences of grace are the inheritance of every saint; and herein there is a sweet communion between Christ and His Church, inasmuch as they both receive the same grace. As we day by day receive grace from Jesus and more constantly recognize it as coming from Him, we shall behold Him in communion with us and enjoy the felicity of communion with Him. Let us make daily use of our riches, taking from Him the supply of all we need with as much boldness as men take money from their own purse.

BE DILIGENT AND PROSPER

He did it with all his heart, and prospered.
2 CHRONICLES 31:21 KJV

It is the general rule of the moral universe that those men prosper who do their work with all their hearts, while those are almost certain to fail who go to their labor leaving half their hearts behind them. God is not pleased to send wealth to those who will not dig in the field to find its hidden treasure.

It is universally confessed that if a man would prosper, he must be diligent in business. It is the same in religion as it is in other things. If you would prosper in your work for Jesus, let it be heart work and let it be done with all your heart. Put as much force, energy, heartiness, and earnestness into religion as you do into business, for it deserves far more. The Holy Spirit helps our infirmities, but He does not encourage our idleness; He loves active believers. Wholeheartedness shows itself in perseverance; there may be failure at first, but the earnest worker will say, "It is the Lord's work, and it must be done; my Lord has bidden me do it, and in His strength I will accomplish it."

Christian, are you "with all your heart" serving your Master? Remember the earnestness of Jesus! Think what heart work was His! When He sweat great drops of blood, it was no light burden He had to carry upon those blessed shoulders; and when He poured out His heart, it was no weak effort He was making for the salvation of His people. Was Jesus in earnest, and are we lukewarm?

Day 226

PEACEMAKERS

"Blessed are the peacemakers, for they will be called children of God."

MATTHEW 5:9 NIV

This is the seventh of the beatitudes, and seven was the number of perfection among the Hebrews. It may be that the Savior placed the peacemaker seventh on the list because he most nearly approaches the perfect man in Christ Jesus.

He who would have perfect blessedness, as far as it can be enjoyed on earth, must become a peacemaker. The verse which precedes it speaks of the blessedness of "the pure in heart, for they shall see God." It is well to understand that we are to be "first pure, then peaceable." Our peaceableness is never to be a compact with sin or toleration of evil. We must set our faces against everything which is contrary to God and His holiness: Purity being in our souls a settled matter, we can go on to peaceableness.

The verse that follows seems to have been put there on purpose. However peaceable we may be in this world, yet we shall be misrepresented and misunderstood; and no marvel, for even the Prince of Peace, by His very peacefulness, brought fire upon the earth. He Himself, though He loved mankind and did no ill, was "despised and rejected of men, a man of sorrows and acquainted with grief." Lest, therefore, the peaceable in heart should be surprised when they meet with enemies, it is added in the following verse, "Blessed are they who are persecuted for righteousness' sake, for theirs is the kingdom of heaven." Thus the peacemakers are not only pronounced to be blessed but they are compassed about with blessings.

GOD OUR FATHER

For you are all sons and daughters of
God through faith in Christ Jesus.
GALATIANS 3:26 NASB

The Fatherhood of God is common to all His children. Peter and Paul, the highly favored apostles, were of the family of the Most High, and so are you also, the weak Christian is as much a child of God as the strong one.

All the names are in the same family register. One may have more grace than another, but God our heavenly Father has the same tender heart toward all. One may do more mighty works and may bring more glory to his Father, but he whose name is the least in the kingdom of heaven is as much the child of God as he who stands among the King's mighty men. Let this cheer and comfort us when we draw near to God and say, "Our Father."

Yet while we are comforted by knowing this, let us not rest contented with weak faith but ask, like the apostles, to have it increased. However feeble our faith may be, if it be real faith in Christ, we shall reach heaven at last; but we shall not honor our Master much on our pilgrimage, neither shall we abound in joy and peace. If then you would live to Christ's glory and be happy in His service, seek to be filled with the Spirit of adoption more and more completely, until perfect love shall cast out fear.

CRUCIFIED WITH CHRIST

I have been crucified with Christ.
GALATIANS 2:20 NKJV

The Lord Jesus Christ acted in what He did as a great public representative person, and His dying upon the cross was the virtual dying of all His people. Then all His saints rendered unto justice what was due and made a reparation to divine vengeance for all their sins. The apostle of the Gentiles delighted to think that as one of Christ's chosen people he died upon the cross in Christ. He did more than believe this doctrinally; he accepted it confidently, resting his hope upon it. He believed that by virtue of Christ's death he had satisfied divine justice and found reconciliation with God.

Beloved, what a blessed thing it is when the soul can, as it were, stretch itself upon the cross of Christ and feel "I am dead; the law has slain me, and I am therefore free from its power, because in my Surety I have borne the curse and in the person of my Substitute the whole that the law could do by way of condemnation has been executed upon me, for I am crucified with Christ."

The Christian's life is a matchless riddle. No human can comprehend it; even the believer himself cannot understand it. Dead, yet alive! Crucified with Christ, and yet at the same time risen with Christ in newness of life! Union with the suffering, bleeding Savior and death to the world and sin are soul-cheering things. Oh, for more enjoyment of them!

Day 229

INCOMPREHENSIBLE LOVE

The love of Christ which surpasses knowledge. . .
EPHESIANS 3:19 NASB

The love of Christ in its sweetness, its fullness, its greatness, its faithfulness passes all human comprehension. Where shall language be found which shall describe His matchless, His unparalleled love toward the children of men? For this love of Christ is indeed measureless and fathomless; none can attain unto it.

Before we can have any right idea of the love of Jesus, we must understand His previous glory in its height of majesty and His incarnation upon the earth in all its depths of shame. But who can tell us the majesty of Christ? When He was enthroned in the highest heavens, He was very God of very God; by Him were the heavens made, and all the hosts of it. His own almighty arm upheld the spheres, the praises of cherubim and seraphim perpetually surrounded Him, the full chorus of the hallelujahs of the universe unceasingly flowed to the foot of His throne—He reigned supreme above all His creatures, God over all, blessed forever. Who can tell His height of glory then? And who, on the other hand, can tell how low He descended?

To be a man was something, to be a man of sorrows was far more; to bleed and die and suffer, these were much for Him who was the Son of God; but to suffer such unparalleled agony—to endure a death of shame and desertion by His Father, this is a depth of condescending love which the most inspired mind must utterly fail to fathom. This is love! Oh, let this love fill our hearts with adoring gratitude.

Let us search and try our ways,
and turn again to the LORD.

LAMENTATIONS 3:40 KJV

The spouse who fondly loves her absent husband longs for his return; an extended separation is a semideath to her spirit. And so with souls who love the Savior greatly, they must see His face; they cannot bear that He should be away and no more hold communion with them. A reproaching glance, an uplifted finger will be grievous to loving children who fear to offend their tender Father and are only happy in His smile. It was so once with you.

A scripture, a threatening, a touch of the rod of affliction, and you went to your Father's feet, crying, "Show me wherefore You contendest with me?" Is it so now? Are you content to follow Jesus from a distance? Can you contemplate suspended communion with Christ? Can you bear to have your Beloved walking contrary to you because you walk contrary to Him? Have your sins separated you and your God?

Let me affectionately warn you, for it is a grievous thing when we can live contentedly without the present enjoyment of the Savior's face. No matter how hard, how insensible, how dead we may have become, let us go again in all the rags and poverty and defilement of our natural condition. Let us clasp that cross, let us look into those languid eyes, let us bathe in that fountain filled with blood—this will bring back to us our first love; this will restore the simplicity of our faith and the tenderness of our heart.

HIS WOUNDS
REMOVED OUR SIN

By his wounds we are healed.
ISAIAH 53:5 NIV

Pilate delivered our Lord to the lictors to be scourged. The Roman scourge was a most dreadful instrument of torture. It was made of the sinews of oxen, and sharp bones were intertwined among the sinews; so that every time the lash came down, these pieces of bone inflicted fearful laceration and tore off the flesh from the bone. The Savior was, no doubt, bound to the column and thus beaten. He had been beaten before; but this of the Roman lictors was probably the most severe of His scourgings.

My soul, stand here and weep over His poor stricken body. Believer, can you gaze upon Him without tears as He stands before you, the mirror of agonizing love? He is at once fair as the lily for innocence and red as the rose with the crimson of His own blood. As we feel the sure and blessed healing that His stripes have wrought in us, does not our heart melt at once with love and grief? If ever we have loved our Lord Jesus, surely we must feel that affection glowing now within our bosoms.

We would be compelled to go to our chambers and weep, but since our business calls us away, we will first pray our Beloved to print the image of His bleeding self upon the tablets of our hearts all the day; and at nightfall we will return to commune with Him and sorrow that our sin should have cost Him so dearly.

THE KINGDOM OF GOD

He will see his offspring and prolong his days,
and the will of the LORD will prosper in his hand.
ISAIAH 53:10 NIV

Whenever you are praying for the kingdom of Christ, let your eyes behold the dawning of the blessed day which draws near, when the Crucified shall receive His coronation in the place where men rejected Him.

Courage, you who prayerfully work and toil for Christ with success of the very smallest kind, it shall not be so always; better times are before you. Your eyes cannot see the blissful future: Borrow the telescope of faith, wipe the misty breath of your doubts from the glass, look through it and behold the coming glory. Do you make this your constant prayer? Remember that the same Christ who tells us to say, "Give us this day our daily bread," had first given us this petition: "Hallowed be Your name, Your kingdom come, Your will be done on earth as it is in heaven."

Let not your prayers be all concerning your own sins, your own wants, your own imperfections, your own trials, but let them climb the starry ladder and get up to Christ Himself; and then, as you draw nigh to the mercy seat, offer this prayer continually: "Lord, extend the kingdom of Your dear Son." Such a petition, fervently presented, will elevate the spirit of all your devotions. Mind that you prove the sincerity of your prayer by laboring to promote the Lord's glory.

GRACE TO SOAR

"Come, let's go up to the mountain of the LORD."
ISAIAH 2:3 NASB

It is exceedingly beneficial to our souls to mount above this present evil world to something nobler and better. The cares of this world and the deceitfulness of riches are apt to choke everything good within us, and we grow fretful, desponding, perhaps proud and carnal. It is well for us to cut down these thorns and briers, for heavenly seed sown among them is not likely to yield a harvest; and where shall we find a better sickle with which to cut them down than communion with God and the things of the kingdom?

May the Spirit of God assist us to leave the mists of fear and the fevers of anxiety, and all the ills that gather in this valley of earth, and to ascend the mountains of anticipated joy and blessedness. May God the Holy Spirit cut the cords that keep us here below and assist us to mount! We sit too often like chained eagles fastened to the rock; only that, unlike the eagle, we begin to love our chain, and would perhaps, if it came really to the test, be reluctant to have it snapped. May God now grant us grace, if we cannot escape from the chain as to our flesh, yet to do so as to our spirits; and leaving the body, like a servant, at the foot of the hill, may our soul, like Abraham, attain the top of the mountain, there to indulge in communion with the Most High.

HUMILITY

Before honor comes humility.
PROVERBS 15:33 NASB

Humiliation of soul always brings a positive blessing with it. If we empty our hearts of self, God will fill them with His love. Stoop if you would climb to heaven. You must grow downward that you may grow upward; for the sweetest fellowship with heaven is to be had by humble souls, and by them alone.

God will deny no blessing to a thoroughly humbled spirit. "Blessed are the poor in spirit, for theirs is the kingdom of heaven" with all its riches and treasures. God blesses us all up to the full measure and extremity of what it is safe for Him to do. If you do not get a blessing, it is because it is not safe for you to have one. If our heavenly Father were to let your unhumbled spirit win a victory in His holy war, you would pilfer the crown for yourself; and meeting with a fresh enemy, you would fall a victim, so that you are kept low for your own safety.

When a man is sincerely humble and never ventures to touch so much as a grain of the praise, there is scarcely any limit to what God will do for him. Humility makes us ready to be blessed by the God of all grace and fits us to deal efficiently with our fellowmen. True humility is a flower that will adorn any garden. Whether it is prayer or praise, whether it is work or suffering, the genuine salt of humility cannot be used in excess.

A PRAYER OF REPENTANCE

Deliver me from bloodguiltiness, O God,
thou God of my salvation: and my tongue
shall sing aloud of thy righteousness.
PSALM 51:14 KJV

In this solemn confession, observe that David plainly names his sin. He does not call it manslaughter nor speak of it as an imprudence by which an unfortunate accident occurred to a worthy man, but he calls it by its true name: bloodguiltiness. He did not actually kill the husband of Bathsheba; but still it was planned in David's heart that Uriah should be slain, and he was before the Lord his murderer.

Learn in confession to be honest with God. Do not give fair names to foul sins; call them what you will, they will smell no sweeter. What God sees them to be, that do you labor to feel them to be; and with all openness of heart, acknowledge their real character. Observe that David was evidently oppressed with the heinousness of his sin. It is easy to use words, but it is difficult to feel their meaning. The fifty-first Psalm is the photograph of a contrite spirit. Let us seek after like brokenness of heart; for however excellent our words may be, if our heart is not conscious of the hell-deservingness of sin, we cannot expect to find forgiveness.

The psalmist ends with a commendable vow: If God will deliver him, he will "sing aloud." Who can sing in any other style of such a mercy as this! But note the subject of the song—"thy righteousness." We must sing of the finished work of a precious Savior, and he who knows most of forgiving love will sing the loudest.

TRUST IN GOD'S PROTECTION

I will fear no evil; for You are with me.
PSALM 23:4 NKJV

How firm, how happy, how calm, how peaceful we may be, when the world shakes to and fro and the pillars of the earth are removed! Even death itself with all its terrible influences has no power to suspend the music of a Christian's heart but rather makes that music become more sweet, more clear, more heavenly, until the last kind act which death can do is to let the earthly strain melt into the heavenly chorus, the temporal joy into the eternal bliss! Let us have confidence then in the blessed Spirit's power to comfort us.

Are you in poverty? Fear not; the divine Spirit can give you, in your want, a greater plenty than the rich have in their abundance. You do not know what joys may be stored up for you. Are you conscious of a growing failure of your bodily powers? Do you expect to suffer long nights of languishing and days of pain? Do not be sad! That bed may become a throne to you.

You little know how every pang that shoots through your body may be a refining fire to consume your dross—a beam of glory to light up the secret parts of your soul. Are the eyes growing dim? Jesus will be your light. Do the ears fail you? Jesus' name will be your soul's best music, and His person your dear delight. In You, my God, my heart shall triumph, come what ills! By Your power, Oh blessed Spirit, my heart shall be exceedingly glad, though all things should fail me here below.

CALVARY

The place, which is called Calvary. . .
LUKE 23:33 KJV

The hill of comfort is the hill of Calvary, the house of consolation is built with the wood of the cross, the temple of heavenly blessing is founded upon the fractured rock— fractured by the spear that pierced His side. No scene in sacred history ever gladdens the soul like Calvary's tragedy.

Light springs from Golgotha, and every herb of the field blooms sweetly beneath the shadow of the once accursed tree. In that place of thirst, grace has dug a fountain which ever gushes with waters pure as crystal, each drop capable of alleviating the woes of mankind. You who have had your seasons of conflict will confess that it was not at Olivet that you ever found comfort, not on the hill of Sinai nor on Tabor; but Gethsemane and Golgotha have been a means of comfort to you. The bitter herbs of Gethsemane have often taken away the bitters of your life, and the groans of Calvary yield us comfort rare and rich.

We would have never known Christ's love in all its heights and depths if He had not died; nor could we guess the Father's deep affection if He had not given His Son to die. The common mercies we enjoy all sing of love, just as the seashell, when we put it to our ears, whispers of the deep sea; but if we desire to hear the ocean itself, we must not look at everyday blessings but at the transactions of the crucifixion. He who would know love, let him retire to Calvary and see the Man of Sorrows die.

Day 238
FORGIVE MY SINS

Look on my affliction and my pain,
and forgive all my sins.
PSALM 25:18 NKJV

It is good for us when prayers about our sorrows are linked with pleas concerning our sins—when, being under God's hand, we are not wholly taken up with our pain but remember our offences against God. It is good, also, to take both sorrow and sin to the same place. It was to God that David carried his sorrow; it was to God that David confessed his sin. Even your little sorrows you may turn over to God, for He counts the hairs of your head; and your great sorrows you may commit to Him, for He holds the ocean in the hollow of His hand. Go to Him, whatever your present trouble, and you will find Him able and willing to relieve you. But we must take our sins to God too. We must carry them to the cross, that the blood may fall upon them, to purge away their guilt.

We are to go to the Lord with sorrows and with sins in the right spirit. David cries, "Lord, as for my affliction and my pain, I will not dictate to Your wisdom. I will leave them to You; I would be glad if my pain were removed, but do as You will. As for my sins, Lord, I know what I want with them; I must have them forgiven—I cannot endure to lie under their curse for a moment." A Christian counts sorrow lighter in the scale than sin; he can bear that his troubles should continue, but he cannot support the burden of his transgressions.

Day 239

BLESSING FOR THE BLESSED

Say to the righteous that it will go well for them.
ISAIAH 3:10 NASB

From the beginning of the year to the end of the year, from the first gathering of evening shadows until the daystar shines, in all conditions and under all circumstances, it shall be well with the righteous. It is so well with him that we could not imagine it to be better, for he is well fed, he feeds upon the flesh and blood of Jesus; he is well clothed, he wears the imputed righteousness of Christ; he is well housed, he dwells in God; he is well married, his soul is knit in bonds of marriage union to Christ; he is well provided for, for the Lord is his Shepherd; he is well endowed, for heaven is his inheritance. It is well with the righteous—well upon divine authority; the mouth of God speaks the comforting assurance.

Oh beloved, if God declares that all is well, ten thousand devils may declare it to be ill, but we laugh them all to scorn. Blessed be God for a faith that enables us to believe God when the creatures contradict Him. It is, says the Word, at all times well with you, righteous one; then, beloved, if thou cannot see it, let God's Word sustain you instead of sight. Yes, believe it on divine authority more confidently than if your eyes and feelings told it to you. Whom God blesses is blessed indeed, and what His lip declares is truth most sure and steadfast.

Day 240

GOD'S CHILDREN
ENCOURAGED

Lift them up for ever.
PSALM 28:9 KJV

God's people need lifting up. They are very heavy by nature. By nature sparks fly upward, but the sinful souls of men fall downward. O Lord, "lift them up forever!" David himself said, "Unto Thee, O God, do I lift up my soul," and he here feels the necessity that other men's souls should be lifted up as well as his own. When you ask this blessing for yourself, do not forget to seek it for others also.

There are three ways in which God's people require to be lifted up. They require being elevated in character. Lift them up, O Lord; do not let Your people to be like the world's people! The world lies in the wicked one. The world's people are looking after silver and gold, seeking their own pleasures and the gratification of their lusts; but Lord, lift Your people up above all this! Set their hearts upon their risen Lord and the heavenly heritage! Furthermore, believers need to be prospered in conflict. In the battle, if they seem to fall, O Lord, be pleased to give them the victory. If the foot of the foe is upon their necks for a moment, help them to grasp the sword of the Spirit and eventually to win the battle. Lord, lift up Your children's spirits in the day of conflict; let them not sit in the dust, mourning forever. Suffer not the adversary to trouble them and make them fret; but if they have been, like Hannah, persecuted, let them sing of the mercy of a delivering God.

THE BLOOD OF CHRIST

The precious blood of Christ. . .
1 PETER 1:19 NIV

Standing at the foot of the cross, we see hands and feet and side, all pouring forth crimson streams of precious blood. It is "precious" because of its redeeming and atoning efficacy. By it the sins of Christ's people are atoned for; they are redeemed from under the law—they are reconciled to God, made one with Him.

Christ's blood is also "precious" in its cleansing power; it "cleans from all sin." "Though your sins be as scarlet, they shall be as white as snow." Through Jesus' blood there is not a spot left upon any believer; no wrinkle nor any such thing remains. Oh, precious blood which makes us clean, removing the stains of abundant iniquity and permitting us to stand accepted in the Beloved, notwithstanding the many ways in which we have rebelled against our God.

The blood of Christ is likewise "precious" in its preserving power. We are safe from the destroying angel under the sprinkled blood. Remember it is God's seeing the blood that is the true reason for our being spared. Here is comfort for us when the eye of faith is dim, for God's eye is still the same.

The blood of Christ is "precious" also in its sanctifying influence. The same blood that justifies by taking away sin quickens the new nature and leads it onward to subdue sin and to follow out the commands of God. There is no motive for holiness so great as that which streams from the veins of Jesus.

DEATH DEFEATED

*That through death He might destroy
him who had the power of death. . .*
HEBREWS 2:14 NKJV

Oh child of God, death has lost its sting because the devil's power over it is destroyed. Then cease to fear dying. Ask grace from God the Holy Spirit, that by an intimate knowledge and a firm belief of your Redeemer's death, you may be strengthened for that hour.

Living near the cross of Calvary, you may think of death with pleasure and welcome it when it comes with intense delight. It is sweet to die in the Lord: It is a covenant blessing to sleep in Jesus. Death is no longer banishment; it is a return from exile, a going home to the many mansions where the loved ones already dwell.

The distance between glorified spirits in heaven and militant saints on earth seems great, but it is not so. We are not far from home—a moment will bring us there. "Absent from the body, present with the Lord." Think not that a long period intervenes between the instant of death and the eternity of glory. When the eyes close on earth, they open in heaven. Then, child of God, what is there for you to fear in death, seeing that through the death of your Lord its curse and sting are destroyed?

MY REDEEMER

"I know that my Redeemer lives."
JOB 19:25 NKJV

Job's comfort lies in that little word *my*—"my Redeemer"—and in the fact that the Redeemer lives. Oh, to get hold of a living Christ! We must take hold of Him before we can enjoy Him. Do not rest until by faith you can say, "Yes, I cast myself upon my living Lord, and He is mine." It may be you hold Him with a feeble hand; you somewhat think it presumption to say, "He lives as my Redeemer." Yet remember, if you have but faith as a mustard seed, that little faith entitles you to say it.

But there is also another word here, expressive of Job's strong confidence: "I know." To say "I hope so; I trust so" is comfortable, and there are thousands in the fold of Jesus who hardly ever get much further. But to reach the essence of consolation, you must say, "I know." Ifs, buts, and perhapses are sure murderers of peace and comfort. Doubts are dreary things in times of sorrow. Surely if Job, in those ages before the coming and advent of Christ, could say, "I know," we should not speak less positively.

God forbid that our positiveness should be presumption. Let us see that our evidences are right, lest we build upon an ungrounded hope; and then let us not be satisfied with the mere foundation, for it is from the upper rooms that we get the widest prospect. A living Redeemer, truly mine, is joy unspeakable.

THE RIGHT HAND OF GOD

Who is at the right hand of God. . .
ROMANS 8:34 NASB

He who was once despised and rejected of men now occupies the honorable position of a beloved and honored Son. The right hand of God is the place of majesty and favor. Our Lord Jesus is His people's representative. When He died for them, they had rest; when He rose again for them, they had liberty; when He sat down at His Father's right hand, they had favor and honor and dignity. The raising and elevation of Christ is the elevation, the acceptance and enshrinement, the glorifying of all His people, for He is their head and representative. This sitting at the right hand of God then is to be viewed as the acceptance of our souls. Dear saint, see in this your sure freedom from condemnation. "Who is he that condemneth?" Who shall condemn the men who re in Jesus at the right hand of God?

The right hand is the place of power. Christ at the right hand of God has all power in heaven and on earth. Who shall fight against the people who have such power vested in their Captain? Oh my soul, what can destroy you if Omnipotence is your helper? If the protection of the Almighty covers you, what sword can smite you? Rest secure. If Jesus is your all-prevailing King and has trodden your enemies beneath His feet; if sin, death, and hell are all vanquished by Him and you are represented in Him, by no possibility can you be destroyed.

JESUS IS EXALTED

"God exalted him."

ACTS 5:31 NIV

Jesus our Lord, once crucified, dead, and buried, now sits upon the throne of glory. The highest place that heaven affords is His by undisputed right. He is exalted at the Father's right hand, and though as Jehovah He had eminent glories in which finite creatures cannot share, yet as the Mediator, the honors that Jesus wears in heaven are the heritage of all the saints.

We are actually one with Him, we are members of His body, and His exaltation is our exaltation. He cannot be glorified without His bride. Look up to Jesus now, let the eye of your faith behold Him with many crowns upon His head, and remember that you will one day be like Him, when you shall see Him as He is; you shall not be so great as He is, you shall not be so divine, but still you shall, in a measure, share the same honors and enjoy the same happiness and the same dignity which He possesses.

Be content to live unknown for a little while and to walk your weary way through the fields of poverty or up the hills of affliction; for soon you shall reign with Christ, for He has "made us kings and priests unto God, and we shall reign forever and ever." Oh, wonderful thought for the children of God! We have Christ for our glorious representative in heaven's courts now, and soon He will come and receive us to Himself, to be with Him there, to behold His glory, and to share His joy.

Day 246

CALM IN THE
MIDST OF TERROR

You shall not be afraid of the terror by night.
PSALM 91:5 NKJV

What is this terror? It may be the cry of "Fire!" or the noise of thieves or the shriek of sudden sickness or death. We live in the world of death and sorrow. This should not alarm us, for be the terror what it may, the promise is that the believer shall not be afraid.

Why should he? God our Father is here and will be here all through the lonely hours; He is an almighty Watcher, a sleepless Guardian, a faithful Friend. Nothing can happen without His direction, for even hell itself is under His control. Darkness is not dark to Him. He has promised to be a wall of fire around His people—and who can break through such a barrier?

Worldlings might be afraid, for they have an angry God above them, a guilty conscience within them, and a yawning hell beneath them; but we who rest in Jesus are saved from all these through rich mercy. If we give way to foolish fear, we lead others to doubt the reality of godliness. We ought to be afraid of being afraid, lest we should displease the Holy Spirit by foolish distrust.

God has not forgotten to be gracious nor shut up His tender mercies; it may be night in the soul, but there need be no terror, for the God of love changes not. Children of light may walk in darkness, but they are not therefore cast away; no, they are now enabled to prove their adoption by trusting in their heavenly Father as hypocrites cannot do.

Day 247

MORE THAN CONQUERORS

In all these things we are more than
conquerors through him who loved us.
ROMANS 8:37 NIV

We go to Christ for forgiveness and then too often look to the law for power to fight our sins. Take your sins to Christ's cross, for the old man can only be crucified there: We are crucified with Him. The only weapon to fight sin with is the spear that pierced the side of Jesus.

To give an illustration: You want to overcome an angry temper; how do you begin? It is very possible you have never tried the right way of going to Jesus with it. How did I get salvation? I came to Jesus just as I was, and I trusted Him to save me. I must kill my angry temper in the same way. It is the only way in which I can ever kill it. I must go to the cross with it and say to Jesus, "Lord, I trust You to deliver me from it."

Are you covetous? Do you feel the world entangle you? You may struggle against this evil as long as you wish, but if it is your besetting sin, you will never be delivered from it in any way but by the blood of Jesus. Take it to Christ. Tell Him: "Lord, I have trusted You, and Your name is Jesus, for You save Your people from their sins. Lord, this is one of my sins; save me from it!" You must be conquerors through Him who has loved you, if conquerors at all.

Day 248
OPEN THE DOOR TO JESUS

"If anyone hears my voice and opens the door,
I will come in and eat with that person."
REVELATION 3:20 NIV

What is your desire? Is it set upon heavenly things? Do you long to enjoy the high doctrine of eternal love? Do you desire liberty in very close communion with God? Do you aspire to know the heights and depths and lengths and breadths? Then you must draw near to Jesus; you must get a clear sight of Him in His preciousness and completeness: You must view Him in His work, in His offices, in His person. He who understands Christ receives an anointing from the Holy One, by which He knows all things.

Open the door, and He will come into your souls. He has long been knocking. Fling wide then the portals of your soul. He will come with that love which you long to feel, He will come with that joy into which you cannot work your poor depressed spirit, He will bring the peace which now you have not, He will cheer you until you have no other sickness but that of "love o'erpowering, love divine." Only open the door to Him, drive out His enemies, give Him the keys of your heart, and He will dwell there forever.

Oh, wondrous love that brings such a guest to dwell in such a heart!

Day 249

CALL ON GOD

God, even our own God. . .
PSALM 67:6 KJV

It is strange how little use we make of the spiritual blessings which God gives us, but it is stranger still how little use we make of God Himself. Though He is "our own God," we apply ourselves but little to Him and ask but little of Him.

How seldom do we ask counsel at the hands of the Lord! How often do we go about our business without seeking His guidance! In our troubles how constantly do we strive to bear our burdens ourselves, instead of casting them upon the Lord that He may sustain us!

This is not because we may not, for the Lord seems to say, "I am yours, soul, come and make use of Me as you will; you may freely come to My store, and the oftener the more welcome." It is our own fault if we make not free with the riches of our God.

Then since you have such a Friend and He invites you, draw from Him daily. Never want while you have a God to go to, never fear or faint while you have God to help you, go to your treasure and take whatever you need—there is all that you could want. Make use of Him in prayer. Go to Him often because He is your God. Use Him constantly by faith at all times. Whatever you are and wherever you are, remember God is just what you want and just where you want, and that He can do all you want.

PROMISES OF SCRIPTURE

Remember the word unto thy servant,
upon which thou hast caused me to hope.

PSALM 119:49 KJV

Whatever your special need may be, you may readily find some promise in the Bible suited to it.

Are you faint and feeble because your way is rough and you are weary? Here is the promise: "He gives power to the faint." When you read such a promise, take it back to the great Promiser and ask Him to fulfill His own Word. Are you seeking after Christ and thirsting for closer communion with Him? This promise shines like a star upon you: "Blessed are they who hunger and thirst after righteousness, for they shall be filled." Take that promise to the throne continually; do not plead anything else, but go to God over and over again with this: "Lord, You have said it, do as You have said." Are you distressed because of sin and burdened with the heavy load of your iniquities? Listen to these words: "I, even I, am He who blots out your transgressions and will no more remember your sins." You have no merit of your own to plead why He should pardon you, but plead His written engagements and He will perform them. If you have lost the sweet sense of the Savior's presence and are seeking Him with a sorrowful heart, remember the promises: "Return unto Me, and I will return unto you"; "For a small moment have I forsaken you, but with great mercies will I gather you."

MY REFUGE

You are my refuge in the day of disaster.
JEREMIAH 17:17 NIV

The path of the Christian is not always bright with sunshine; he has his seasons of darkness and of storm. At certain periods clouds cover the believer's sun, and he walks in darkness and sees no light. There are many who have rejoiced in the presence of God for a season, they have basked in the sunshine in the earlier stages of their Christian career, they have walked along the "green pastures" by the side of the "still waters," but suddenly they find the glorious sky is clouded; instead of the land of Goshen, they have to tread the sandy desert; in the place of sweet waters, they find troubled streams, bitter to their taste; and they say, "Surely if I were a child of God, this would not happen."

Oh, do not say that, you who are walking in darkness. The best of God's saints must drink the bitterness; the dearest of His children must bear the cross. No Christian has enjoyed perpetual prosperity; no believer can always keep his harp from the willows. Perhaps the Lord allotted you at first a smooth and unclouded path because you were weak and timid. He tempered the wind to the shorn lamb, but now that you are stronger in the spiritual life, you must enter upon the riper and rougher experience of God's full-grown children. We need winds and tempests to exercise our faith, to tear off the rotten bough of self-dependence, and to root us more firmly in Christ. The day of evil reveals to us the value of our glorious hope.

Day 252

GOD'S PLEASURE IN HIS CHILDREN

The LORD takes pleasure in His people.
PSALM 149:4 NKJV

How comprehensive is the love of Jesus! There is no part of His people's interests that He does not consider, and there is nothing that concerns their welfare that is not important to Him. Not merely does He think of you, believer, as an immortal being but as a mortal being too. Do not deny it or doubt it: "The very hairs of your head are all numbered." "The steps of a good man are ordered by the Lord, and he delights in His way."

Believer, rest assured that the heart of Jesus cares about your common affairs. The breadth of His tender love is such that you may resort to Him in all matters; for in all your afflictions, He is afflicted, and like as a father pities his children, so does He pity you. Oh, what a heart is His that does not merely comprehend the persons of His people, but comprehends also the diverse and innumerable concerns of all those persons!

Do you think that you can measure the love of Christ? Think of what His love has brought you—justification, adoption, sanctification, eternal life! The riches of His goodness are unsearchable; you shall never be able to tell them out or even conceive them. Oh, the breadth of the love of Christ! Go to your rest rejoicing, for thou art no desolate wanderer but a beloved child, watched over, cared for, supplied, and defended by your Lord.

PRECIOUS THOUGHTS

How precious to me are your thoughts, God!
PSALM 139:17 NIV

God is always thinking about us, never turns His mind away from us, has us always before His eyes; and this is precisely as we would have it, for it would be dreadful to exist for a moment beyond the observation of our heavenly Father. His thoughts are always tender, loving, wise, prudent, far-reaching; and they bring to us countless benefits: Thus it is a choice delight to remember them.

In all our wanderings the watchful glance of the eternal Watcher is evermore fixed upon us—we never roam beyond the Shepherd's eye. In our sorrows He observes us incessantly, and not a pang escapes Him; in our toils He marks all our weariness and writes in His book all the struggles of His faithful ones. These thoughts of the Lord encompass us in all our paths and penetrate the innermost region of our being. Not a nerve or tissue, valve or vessel of our bodily organization is uncared for; all the inconsequences of our little world are thought upon by the great God.

Is this precious to you? Then hold to it. The notice of a nobleman is valued so highly that he who has it counts his fortune made; but what is it to be thought of by the King of kings! If the Lord thinks of us, all is well and we may rejoice evermore.

A very present help. . .
PSALM 46:1 KJV

Covenant blessings are not meant to be looked at only but to be appropriated. Even our Lord Jesus is given to us for our present use.

Believer, you do not make use of Christ as you ought to. When you are in trouble, why do you not tell Him all your grief? Has He not a sympathizing heart, and can He not comfort and relieve you? No, you rather go to all your friends, except your best Friend, and tell your tale everywhere except to your Lord. Are you burdened with sins? Here is a fountain filled with blood: Use it. Has a sense of guilt returned upon you? The pardoning grace of Jesus may be proved again and again. Come to Him at once for cleansing. Do you lament your weakness? He is your strength. Why not lean upon Him? Do you feel sick? Call to the Beloved Physician! He will give the remedy that will revive you.

You are poor, but you have "a Kinsman, a mighty man of wealth." What! Will you not go to Him and ask Him to give you of His abundance, when He has given you this promise that you shall be joint-heir with Him, and all that He is and all that He has is yours? There is nothing Christ dislikes more than for His people to make a show of Him and not to use Him. He loves to be employed by us. The more burdens we put on His shoulders, the more precious will He be to us.

GOD'S PEOPLE

"I will be their God, and they will be my people."
2 CORINTHIANS 6:16 NIV

What a sweet title: "My people!" All the nations upon earth are His; the whole world is in His power. Yet are His people, His chosen, more especially His possession for He has done more for them than others. He has bought them with His blood, He has brought them near to Himself, He has set His great heart upon them, He has loved them with an everlasting love, a love which many waters cannot quench and which the revolutions of time shall never suffice in the least degree to diminish.

Dear friends, can you by faith see yourselves in that number? Can you look up to heaven and say, "My Lord and my God: mine by that sweet relationship which entitles me to call You Father, mine by that hallowed fellowship which I delight to hold with You when You are pleased to manifest Yourself unto me as You do not unto the world"? Can you read the Book of Inspiration and find there the indentures of your salvation? Can you read your title written in precious blood? Can you, by humble faith, lay hold of Jesus' garments and say, "My Christ"? If you can, then God says of you and of others like you: "My people"; for if God is your God and Christ your Christ, the Lord has a special, peculiar favor in you: You are the object of His choice, accepted in His beloved Son.

WISDOM AND TRUST

He that handleth a matter wisely shall find good: and
whoso trusteth in the LORD, happy is he.
PROVERBS 16:20 KJV

Wisdom is man's true strength, and under its guidance, he best accomplishes the ends of his being. Wisely handling the matter of life gives to man the richest enjoyment and presents the noblest occupation for his powers; hence by it he finds good in the fullest sense. Wisdom is the compass by which man is to steer across the trackless waste of life; without it he is a derelict vessel, the sport of winds and waves. A man must be prudent in such a world as this, or he will find no good but be betrayed into unnumbered ills. If, trained by the Great Teacher, we follow where He leads, we shall find good, even while in this dark abode.

But where shall this wisdom be found? Many have dreamed of it but have not possessed it. Where shall we learn it? Let us listen to the voice of the Lord, for He has declared the secret; He has revealed to the sons of men where true wisdom lies, and we have it in the text, "Whoso trusteth in the Lord, happy is he." The true way to handle a matter wisely is to trust in the Lord. This is the sure clue to the most intricate labyrinths of life; follow it and find eternal bliss. He who trusts in the Lord has a diploma for wisdom granted by inspiration: Happy is he now, and happier shall he be above.

Lord, teach me the wisdom of faith.

OUR DWELLING PLACE

We dwell in him.

1 JOHN 4:13 KJV

Do you want a house for your soul? Do you ask, "What is the cost?" It is something less than proud human nature will like to give. It is without money and without price.

Oh, you would like to pay a respectable rent! You would love to do something to win Christ? Then you cannot have the house, for it is "without price." Will you take my Master's house on a lease for all eternity with nothing to pay for it, nothing but the rent of loving and serving Him forever? Will you take Jesus and "dwell in Him"?

See, this house is furnished with all you want; it is filled with riches more than you will spend as long as you live. Here you can have intimate communion with Christ and feast on His love; here are tables well set with food for you to live on forever; in it, when weary, you can find rest with Jesus; and from it you can look out and see heaven itself. Will you have the house?

Ah, if you are houseless, you will say, "I should like to have the house, but may I have it?" Yes, there is the key—the key is "Come to Jesus." "But," you say, "I am too shabby for such a house." Never mind, there are garments inside. If you feel guilty and condemned, come; and though the house is too good for you, Christ will make you good enough for the house in time.

Day 258

WAITING WITH PATIENCE

All the days of my appointed time will I wait.
JOB 14:14 KJV

A little stay on earth will make heaven more heavenly. Nothing makes rest so sweet as toil; nothing renders security so pleasant as exposure to alarms. Our battered armor and scarred countenances will render more illustrious our victory above, when we are welcomed to the seats of those who have overcome the world.

We should not have full fellowship with Christ if we did not for a while sojourn below, for He was baptized with a baptism of suffering among men, and we must be baptized with the same if we would share His kingdom. Fellowship with Christ is so honorable that the sorest sorrow is a light price by which to procure it.

Another reason for our lingering here is for the good of others. We would not wish to enter heaven until our work is done, and it may be that we are yet ordained to minister to souls lost in the wilderness of sin.

Our prolonged stay here is doubtless for God's glory. A tried saint, like a well-cut diamond, glitters much in the King's crown. We are God's workmanship, in whom He will be glorified by our afflictions. Our time is fixed and settled by eternal decree. Let us not be anxious about it, but wait with patience until the gates of pearl shall open.

LIVES OF BLESSING

Who has blessed us with every spiritual blessing...
EPHESIANS 1:3 NKJV

All the goodness of the past, the present, and the future, Christ bestows upon His people. In the mysterious ages of the past, the Lord Jesus was His Father's first elect, and in His election He gave us an interest, for we were chosen in Him from before the foundation of the world. He had from all eternity the prerogatives of sonship as His Father's only begotten and well-beloved Son; and He has in the riches of His grace, by adoption and regeneration, elevated us to sonship also, so that to us He has given "power to become the sons of God."

The eternal covenant is ours for our strong consolation and security. The marvelous incarnation of the God of heaven, with all the amazing condescension and humiliation which attended it, is ours. The bloody sweat, the scourge, the cross are ours forever. Whatever blissful consequences flow from perfect obedience, finished atonement, resurrection, ascension, or intercession, all are ours by His own gift.

Upon His breastplate He is now bearing our names, and in His authoritative pleadings at the throne, He remembers our persons and pleads our cause. His dominion over principalities and powers and His absolute majesty in heaven, He employs for the benefit of them who trust in Him. His high estate is as much at our service as was His condition of abasement. He who gave Himself for us in the depths of woe and death does not withdraw the grant now that He is enthroned in the highest heavens.

THE RISEN CHRIST

But the fact is, Christ has been raised from the dead.
1 CORINTHIANS 15:20 NASB

The whole system of Christianity rests upon the fact that "Christ is risen from the dead"; for "If Christ be not risen, then is our preaching vain and your faith is also vain: You are yet in your sins."

The divinity of Christ finds its surest proof in His resurrection. It would not be unreasonable to doubt His Deity if He had not risen. Moreover, Christ's sovereignty depends upon His resurrection, "For to this end Christ died and rose and revived, that He might be Lord both of the dead and the living." Again our justification, that choice blessing of the covenant, is linked with Christ's triumphant victory over death and the grave. Further, our very regeneration is connected with His resurrection, for we are "begotten again unto a lively hope by the resurrection of Jesus Christ from the dead." And most certainly our ultimate resurrection rests here, for "If the Spirit of Him who raised up Jesus from the dead dwell in you, He who raised up Christ from the dead shall also quicken your mortal bodies by His Spirit which dwells in you."

If Christ is not risen, then we shall not rise; but if He is risen, then they who are asleep in Christ have not perished, but in their flesh shall surely behold their God. Thus the silver thread of resurrection runs through all the believer's blessings, from his regeneration onward to his eternal glory, and binds them together. How important then will this glorious fact be in his estimation, and how will he rejoice that beyond a doubt it is established, that "now is Christ risen from the dead."

HE WILL NEVER LEAVE

"I am with you always."
MATTHEW 28:20 NKJV

There is One who is ever the same and who is ever with us. There is one stable Rock amidst the billows of the sea of life.

Oh my soul, set not your affections upon rusting, moth-eaten, decaying treasures, but set your heart upon Him who abides forever faithful to you. Do not build your house upon the moving quicksand of a deceitful world, but found your hopes upon this Rock which, amidst descending rain and roaring floods, shall stand immovably secure. My soul, lay up your treasure in the only secure cabinet; store your jewels where you can never lose them. Put your all in Christ; set all your affections on His person, all your hope in His merit, all your trust in His efficacious blood, all your joy in His presence, and so you may laugh at loss and defy destruction.

The dark flood must soon roll between you and all you have; then wed your heart to Him who will never leave you; trust yourself with Him who will go with you through the black and surging current of death's stream and who will land you safely on the celestial shore and seat you with Him in heavenly places forever. Tell your secrets to the Friend who sticks closer than a brother. Trust all your concerns with Him who never can be taken from you, who will never leave you, and who will never let you leave Him, even "Jesus Christ, the same yesterday and today and forever."

Day 262
HAVE COURAGE!

"Be strong and very courageous."
JOSHUA 1:7 NIV

Our God's tender love for His servants makes Him concerned for the state of their inward feelings. He desires them to be of good courage.

It is plain that our Master would not have us entangled with fears. Our Lord does not love to see our countenance sad. It was a law of Ahasuerus that no one should come into the king's court dressed in mourning. This is not the law of the King of kings, for we may come mourning as we are; but still He would have us put off the spirit of heaviness and put on the garment of praise, for there is much reason to rejoice. The Christian man ought to be of a courageous spirit in order that he may glorify the Lord; if he is fearful and fainthearted, it will dishonor his God.

Besides, what a bad example it is. This disease of doubtfulness and discouragement is an epidemic that soon spreads among the Lord's flock. One downcast believer makes twenty souls sad. Moreover, unless your courage is kept up, Satan will be too much for you. Let your spirit be joyful in God your Savior, the joy of the Lord shall be your strength, and no fiend of hell shall make headway against you; but cowardice throws down the banner. Moreover, labor is light to a man of cheerful spirit; and success waits upon cheerfulness.

The man who toils rejoicing in his God, believing with all his heart has success guaranteed. He who sows in hope shall reap in joy; therefore "be thou strong and very courageous."

JOY FOLLOWS PAIN

Weeping may endure for a night,
but joy cometh in the morning.
PSALM 30:5 KJV

If you are in a night of trial, think of tomorrow; cheer your heart with the thought of the coming of the Lord. Be patient, for "He comes with clouds descending." Be patient! The Husbandman waits until He reaps His harvest. Be patient, for you know who has said, "Behold, I come quickly, and my reward is with me, to give to every man according as his work shall be."

Your head may be crowned with thorny troubles now, but it shall wear a starry crown before long; your hand may be filled with cares—it shall sweep the strings of the harp of heaven soon. Your garments may be soiled with dust now; they shall be white in a short time. Wait a little longer. How despicable our troubles and trials will seem when we look back upon them! Looking at them presently, they seem immense; but when we get to heaven, we shall then "with transporting joys recount the labors of our feet." Our trials will then seem light and momentary afflictions.

Let us go on boldly; after the dark of night the morning comes, which is more than they can say who are shut up in the darkness of hell. Do you know what it is to live in the future—to live on expectation—to antedate heaven? It may be dark now, but it will soon be light; it may be all trial now, but it will soon be all happiness. What does it matter if "weeping may endure for a night," when "joy comes in the morning"?

Day 264
GOD, MY PORTION

You are my portion, LORD.
PSALM 119:57 NIV

Look at your possessions and compare your portion with the lot of other men. Some of them have their portion in the field; they are rich, and their harvests yield them a golden increase—but what are harvests compared with your God, who is the God of harvests? What are bursting granaries compared with Him, who is the Husbandman and feeds you with the bread of heaven?

Some have their portion in the city; their wealth is abundant and flows to them in constant streams, until they become a very reservoir of gold—but what is gold compared with God? You could not live on it; your spiritual life could not be sustained by it. But you have God, and in Him you have more than gold or riches ever could buy.

Some have their portion in that which most men love—applause and fame—but is not God more to you than that? There are griefs in life that wealth cannot alleviate, and there is the deep need of a dying hour for which no riches can provide. But when you have God for your portion, you have more than all else put together. In Him every want is met, whether in life or in death. With God for your portion you are rich indeed, for He will supply your need, comfort your heart, ease your grief, guide your steps, be with you in the dark valley, and then take you home to enjoy Him as your portion forever.

SHARING WITH HIS PEOPLE

Joint-heirs with Christ. . .
ROMANS 8:17 KJV

The boundless realms of His Father's universe are Christ's by prescriptive right. He is the sole proprietor of the vast creation of God, and He has admitted us to claim the whole as ours. The golden streets of paradise, the pearly gates, the river of life, the transcendent bliss, and the unutterable glory are, by our blessed Lord, offered to us for our everlasting possession. All that He has, He shares with His people.

The crown royal He has placed upon the head of His Church, appointing her a kingdom and calling her sons a royal priesthood, a generation of priests and kings. He uncrowned Himself that we might have a coronation of glory; He would not sit upon His own throne until He had procured a place upon it for all who overcome by His blood. Behold the reward of every Christian conqueror! Christ's throne, crown, scepter, palace, treasure, robes, heritage are yours.

Far superior to the jealousy, selfishness, and greed, which admit of no participation of their advantages, Christ deems His happiness completed by His people sharing it. The smiles of His Father are all the sweeter to Him because His people share them. The honors of His kingdom are more pleasing because His people appear with Him in glory. He delights in His throne because on it there is a place for them. He rejoices in His royal robes since over them His skirts are spread. He delights the more in His joy because He calls them to enter into it.

THE GOOD SHEPHERD

He shall gather the lambs with his arm,
and carry them in his bosom.
ISAIAH 40:11 KJV

Who is He of whom such gracious words are spoken? He is the Good Shepherd. Why does He carry the lambs in His bosom? Because He has a tender heart, and any weakness at once melts His heart. It is His position as a faithful High Priest to consider the weak. Besides, He purchased them with blood; they are His property. He must and will care for those who cost Him so dearly. He is responsible for each lamb, bound not to lose one; they are all a part of His glory and reward.

But how may we understand "He will carry them"? Sometimes He carries them by not permitting them to endure much trial. Providence deals tenderly with them. Often they are "carried" by being filled with an unusual degree of love, so that they bear up and stand fast. Though their knowledge may not be deep, they have great sweetness in what they do know. Frequently He "carries" them by giving them a very simple faith, which takes the promise just as it stands and believingly runs with every trouble straight to Jesus.

"He carries the lambs in His bosom." Here is boundless affection. Would He put them in His bosom if He did not love them? Here is tender nearness: So near are they that they could not possibly be nearer. Here is perfect safety: In His bosom who can hurt them? They must hurt the Shepherd first. Here is perfect rest and sweetest comfort. We are not sufficiently sensible of the infinite tenderness of Jesus!

LIMITLESS RICHES

Who richly supplies us with all things to enjoy.
1 TIMOTHY 6:17 NASB

Our Lord Jesus is ever giving and does not for a solitary instant withdraw His hand. As long as there is a vessel of grace not yet full to the brim, the oil shall not be stayed. He is a sun ever shining, He is manna always falling round the camp, He is a rock in the desert ever sending out streams of life from His smitten side; the rain of His grace is always dropping, the river of His bounty is ever flowing, and the wellspring of His love is constantly overflowing.

As the King can never die, so His grace can never fail. His mercies are new every morning and fresh every evening. Who can know the number of His benefits or recount the list of His bounties? The countless stars are but as the standard-bearers of a more innumerable host of blessings. How shall my soul extol Him who daily loads us with benefits and who crowns us with loving-kindness? Oh, that my praise could be as ceaseless as His bounty!

FOLLOW CHRIST'S FOOTPRINTS

Whoever claims to live in him must live as Jesus did.
1 JOHN 2:6 NIV

Why should Christians imitate Christ? They should do it for their own sakes. If they desire to be in a healthy state of soul, if they would escape the sickness of sin and enjoy the vigor of growing grace, let Jesus be their model. If they would enjoy holy and happy communion with Jesus, if they would be lifted up above the cares and troubles of this world, let them walk even as He walked. There is nothing that can so assist you to walk toward heaven with good speed as wearing the image of Jesus on your heart to rule all its motions. It is when, by the power of the Holy Spirit, you are enabled to walk with Jesus in His very footsteps that you are most happy and most known to be the sons of God.

Strive to be like Jesus. Imitate His example. Christian, do you love the Savior? Is His name precious to you? Is His cause dear to you? Is it your desire that He should be glorified? Are you longing for souls to be won to Him? If so, imitate Jesus.

Day 269

AFTERWARD

Afterward it yieldeth the peaceable fruit.
HEBREWS 12:11 KJV

How happy are tried Christians afterward. There is no calm more deep than that which succeeds a storm. Who has not rejoiced in clear skies after rain? Our sorrows, like the passing keels of the vessels upon the sea, leave a silver line of holy light behind them "afterward." It is peace—sweet, deep peace—which follows the horrible turmoil which once reigned in our tormented, guilty souls.

The Christian has his best things last, and he therefore in this world receives his worst things first. But even his worst things are "afterward" good things. Even now he grows rich by his losses, he rises by his falls, he lives by dying, and becomes full by being emptied; if then his grievous afflictions yield him so much peaceable fruit in this life, what shall be the full vintage of joy "afterward" in heaven?

If his dark nights are as bright as the world's days, what shall his days be? If even his starlight is more splendid than the sun, what must his sunlight be? If he can sing in a dungeon, how sweetly will he sing in heaven? If he can praise the Lord in the fires, how will he extol Him before the eternal throne? If evil be good to him now, what will the overflowing goodness of God be to him then? Who would not choose to be a Christian? Who would not bear the present cross for the crown which cometh afterward? Wait, dear soul, and let patience have her perfect work.

DRAWING CLOSE TO GOD

"I drew them with gentle cords, with bands of love."
HOSEA 11:4 NKJV

Our heavenly Father often draws us with the cords of love, but how backward we are to run toward Him! How slowly we respond to His gentle impulses! He draws us to exercise a more simple faith in Him; but we do not leave our worldly cares with God, but like Martha we cumber ourselves with much serving. Does not this draw us to trust Him? Can we not hear Him say, "Come, My child, and trust Me. The veil is rent; enter into My presence and approach boldly to the throne of My grace. I am worthy of your fullest confidence; cast your cares on Me."

But although called with tones of love to the blessed exercise of this comforting grace, we will not come. At another time He draws us to closer communion with Himself. There are secret rooms not yet opened to us; Jesus invites us to enter them, but we hold back. Shame on our cold hearts! We are but poor lovers of our sweet Lord Jesus, not fit to be His servants, much less to be His brides, and yet He has exalted us to be bone of His bone and flesh of His flesh, married to Him by a glorious marriage covenant.

Herein is love! But if we obey not the gentle drawings of His love, He will send affliction to drive us into closer intimacy with Himself. Have us nearer He will.

A PURPOSE FULFILLED

The LORD will perfect that which concerneth me.
PSALM 138:8 KJV

The confidence that the psalmist expressed was a divine confidence. His dependence was on the Lord alone. The psalmist was wise; he rested upon nothing short of the Lord's work.

It is the Lord who has begun the good work within us; it is He who has carried it on, and if He does not finish it, it never will be complete. If there be one stitch in the celestial garment of our righteousness which we are to insert ourselves, then we are lost; but this is our confidence: The Lord who began will perfect. He has done it all, must do it all, and will do it all. Our confidence must not be in what we have done nor in what we have resolved to do, but entirely in what the Lord will do.

Unbelief insinuates: "You will never be able to stand. Look at the evil of your heart; you can never conquer sin. Remember the sinful pleasures and temptations of the world that beset you; you will be certainly allured by them and led astray." Yes, we should indeed perish if left to our own strength. But thanks be to God, He will perfect that which concerns us and bring us to the desired haven. We can never be too confident when we confide in Him alone and never too much concerned to have such a trust.

CONVERSATION

*Only let your conversation be as
it becometh the gospel of Christ.*
PHILIPPIANS 1:27 KJV

The word *conversation* does not merely mean our talk with one another, but the whole course of our life and behavior in the world. What sort of conversation is this? In the first place, the Gospel is very simple. So Christians should be simple and plain in their habits. There should be about our manner, our speech, our dress, our whole behavior that simplicity which is the very soul of beauty.

The Gospel is a very fearless Gospel; it boldly proclaims the truth, whether men like it or not: We must be equally faithful and unflinching. But the Gospel is also very gentle. Mark this spirit in its Founder: "A bruised reed He will not break." Let us seek to win others by the gentleness of our words and acts.

The Gospel is very loving. It is the message of the God of love to a lost and fallen race. Christ's last command to His disciples was "Love one another." Oh, for more real, hearty union and love for all the saints, for more tender compassion toward the souls of the worst and vilest of men!

We must not forget that the Gospel of Christ is holy. It never excuses sin: It pardons it but only through an atonement. If our life is to resemble the Gospel, we must shun everything that would hinder our perfect conformity to Christ. For His sake, for our own sakes, and for the sakes of others, we must strive day by day to let our conversation be more in accordance with His Gospel.

Day 273
REST IN CHRIST

Come unto me, all ye that labour and are heavy
laden, and I will give you rest. Take my yoke upon
you, and learn of me; for I am meek and lowly
in heart: and ye shall find rest unto your souls.
For my yoke is easy, and my burden is light.
MATTHEW 11:28–30 KJV

"I will give you rest" comes before "Ye shall find rest." It is the rest of a man who is already at rest, the repose of a man who has received a "given" rest and now "discovers" the found rest. It is the rest of a learner—"Learn of Me, and you shall find rest." It is not so much the rest of one who was until now laboring and heavy laden, as of one who is today learning at the Savior's feet. It is the rest of a seeker evidently, for finding usually implies a search.

Having been pardoned and saved, the saved man in the course of his experience discovers more and more reason for peace; he is learning and seeking, and he finds. The rest is evidently touched upon, however, as a thing unknown, which becomes the subject of discovery. The man had a rest from his burden; now he finds a rest in Christ which exceeds what he asked or even thought.

PERSEVERANCE

Remain true to the faith.
ACTS 14:22 NIV

Perseverance is the badge of true saints. The Christian life is not a beginning only in the ways of God, but also a continuance in the same as long as life lasts. It is with a Christian as it was with the great Napoleon: He said, "Conquest has made me what I am, and conquest must maintain me." So under God, conquest has made you what you are, and conquest must sustain you.

He only is a true conqueror and shall be crowned at the last who continues until war's trumpet is blown no more. Perseverance is, therefore, the target of all our spiritual enemies. The world does not object to your being a Christian for a time, if she can but tempt you to cease your pilgrimage. The flesh will seek to ensnare you and to prevent your pressing on to glory: "It is weary work being a pilgrim; come, give it up. Am I always to be affronted? Am I never to be indulged? Give me at least a leave from this constant warfare." Satan will make many a fierce attack on your perseverance; it will be the mark for all his arrows. He will strive to hinder you in service: He will insinuate that you are doing no good and that you want rest. He will endeavor to make you weary of suffering; he will whisper, "Curse God, and die." Or he will attack your steadfastness. Or he will attack your doctrinal sentiments. Wear your shield close upon your armor, and cry mightily unto God that by His Spirit you may endure to the end.

Day 275
A WORD OF
ENCOURAGEMENT

Those he justified, he also glorified.
ROMANS 8:30 NIV

Here is a precious truth for you. You may be poor or in suffering or unknown; but for your encouragement take a review of your "calling" and the consequences that flow from it, and especially that blessed result here spoken of. As surely as you are God's child today, so surely shall all your trials soon be at an end, and you shall be rich to all the intents of bliss. Wait awhile, and that weary head shall wear the crown of glory; and that hand of labor shall grasp the palm branch of victory.

Do not lament your troubles, but rather rejoice that before long you will be where "there shall be neither sorrow nor crying, neither shall there be any more pain." The everlasting song is almost on your lips. The portals of heaven stand open for you. Think not that you can fail to enter into rest. If He has called you, nothing can divide you from His love. Distress cannot sever the bond, the fire of persecution cannot burn the link, the hammer of hell cannot break the chain. You are secure; that voice which called you at first shall call you yet again from earth to heaven, from death's dark gloom to immortality's unuttered splendors.

Rest assured; the heart of Him who has justified you beats with infinite love toward you. You will soon be with the glorified; you are only waiting here to be made meet for the inheritance, and that done, the wings of angels shall carry you far away, to the mount of peace and joy and blessedness.

THE GREAT PHYSICIAN

Who heals all your diseases. . .
PSALM 103:3 NASB

What a comfort to know that we have a Great Physician who is both able and willing to heal us! His cures are very speedy—there is life in a look at Him; His cures are radical—He strikes at the center of the disease; and therefore His cures are sure and certain—He never fails, and the disease never returns. There is no relapse where Christ heals, no fear that His patients should be merely patched up for a season. He makes new men of them: He also gives them a new heart, and He puts a right spirit within them. He is well skilled in all diseases.

Physicians generally have some specialty. Although they may know a little about almost all our pains and ills, there is usually one disease that they have studied above all others; but Jesus Christ is thoroughly acquainted with the whole of human nature. He is as much at home with one sinner as with another, and never yet did He meet with a case that was difficult for Him. He has had extraordinary complications of strange diseases to deal with, but He knows how to treat the patient. The medicine He gives is the only true potion, healing in every instance. Whatever our spiritual malady may be, we should request at once of the Divine Physician. There is no brokenness of heart that Jesus cannot bind up.

We trust Him, and sin dies; we love Him, and grace lives; we wait for Him, and grace is strengthened; we see Him as He is, and grace is perfected forever.

SHARE CHRIST WITH ZEAL

Be zealous.
REVELATION 3:19 KJV

If you would see souls converted, if you would place crowns upon the head of the Savior, and His throne lifted high, then be filled with zeal. Every grace will have accomplishments, but this will be first; prudence, knowledge, patience, and courage will follow in their places, but zeal must lead the van.

This zeal is the fruit of the Holy Spirit: It draws its vital force from the continued operations of the Holy Spirit in the soul. If our inner life dwindles, if our heart beats slowly before God, we shall not know zeal; but if all be strong and vigorous within, then we cannot but feel a loving anxiety to see the kingdom of Christ come and His will done on earth, even as it is in heaven.

A deep sense of gratitude will nourish Christian zeal. We find abundant reason why we should spend and be spent for God. And zeal is also stimulated by the thought of the eternal future. It looks with tearful eyes down to the flames of hell, and it cannot slumber: It looks up with anxious gaze to the glories of heaven, and it cannot but bestir itself. It feels that time is short compared with the work to be done, and therefore it devotes all that it has to the cause of its Lord. And it is ever strengthened by the remembrance of Christ's example.

Let us prove that we are His disciples by manifesting the same spirit of zeal.

GREAT THINGS

The LORD hath done great things
for us; whereof we are glad.
PSALM 126:3 KJV

Some Christians are prone to look on the dark side of everything and to dwell more upon what they have gone through than upon what God has done for them. Ask for their impression of the Christian life, and they will describe their continual conflicts, their deep afflictions, their sad adversities, and the sinfulness of their hearts, yet with scarcely any allusion to the mercy and help that God has granted them. But a Christian whose soul is in a healthy state will come forward joyously and say, "I will speak not about myself but to the honor of my God. He has brought me up out of a horrible pit and out of the miry clay and set my feet upon a rock and established my goings; and He has put a new song in my mouth, even praise unto our God. The Lord has done great things for me, whereof I am glad."

It is true that we endure trials, but it is just as true that we are delivered out of them. It is true that we have our corruptions, and mournfully we know this; but it is quite as true that we have an all-sufficient Savior who overcomes these corruptions and delivers us from their dominion. The deeper our troubles, the louder our thanks to God who has led us through and preserved us. Our griefs cannot mar the melody of our praise; we reckon them to be the bass part of our life's song: "He has done great things for us, whereof we are glad."

EXPLORE GOD'S WORD

Search the scriptures.
JOHN 5:39 KJV

The Greek word here rendered *search* signifies a strict, close, diligent, curious search, such as men make when they are seeking gold, or hunters when they are in earnest after game. We must not rest content with having given a superficial reading to a chapter or two, but with the candle of the Spirit, we must deliberately seek out the hidden meaning of the Word.

Holy scripture requires searching—much of it can only be learned by careful study. There is milk for babes but also meat for strong men. No man who merely skims the book of God can profit from it; we must dig and mine until we obtain the hidden treasure. The door of the Word only opens to the key of diligence. The scriptures claim searching. They are the writings of God—who shall dare to treat them with levity? He who despises them despises the God who wrote them. God forbid that any of us should leave our Bibles to become swift witnesses against us in the great day of account. The Word of God will repay searching. Scripture grows upon the student. It is full of surprises.

The scriptures reveal Jesus: "They are they which testify of Me." No more powerful motive can be urged upon Bible readers than this: He who finds Jesus finds life, heaven, all things. Happy is he who, searching his Bible, discovers his Savior.

HONOR CHRIST IN YOUR DAILY LIFE

We live unto the Lord.
ROMANS 14:8 KJV

If God had willed it, each of us might have entered heaven at the moment of conversion. It was not absolutely necessary for our preparation for immortality that we should linger here. It is possible for a man to be taken to heaven though he has just placed his faith in Jesus. It is true that our sanctification is a long and continued process, and we shall not be perfected until we lay aside our bodies and enter within the veil; but nevertheless, had the Lord so willed it, He might have changed us from imperfection to perfection and have taken us to heaven at once.

Why then are we here? Would God keep His children out of paradise a single moment longer than was necessary? Why is the army of the living God still on the battlefield when one charge might give them the victory? Why are His children still wandering through a maze, when a solitary word from His lips would bring them into the center of their hopes in heaven? They are here that they may "live unto the Lord" and may bring others to know His love.

We remain on earth as sowers to scatter good seed, as ploughmen to break up the fallow ground, as heralds publishing salvation. We are here as the "salt of the earth," to be a blessing to the world. We are here to glorify Christ in our daily life. We are here as workers for Him and as "workers together with Him." Let us live earnest, useful, holy lives to "the praise of the glory of His grace."

THE WARMTH OF THE SON

We love Him because He first loved us.
1 JOHN 4:19 NKJV

There is no light in the planet but that which proceeds from the sun, and there is no true love for Jesus in the heart but that which comes from the Lord Jesus Himself. From this overflowing fountain of the infinite love of God, all our love for God must spring.

This must ever be a great and certain truth, that we love Him for no other reason than because He first loved us. Our love for Him is the fair offspring of His love to us. Anyone may have cold admiration when studying the works of God, but the warmth of love can only be kindled in the heart by God's Spirit. How great the wonder that we should ever have been brought to love Jesus at all! How marvelous that when we had rebelled against Him, He should by a display of such amazing love seek to draw us back.

Love then has for its parent the love of God shed abroad in the heart: But after it is thus divinely born, it must be divinely nourished. Love is an exotic; it is not a plant that will flourish naturally in human soil—it must be watered from above. Love for Jesus is a flower of a delicate nature, and if it received no nourishment but that which could be drawn from the rock of our hearts, it would soon wither. Love must feed on love. The very soul and life of our love to God is His love to us.

A HOLY CALLING

Who has saved us and called us with a holy calling. . .
2 TIMOTHY 1:9 NKJV

Believers in Christ Jesus are saved. They are not looked upon as persons who are in a hopeful state and may ultimately be saved, but they are already saved. Salvation is not a blessing to be enjoyed upon the deathbed and to be sung of in a future state above, but a matter to be obtained, received, promised, and enjoyed now. The Christian is saved in God's purpose; God has ordained him unto salvation, and that purpose is complete. This complete salvation is accompanied by a holy calling.

Those whom the Savior saved are in due time effectually called by the power of God unto holiness: They leave their sins; they endeavor to be like Christ; they choose holiness, not out of any compulsion but of a new nature which leads them to rejoice in holiness just as naturally as before they delighted in sin. God neither chose them nor called them because they were holy, but He called them that they might be holy.

The excellencies which we see in a believer are as much the work of God as the atonement itself. Thus is brought out very sweetly the fullness of the grace of God. Salvation must be of grace because the Lord is the author of it, and what motive but grace could move Him to save the guilty? Salvation must be of grace because the Lord works in such a manner that our righteousness is forever excluded. Such is the believer's privilege—a present salvation; such is the evidence that he is called to it—a holy life.

DELIGHT IN CHRISTIANITY

Take delight in the LORD.
PSALM 37:4 NIV

The life of the believer is described as a delight in God, and we are thus certified of the great fact that true religion overflows with happiness and joy. Ungodly persons and mere professors never look upon religion as a joyful thing; to them it is service, duty, or necessity, but never pleasure or delight. If they attend to religion at all, it is either that they may gain from it, or else because they dare not do otherwise.

The thought of delight in religion is so strange to most men that no two words in their language stand further apart than *holiness* and *delight*. But believers who know Christ understand that delight and faith are so blessedly united that the gates of hell cannot prevail to separate them. Those who love God with all their hearts find that His ways are ways of pleasantness and all His paths are peace. Such joys, such brimful delights, such overflowing blessed-nesses do the saints discover in their Lord, that so far from serving Him from custom, they would follow Him though all the world cast out His name as evil.

We fear not God because of any compulsion; our faith is no fetter, our profession is no bondage, we are not dragged to holiness nor driven to duty. No, our piety is our pleasure, our hope is our happiness, our duty is our delight. Delight and true religion are as allied as root and flower, as indivisible as truth and certainty; they are, in fact, two precious jewels glittering side by side in a setting of gold.

TRIUMPH OVER FEAR

The LORD is my light and my salvation;
whom shall I fear? The LORD is the strength
of my life; of whom shall I be afraid?
PSALM 27:1 KJV

Into the soul at the new birth, divine light is poured as the precursor of salvation; where there is not enough light to reveal our own darkness and to make us long for the Lord Jesus, there is no evidence of salvation. After conversion our God is our joy, comfort, guide, teacher, and in every sense our light: He is light within, light around, light reflected from us, and light to be revealed to us.

It is not said merely that the Lord gives light but that He *is* light, nor that He gives salvation but that He *is* salvation; he then who by faith has laid hold upon God has all covenant blessings in his possession. This established as fact, the argument drawn from it is put in the form of a question: "Whom shall I fear?"—a question that is its own answer. The powers of darkness are not to be feared for the Lord, our light, destroys them; and the damnation of hell is not to be dreaded by us for the Lord is our salvation.

Our life derives all its strength from God; and if He deigns to make us strong, we cannot be weakened by the adversary. "Of whom shall I be afraid?" The bold question looks into the future as well as the present. "If God be for us," who can be against us, either now or in time to come?

A CRY FOR HELP

Help, LORD.
PSALM 12:1 NIV

The prayer itself is remarkable, for it is short but seasonable, sententious, and suggestive. David mourned the fewness of faithful men, and therefore lifted up his heart in supplication—when the creature failed, he flew to the Creator. He evidently felt his own weakness, or he would not have cried for help; but at the same time he intended honestly to exert himself for the cause of truth, for the word *help* is inapplicable where we ourselves do nothing. There is much of directness, clearness of perception, and distinctness of utterance in this petition of two words. The psalmist runs directly to his God with a well-considered prayer; he knows what he is seeking and where to seek it. Lord, teach us to pray in the same blessed manner.

Spiritual warriors in inward conflicts may send to the throne for reinforcements, and this will be a model for their request. Workers in heavenly labor may obtain grace in time of need. Seeking sinners may offer up the same supplication; in all these cases, times, and places, this will serve the turn of needy souls. "Help, Lord" will suit us living and dying, suffering or laboring, rejoicing or sorrowing. In Him our help is found; let us not be slow to cry to Him.

The answer to the prayer is certain, if it is sincerely offered through Jesus. The Lord's character assures us that He will not leave His people, His relationship as Father and Husband guarantees us His aid, His gift of Jesus is a pledge of every good thing, and His sure promise stands: "Fear not, I will help thee."

Thy Redeemer. . .
ISAIAH 54:5 KJV

Jesus, the Redeemer, is altogether ours and ours forever. All the offices of Christ are held on our behalf. He is king for us, priest for us, and prophet for us. Whenever we read a new title of the Redeemer, let us appropriate Him as ours under that name as much as under any other. The shepherd's staff, the father's rod, the captain's sword, the priest's miter, the prince's scepter, the prophet's mantle—all are ours. Jesus has no dignity that He will not employ for our exaltation and no prerogative which He will not exercise for our defense. His fullness of Godhead is our unfailing, inexhaustible treasure house.

His manhood also, which He took upon Him for us, is ours in all its perfection. To us our gracious Lord communicates the spotless virtue of a stainless character, to us He gives the meritorious efficacy of a devoted life, on us He bestows the reward procured by obedient submission and incessant service. He bequeaths us His manger, from which to learn how God came down to man, and His cross to teach us how man may go up to God. All His thoughts, emotions, actions, utterances, miracles, and intercessions were for us. He trod the road of sorrow on our behalf. Christ everywhere and every way is our Christ, forever most richly to enjoy. Oh my soul, by the power of the Holy Spirit, call Him "thy Redeemer."

BUILDING ON THE
SURE FOUNDATION

The firm foundation of God stands.
2 TIMOTHY 2:19 NASB

The foundation upon which our faith rests is this, that "God was in Christ reconciling the world unto Himself, not imputing their trespasses unto them." The great fact on which genuine faith relies is that "the Word was made flesh and dwelt among us" and that "Christ also has suffered for sin, the just for the unjust, that He might bring us to God"; "Who Himself bore our sins in His own body on the tree"; "For the chastisement of our peace was upon Him, and by His stripes we are healed."

In one word, the great pillar of the Christian's hope is *substitution.* The vicarious sacrifice of Christ for the guilty, Christ being made sin for us that we might be made the righteousness of God in Him, Christ offering up a true and proper expiatory and substitutionary sacrifice in the room, place, and stead of as many as the Father gave Him, who are known to God by name and are recognized in their own hearts by their trusting in Jesus—this is the cardinal fact of the Gospel.

If this foundation were removed, what could we do? But it stands firm as the throne of God. We know it, we rest on it, we rejoice in it; and our delight is to hold it, to meditate upon it, and to proclaim it, while we desire to be actuated and moved by gratitude for it in every part of our life and conversation.

PERMANENCE IN CHRIST

The things which cannot be shaken may remain.
HEBREWS 12:27 NKJV

Whatever your losses have been or may be, you enjoy present salvation. You are standing at the foot of His cross, trusting alone in the merit of Jesus' precious blood, and no rise or fall of the markets can interfere with your salvation in Him; no breaking of banks, no failures and bankruptcies can touch that. Then you are a child of God. God is your Father. No change of circumstances can ever rob you of that. Although by losses brought to poverty and stripped bare, you can say, "He is my Father still. In my Father's house are many mansions; therefore will I not be troubled."

You have another permanent blessing, namely, the love of Jesus Christ. He who is God and man loves you with all the strength of His affectionate nature—nothing can affect that. The fig tree may not blossom, and the flocks may cease from the field; it matters not to the man who can sing, "My Beloved is mine, and I am His." Our best portion and richest heritage we cannot lose.

Whatever troubles come, let us act as men; let us show that we are not such little children as to be cast down by what may happen in this poor fleeting state of time. Our country is Immanuel's land, our hope is above the sky and therefore calm as the summer's ocean; we will see the wreck of everything earthborn and yet rejoice in the God of our salvation.

PROPER SERVICE

---

*Let every man abide in the same
calling wherein he was called.*

1 CORINTHIANS 7:20 KJV

Beloved, it is not office, it is earnestness; it is not position, it is grace that will enable us to glorify God. God is most surely glorified in that cobbler's stall, where the godly worker, as he plies the awl, sings of the Savior's love. The name of Jesus is glorified by the poor, unlearned carter as he drives his horse and blesses his God or speaks to his fellow laborer by the roadside, as much as by the popular divine who throughout the country is thundering out the Gospel.

God is glorified by our serving Him in our proper vocations. Take care that you do not forsake the path of duty by leaving your occupation, and take care you do not dishonor your profession while in it. Think little of yourselves, but do not think too little of your callings. Every lawful trade may be sanctified by the Gospel to noblest ends. Turn to the Bible, and you will find the most menial forms of labor connected either with most daring deeds of faith or with persons whose lives have been illustrious for holiness.

Therefore be not discontented with your calling. Whatever God has made your position or your work, abide in that unless you are quite sure that He calls you to something else. Let your first care be to glorify God to the utmost of your power where you are. Fill your present sphere to His praise, and if He needs you in another, He will show it to you. Lay aside vexatious ambition, and embrace peaceful content.

Day 290

KEEP YOUR
EYES ON JESUS

Fixing our eyes on Jesus. . .
HEBREWS 12:2 NIV

It is the Holy Spirit's constant work to turn our eyes away from self to Jesus; but Satan's work is just the opposite of this, for he is constantly trying to make us regard ourselves instead of Christ. He insinuates: "Your sins are too great for pardon, you have no faith, you do not repent enough, you will never be able to endure, you have not the joy of His children, you have a wavering hold of Jesus." All these are thoughts about self, and we shall never find comfort or assurance by looking within. But the Holy Spirit turns our eyes entirely away from self: He tells us that we are nothing, but that "Christ is all in all."

It is not your hold of Christ that saves you—it is Christ; it is not your joy in Christ that saves you—it is Christ; it is not even faith in Christ, though that be the instrument—it is Christ's blood and merits; therefore, look not to your hope, but to Jesus, the source of your hope; look not to your faith, but to Jesus, the author and finisher of your faith. It is what Jesus is, not what we are, that gives rest to the soul.

Keep your eye simply on Him; let His death, His sufferings, His merits, His glories, His intercession be fresh upon your mind; when you wake in the morning, look to Him; when you lie down at night, look to Him. Do not let your hopes or fears come between you and Jesus; follow Him, and He will never fail you.

HEARTS OF GLADNESS

In him our hearts rejoice, for we trust in his holy name.
PSALM 33:21 NIV

Christians can rejoice even in the deepest distress. Although trouble may surround them, they still sing; and, like many birds, they sing best in their cages. The waves may roll over them, but their souls soon rise to the surface and see the light of God's countenance. Trouble does not necessarily bring consolation with it to the believer, but the presence of the Son of God in the fiery furnace with him fills his heart with joy. He is sick and suffering, but Jesus visits him and makes his bed for him. He is dying, but Jesus puts His arms around him and cries, "Fear not, beloved, to die is to be blessed; the waters of death have their fountainhead in heaven. They are not bitter; they are sweet as nectar, for they flow from the throne of God."

As the departing saint wades through the stream and the billows gather around him, the same voice sounds in his ears, "Fear not, I am with thee; be not dismayed, I am your God." As he nears the borders of the infinite unknown, Jesus says, "Fear not, it is your Father's good pleasure to give you the kingdom." Thus strengthened and consoled, the believer is not afraid to die; no, he is even willing to depart, for since he has seen Jesus as the Morning Star, he longs to gaze upon Him as the sun in his strength. Truly the presence of Jesus is all the heaven we desire.

Trust in the LORD forever, for the LORD,
the LORD, himself is the Rock eternal.
ISAIAH 26:4 NIV

Seeing that we have such a God to trust, let us rest upon Him with all our weight; let us resolutely drive out all unbelief and endeavor to get rid of doubts and fears, which so much mar our comfort since there is no excuse for fear where God is the foundation of our trust.

How unkind is our conduct when we put so little confidence in our heavenly Father who has never failed us and who never will. It were well if doubting were banished from the household of God; but it is to be feared that old Unbelief is as nimble nowadays as when the psalmist asked, "Is his mercy clean gone forever? Will he be favorable no more?" David had not made any very lengthy trial of the mighty sword of the giant Goliath, and yet he said, "There is none like it." He had tried it once in the hour of his youthful victory, and it had proved itself to be of the right metal, and therefore he praised it ever afterward; even so should we speak well of our God—there is none like unto Him in the heaven above or the earth beneath.

We have been in many trials, but we have never yet been cast where we could not find in our God all that we needed. Let us then be encouraged to trust in the Lord forever, assured that His everlasting strength will be, as it has been, our succor and stay.

A SAFE SHELTER

"Whoever listens to me will dwell safely,
and will be secure, without fear of evil."
PROVERBS 1:33 NKJV

Divine love is rendered conspicuous when it shines in the midst of judgments. Fair is that lone star which smiles through the rifts of the thunderclouds, bright is the oasis which blooms in the wilderness of sand, so fair and so bright is love in the midst of wrath.

When the Israelites provoked the Most High by their continued idolatry, He punished them by withholding both dew and rain, so that their land was visited by a sore famine; but while He did this, He took care that His own chosen ones should be secure. Come what may, God's people are safe. Let convulsions shake the solid earth, let the skies themselves be rent in two, yet amid the wreck of worlds the believer shall be as secure as in the calmest hour of rest.

If God cannot save His people under heaven, He will save them in heaven. If the world becomes too hot to hold them, then heaven shall be the place of their reception and their safety. Be confident, when you hear of wars and rumors of wars. Let no agitation distress you, but be quiet from fear of evil. Whatever comes upon the earth, you, beneath the broad wings of Jehovah, will be secure. Stay yourself upon His promise; rest in His faithfulness, and bid defiance to the blackest future for there is nothing in it direful for you. Your sole concern should be to show forth to the world the blessedness of hearkening to the voice of wisdom.

AWAITING INSTRUCTION

Lead me in thy truth, and teach me: for thou art the
God of my salvation; on thee do I wait all the day.
PSALM 25:5 KJV

When the believer has begun with trembling feet to walk in the way of the Lord, he asks to be still led onward like a little child upheld by its parent's helping hand, and he craves to be further instructed in the alphabet of truth. Jehovah is the Author and Perfecter of salvation to His people. Reader, is He the God of your salvation? Do you find in the Father's election, in the Son's atonement, and in the Spirit's quickening all the grounds of your eternal hopes? If so, you may use this as an argument for obtaining further blessings; if the Lord has ordained to save you, surely He will not refuse to instruct you in His ways.

It is a happy thing when we can address the Lord with the confidence that David here manifests; it gives us great power in prayer and comfort in trial. "On You do I wait all the day." Patience is the fair handmaid and daughter of faith; we cheerfully wait when we are certain that we shall not wait in vain. It is our duty and our privilege to wait upon the Lord in service, in worship, in expectancy, in trust all the days of our life. Our faith will be tried faith, and if it is of the true kind, it will bear continued trial without yielding. We shall not grow weary of waiting upon God if we remember how long and how graciously He once waited for us.

CHRISTIAN CHARACTER

May the God of all grace. . .
after you have suffered a while,
perfect, establish, strengthen, and settle you.
1 PETER 5:10 NKJV

You have seen the rainbow as it spans the plain: Glorious are its colors and rare its hues. It is beautiful, but it passes away. The colors give way to the fleecy clouds, and the sky is no longer brilliant with the tints of heaven. It is not established. How can it be? A glorious show made up of transitory sunbeams and passing raindrops, how can it abide?

The graces of the Christian character must not resemble the rainbow in its transitory beauty but, on the contrary, must be established, settled, abiding. Seek that every good thing you have may be an abiding thing. May your character not be writing in the sand but an inscription upon the rock! May your faith be no "baseless fabric of a vision," but may it be built of material able to endure that awful fire which shall consume the wood, hay, and stubble of the hypocrite. May you be rooted and grounded in love. May your convictions be deep, your love real, your desires earnest. May your whole life be so settled and established that all the blasts of hell and all the storms of earth shall never be able to remove you.

GOD IS FOR US

When I cry unto thee, then shall mine enemies
turn back: this I know; for God is for me.
PSALM 56:9 KJV

It is impossible for any human speech to express the full meaning of this delightful phrase: "God is for me." He was "for us" before the worlds were made; He was "for us," or He would not have given His well-beloved Son; He was "for us" when He smote the Only Begotten and laid the full weight of His wrath upon Him—He was "for us" though He was against Him; He was "for us" when we were ruined in the Fall—He loved us notwithstanding all; He was "for us" when we were rebels against Him and with a high hand were bidding Him defiance; He was "for us," or He would not have brought us humbly to seek His face.

He has been "for us" in many struggles, we have been summoned to encounter hosts of dangers, we have been assailed by temptations from without and within—how could we have remained unharmed to this hour if He had not been "for us"? He is "for us" with all the infinity of His being, with all the omnipotence of His love, with all the infallibility of His wisdom; arrayed in all His divine attributes, He is "for us"—eternally and immutably "for us," "for us" when yonder blue skies shall be rolled up like a worn-out vesture, "for us" throughout eternity. And because He is "for us," the voice of prayer will always ensure His help.

THE GLORY OF GOD

"The LORD our God has shown us his glory."
DEUTERONOMY 5:24 NIV

God's great design in all His works is the manifestation of His own glory. Any aim less than this would be unworthy of Himself. But how shall the glory of God be manifested to such fallen creatures as we are? Self must stand out of the way that there may be room for God to be exalted; and this is the reason why He often brings His people into difficulties: That being made conscious of their own folly and weakness, they may be fitted to behold the majesty of God when He comes forth to work their deliverance.

He whose life is one even and smooth path will see but little of the glory of the Lord, for he has few occasions of self-emptying and little fitness for being filled with the revelation of God. They who navigate little streams and shallow creeks know but little of the God of tempests; but they who "do business in great waters," these see His "wonders in the deep." Among the huge waves of bereavement, poverty, temptation, and reproach, we learn the power of Jehovah because we feel the littleness of man.

Thank God then if you have been led by a rough road. It is this which has given you your experience of God's greatness and loving-kindness. Your troubles have enriched you with a wealth of knowledge to be gained by no other means: Your trials have been the cleft of the rock in which Jehovah has set you that you might behold His glory as it passed by.

Day 298

OUR INHERITANCE IN CHRIST

The earnest of our inheritance...
EPHESIANS 1:14 KJV

What enlightenment, what joys, what consolation, what delight of heart is experienced by that man who has learned to feed on Jesus, and on Jesus alone. Yet the realization that we have of Christ's preciousness is, in this life, imperfect at the best. We have tasted "that the Lord is gracious," but we do not yet know how good and gracious He is although what we know of His sweetness makes us long for more. We are but beginners now in spiritual education: For although we have learned the first letters of the alphabet, we cannot read words yet, much less can we put sentences together; but as one says, "He who has been in heaven but five minutes knows more than the general assembly of divines on earth." We have many ungratified desires at present, but soon every wish will be satisfied; and all our powers shall find the sweetest employment in that eternal world of joy.

Oh Christian, within a very little time you will be rid of all your trials and your troubles. Your eyes now suffused with tears will weep no longer. You will gaze in ineffable rapture upon the splendor of Him who sits upon the throne. Even more, upon His throne you will sit. The triumph of His glory you will share; His crown, His joy, His paradise, these will be yours, and you will be coheir with Him who is the heir of all things.

A WITNESS OF JOY

They. . .rejoiced: for God had made
them rejoice with great joy.
NEHEMIAH 12:43 KJV

They "rejoiced for God had made them rejoice with great joy." It was not all singing and giving. When the wheels of the machine are well oiled, the whole machine goes easily; and when the man has the oil of joy, then in his business and in his family, the wheels of his nature glide along sweetly and harmoniously because he is a glad and a happy man. Oh, happy households where the joy is not confined to one but where all partake of it!

Too many need all the religion they can get to cheer their own hearts, and their poor families and neighbors sit shivering in the cold of ungodliness. Be like those well-constructed stoves of our own houses which send out all the heat into the room. Send out the heat of piety into your house, and let all the neighbors participate in the blessing, for so the text finishes: "The joy of Jerusalem was heard afar off." The joy of the Lord should be observed throughout our neighborhood, and many who might otherwise have been careless of true religion will then enquire, "What makes these people glad and creates such happy households?" Your joy shall thus be God's missionary.

BE THANKFUL
AND PRAISE HIM

Forget not all his benefits.
PSALM 103:2 NIV

It is delightful and profitable to mark the hand of God in the lives of ancient saints and to observe His goodness in delivering them, His mercy in pardoning them, and His faithfulness in keeping His covenant with them. But would it not be even more profitable for us to observe the hand of God in our own lives? Should we not look upon our own history as being at least as full of God, as full of His goodness and truth, as much a proof of His faithfulness and veracity as the lives of any of the saints who have gone before?

We do our Lord an injustice when we suppose that He wrought all His mighty acts and showed Himself strong for those before but does not perform wonders for the saints who are now upon the earth. Have you had no deliverances? Have you passed through no rivers, supported by the divine presence? Have you walked through no fires unharmed? he God who gave Solomon the desire of his heart, has He never listened to you and answered your requests? Have you never been made to lie down in green pastures? Have you never been led by the still waters?

Surely the goodness of God has been the same to us as to the saints of old. Let us then weave His mercies into a song. Let us take the pure gold of thankfulness and the jewels of praise and make them into another crown for the head of Jesus. Let our souls give forth music while we praise the Lord whose mercy endures forever.

REMEMBER
GOD'S PROMISES

Exceedingly great and precious promises. . .
2 PETER 1:4 NKJV

If you would know experimentally the preciousness of the promises and enjoy them in your own heart, meditate upon them. Thinking over the hallowed words will often be the prelude to their fulfillment. While you are considering them, the blessing that you are seeking will insensibly come to you. Many a Christian who has thirsted for the promise has found the favor that it ensured gently distilling into his soul even while he has been considering the divine record; and he has rejoiced that he was led to lay the promise near his heart.

But besides meditating upon the promises, seek to receive them as being the very words of God. My soul, it is God, even your God, God who cannot lie, who speaks to you. This Word of His that you are now considering is as true as His own existence. He is a God unchangeable. He has not altered a word that has gone out of His mouth, nor called back one single consolatory sentence. Nor does He lack any power; it is the God who made the heavens and the earth who has spoken. Nor can He fail in wisdom as to the time when He will bestow the favors, for He knows when it is best to give and when better to withhold. Therefore, seeing that it is the Word of a God so true, so immutable, so powerful, so wise, I will and must believe the promise.

If we thus meditate upon the promises and consider the Promiser, we shall experience their sweetness and obtain their fulfillment.

CONTINUALLY WITH YOU

Nevertheless I am continually with You.
PSALM 73:23 NKJV

"Nevertheless"—as if, notwithstanding all the foolishness and ignorance that David had just been confessing to God, not one atom the less was it true and certain that David was saved and accepted, and that the blessing of being constantly in God's presence was undoubtedly his. Fully conscious of his own lost estate and of the deceitfulness and vileness of his nature, yet by a glorious outburst of faith, he sings, "Nevertheless I am continually with Thee."

Believer, endeavor in like spirit to say, "Nevertheless, since I belong to Christ, I am continually with God!" By this is meant continually upon His mind; He is always thinking of me for my good. Continually before His eye—the eye of the Lord never sleeps but is perpetually watching over my welfare. Continually in His hand—so that none will be able to pluck me out from it. Continually on His heart—worn there as a memorial, even as the High Priest bore the names of the twelve tribes upon his heart forever. "You always think of me, O God. You are always making providence work for my good. You have set me as a signet upon Your arm. Your love is strong as death; many waters cannot quench it, neither can the floods drown it. You see me in Christ, and though in myself despised, You behold me as wearing Christ's garments and washed in His blood; and thus I stand accepted in Your presence. I am thus continually in Your favor—'continually with You.'"

THE STRENGTH OF SPIRITUAL KNOWLEDGE

The people that do know their God shall be strong.
DANIEL 11:32 KJV

Every believer understands that to know God is the highest and best form of knowledge; and this spiritual knowledge is a source of strength to the Christian. It strengthens his faith. Believers are constantly spoken of in the scriptures as being persons who are enlightened and taught of the Lord; they are said to "have an unction from the Holy One," and it is the Spirit's peculiar office to lead them into all truth, and all this for the increase and the fostering of their faith. Knowledge strengthens love, as well as faith. Knowledge opens the door, and then through that door we see our Savior. If we know but little of the excellences of Jesus, what He has done for us and what He is doing now, we cannot love Him much; but the more we know Him, the more we shall love Him. Knowledge also strengthens hope. How can we hope for a thing if we do not know of its existence?

Knowledge supplies us reasons for patience. How shall we have patience unless we know something of the sympathy of Christ and understand the good which is to come out of the correction which our heavenly Father sends us? Nor is there one single grace of the Christian which, under God, will not be fostered and brought to perfection by holy knowledge. How important then it is that we should grow not only in grace but also in the "knowledge" of our Lord and Savior Jesus Christ.

ALL THINGS WORK
TOGETHER FOR GOOD

---

*We know that all things work together
for good to them that love God.*
ROMANS 8:28 KJV

Upon some points a believer is absolutely sure. He knows, for instance, that God sits in the stern sheets of the vessel when it rocks most. He believes that an invisible hand is always on the world's rudder, and that wherever providence may drift, Jehovah steers it. That reassuring knowledge prepares him for everything. He knows that God is always wise, and knowing this he is confident that there can be no accidents, no mistakes—that nothing can occur which ought not to arise. He can say, "If I should lose all I have, it is better that I should lose than have if God so wills: The worst calamity is the wisest and the kindest thing that could befall me if God ordains it."

"We know that all things work together for good to them who love God." The Christian does not merely hold this as a theory, but he knows it as a matter of fact. Everything has worked for good as yet. Every event as yet has worked out the most divinely blessed results; and so believing that God rules all, that He governs wisely, that He brings good out of evil, the believer's heart is assured, and he is enabled calmly to meet each trial as it comes. The believer can in the spirit of true resignation pray, "Send me what You will, my God, as long as it comes from You; there has never come an ill portion from Your table to any of Your children."

A DEEP LOVE

The upright love thee.
SONG OF SOLOMON 1:4 KJV

Believers love Jesus with a deeper affection than they dare to give to any other being. They would sooner lose father and mother than part with Christ. They hold all earthly comforts with a loose hand, but they carry Him fast locked in their bosoms. They voluntarily deny themselves for His sake, but they are not to be driven to deny Him.

It is scant love that the fire of persecution can dry up; the true believer's love is a deeper stream than this. Men have labored to divide the faithful from their Master, but their attempts have been fruitless in every age. This is no everyday attachment which the world's power may at length dissolve. Neither man nor devil has found a key which opens this lock. Never has the craft of Satan been more at fault than when he has exercised it in seeking to break this union of two divinely welded hearts.

The intensity of the love of the upright, however, is not so much to be judged by what it appears as by what the upright long for. It is our daily lament that we cannot love enough. Would that our hearts were capable of holding more and reaching further. Our longest reach is but a span of love, and our affection is but as a drop in a bucket compared with His deserts. Measure our love by our intentions, and it is high indeed. Oh, that we could give all the love in all hearts in one great mass, a gathering together of all loves to Him who is altogether lovely!

CHRIST, OUR LIFE

Christ, who is your life. . .
COLOSSIANS 3:4 NIV

Paul's marvelously rich expression indicates that Christ is the source of our life. That same voice which brought Lazarus out of the tomb raised us to newness of life. He is now the substance of our spiritual life. It is by His life that we live; He is in us, the hope of glory, the spring of our actions, the central thought which moves every other thought. Christ is the sustenance of our life. You never get a morsel to satisfy the hunger of your spirit except you find it in Him! Christ is the solace of our life. All our true joys come from Him; and in times of trouble, His presence is our consolation. There is nothing worth living for but Him, and His loving-kindness is better than life! Christ is the object of our life. As the ship speeds toward the port, so hastens the believer toward the haven of his Savior's bosom. As the soldier fights for his captain and is crowned in his captain's victory, so the believer contends for Christ and gets his triumph out of the triumphs of his Master.

Where there is the same life within, there must be to a great extent the same developments without; and if we live in near fellowship with the Lord Jesus, we shall grow like Him. We shall set Him before us as our divine copy, and we shall seek to walk in His footsteps until He becomes the crown of our life in glory. How safe, how honored, how happy is the Christian, since Christ is our life!

THE POWER TO FORGIVE

"The Son of Man has power on earth to forgive sins."
MATTHEW 9:6 NKJV

Behold one of the Great Physician's mightiest arts: He has power to forgive sin! While He lived here below, before the ransom had been paid, before the blood had been literally sprinkled on the mercy seat, He had power to forgive sin. Does He not have the power to do it now that He has died? What power must dwell in Him who has faithfully discharged the debts of His people! He has boundless power now that He has finished transgression and made an end of sin.

If you doubt it, see Him rising from the dead! Behold Him in ascending splendor raised to the right hand of God! Hear Him pleading before the eternal Father, pointing to His wounds, urging the merit of His sacred passion! What power to forgive is here! The most crimson sins are removed by the crimson of His blood. At this moment, whatever your sinfulness, Christ has power to pardon, power to pardon you and millions akin to you. A word will speak it. He has nothing more to do to win your pardon; all the atoning work is done. He can, in answer to your tears, forgive your sins today and make you know it. He can breathe into your soul at this very moment a peace with God which passes all understanding, which shall spring from perfect remission of your manifold iniquities.

May you now experience the power of Jesus to forgive sin!

OUR EVERLASTING CONSOLATION

Everlasting consolation. . .
2 THESSALONIANS 2:16 KJV

"Everlasting consolation"—here is the most excellent of all, for the eternity of comfort is the crown and glory of it. What is this "everlasting consolation"?

It includes a sense of pardoned sin. A Christian has received in his heart the witness of the Spirit that his iniquities are put away like a cloud, and his transgressions like a thick cloud. If sin is pardoned, is not that an everlasting consolation?

Next, the Lord gives His people an abiding sense of acceptance in Christ. The Christian knows that God looks upon him as standing in union with Jesus. Union to the risen Lord is a consolation of the most abiding order; it is in fact everlasting. Let sickness prostrate us; have we not seen hundreds of believers as happy in the weakness of disease as they would have been in blooming health? Let death's arrows pierce us to the heart; our comfort does not die, for have not we often heard the songs of saints as they have rejoiced because the living love of God was shed abroad in their hearts in dying moments? Yes, a sense of acceptance in the Beloved is an everlasting consolation.

Moreover, the Christian has a conviction of his security. God has promised to save those who trust in Christ: The Christian does trust in Christ, and he believes that God will be as good as His word and will save him. He feels that he is safe by virtue of his being bound up with the person and work of Jesus.

Day 309
A GRATEFUL HEART

You make me glad by your deeds, LORD.
PSALM 92:4 NIV

Do you believe that your sins are forgiven and that Christ has made a full atonement for them? Then what a joyful Christian you ought to be! How you should live above the common trials and troubles of the world! Since sin is forgiven, can it matter what happens to you now?

Christian, if you are saved, while you are glad, be grateful and loving. Cling to that cross that took your sin away; serve Him who served you. "I beseech you therefore by the mercies of God that you present your bodies a living sacrifice, holy, acceptable unto God, which is your reasonable service." Let not your zeal evaporate in some little outburst of song. Show your love in expressive tokens. Love the brethren of Him who loved you. If there is a poor tried believer, weep with him and bear his cross for the sake of Him who wept for you and carried your sins. Since you are forgiven freely for Christ's sake, go and tell others the joyful news of pardoning mercy. Do not be content with this unspeakable blessing for yourself alone but make known abroad the story of the cross.

Holy gladness and holy boldness will make you a good preacher, and all the world will be a pulpit for you to preach in. Cheerful holiness is the most forcible of sermons, but the Lord must give it to you. When it is the Lord's work in which we rejoice, we need not be afraid of being too glad.

GOD'S GRACIOUS MERCY

The mercy of God. . .
PSALM 52:8 NKJV

Meditate on this mercy of the Lord. It is tender mercy. With gentle, loving touch, He heals the brokenhearted and binds up their wounds. He is as gracious in the manner of His mercy as in the matter of it. It is great mercy. There is nothing little in God; His mercy is like Himself—it is infinite. You cannot measure it. His mercy is so great that it forgives great sins of great sinners, after great lengths of time, and then gives great favors and great privileges and raises us up to great enjoyments in the great heaven of the great God. It is undeserved mercy as indeed all true mercy must be, for deserved mercy is only a misnomer for justice.

There is no single mercy. You may think you have but one mercy, but you shall find it to be a whole cluster of mercies. It is abounding mercy. Millions have received it, yet far from its being exhausted, it is as fresh, as full, and as free as ever. It is unfailing mercy. It will never leave you. If mercy is your friend, mercy will be with you in temptation to keep you from yielding, with you in trouble to prevent you from sinking, with you living to be the light and life of your countenance, and with you dying to be the joy of your soul when earthly comfort is ebbing fast.

Day 311

SHEEP PRAISING THEIR SHEPHERD

He shall stand and feed in the strength of the LORD.
MICAH 5:4 KJV

Christ's reign in His Church is that of a shepherd-king. He has supremacy, but it is the superiority of a wise and tender shepherd over his needy and loving flock; He commands and receives obedience, but it is the willing obedience of the well-cared-for sheep, rendered joyfully to their beloved Shepherd whose voice they know so well. He rules by the force of love and the energy of goodness.

His reign is practical in its character. The great Head of the Church is actively engaged in providing for His people. He does not sit down upon the throne in empty state or hold a scepter without wielding it in government. No, He stands and feeds.

His reign is continual in its duration. His eyes never slumber, and His hands never rest; His heart never ceases to beat with love, and His shoulders are never weary of carrying His people's burdens.

His reign is effectually powerful in its action. Wherever Christ is, there is God; and whatever Christ does is the act of the Most High. It is a joyful truth to consider that He who stands today representing the interests of His people is very God of very God to whom every knee shall bow. Happy are we who belong to such a Shepherd, whose humanity communes with us and whose divinity protects us. Let us worship and bow down before Him as the people of His pasture.

RECEIVING THROUGH GIVING

Whoever refreshes others will be refreshed.
PROVERBS 11:25 NIV

To get, we must give; to accumulate, we must scatter; to make ourselves happy, we must make others happy; and in order to become spiritually vigorous, we must seek the spiritual good of others. In watering others, we are ourselves watered.

How? Our efforts to be useful bring out our powers for usefulness. We have latent talents and dormant faculties which are brought to light by exercise. Our strength for labor is hidden even from ourselves, until we venture forth to fight the Lord's battles or to climb the mountains of difficulty. We often find in attempting to teach others that we gain instruction for ourselves.

Oh, what gracious lessons some of us have learned at sickbeds! We went to teach the scriptures; we came away blushing that we knew so little of them. In our conversation with poor saints, we are taught the way of God more perfectly for ourselves and get a deeper insight into divine truth—so that watering others makes us humble. We discover how much grace there is where we had not looked for it and how much the poor saint may surpass us in knowledge. Our own comfort is also increased by our working for others. We endeavor to cheer them, and the consolation gladdens our own heart. Like the two men in the snow—one chafed the other's limbs to keep him from dying and in so doing kept his own blood in circulation and saved his own life. Give then, and it shall be given unto you, good measure, pressed down, and running over.

Day 313
NO MORE GRIEF

"The voice of weeping shall no longer be heard."
ISAIAH 65:19 NKJV

The glorified weep no more, for all outward causes of grief are gone. There are no broken friendships in heaven. Poverty, famine, peril, persecution, and slander are unknown there. No pain distresses; no thought of death or bereavement saddens. They weep no more for they are perfectly sanctified. They are without fault before His throne and are fully conformed to His image.

Well may they cease to mourn who have ceased to sin. They weep no more because all fear of change is past. They know that they are eternally secure. Sin is shut out, and they are shut in. Countless cycles may revolve, but eternity shall not be exhausted; and while eternity endures, their immortality and blessedness shall coexist with it. They are forever with the Lord.

They weep no more because every desire is fulfilled. They cannot wish for anything that they have not in possession. Eye and ear, heart and hand, judgment, imagination, hope, desire, will, all the faculties are completely satisfied; and imperfect as our present ideas are of the things who God has prepared for them who love Him, yet we know enough by the revelation of the Spirit that the saints above are supremely blessed. The joy of Christ, which is an infinite fullness of delight, is in them. That same joyful rest remains for us. It may not be far distant. "Wherefore comfort one another with these words."

FAITH GENERATES LOVE

That Christ may dwell in your hearts by faith.
EPHESIANS 3:17 KJV

Beyond measure it is desirable that we as believers should have the person of Jesus constantly before us, to inflame our love toward Him and to increase our knowledge of Him. I would to God that my readers were all diligent in the learning of the cross. To have Jesus ever near, the heart must be full of Him, welling up with His love even to overrunning; thus the apostle prays "that Christ may dwell in your hearts." See how near he would have Jesus to be! You cannot get a subject closer to you than to have it in the heart itself.

We should pant after love for Christ of a most abiding character; not a love that flames up and then dies out into the darkness of a few embers, but a constant flame fed by sacred fuel, like the fire upon the altar which never went out. This cannot be accomplished except by faith. Faith must be strong, or love will not be fervent; the root of the flower must be healthy, or we cannot expect the bloom to be sweet. Faith is the lily's root, and love is the lily's bloom. Jesus cannot be in your heart's love except you have a firm hold of Him by your heart's faith, and therefore always trust Christ in order that you may always love Him. If love is cold, be sure that faith is drooping.

Day 315

COMMITTING YOUR
SOUL TO GOD

Into your hands I commit my spirit;
deliver me, LORD, my faithful God.
PSALM 31:5 NIV

These words have been frequently used by holy men in their hour of departure. The object of the faithful man's solicitude in life and death is not his body or his estate but his spirit; this is his choice treasure—if this be safe, all is well. What is this mortal state compared with the soul? The believer commits his soul to the hand of his God; it came from Him, it is His own, He has afore time sustained it, He is able to keep it, and it is most fit that He should receive it. All things are safe in Jehovah's hands; what we entrust to the Lord will be secure, both now and in that day of days toward which we are hastening. It is peaceful living and glorious dying to repose in the care of heaven. At all times we should commit our all to Jesus' faithful hands; then though life may hang on a thread and adversities may multiply as the sands of the sea, our soul shall dwell at ease and delight itself in quiet resting places.

Redemption is a solid basis for confidence. David had not known Calvary as we do now, but temporal redemption cheered him; and shall not eternal redemption yet more sweetly console us? Past deliverances are strong pleas for present assistance. What the Lord has done, He will do again, for He changes not. He is faithful to His promises and gracious to His saints; He will not turn away from His people.

HOPE FOR THE BARREN

"Sing, O barren!"
ISAIAH 54:1 NKJV

There are times when we feel very barren. Prayer is lifeless, love is cold, faith is weak; each grace in the garden of our heart languishes and droops. In such a condition, what are we to do?

I can sing of Jesus Christ. I can talk of visits which the Redeemer has paid to me. I can magnify the great love with which He loved His people when He came from the heights of heaven for their redemption. I will go to the cross again. Come, my soul, heavy laden you once were and lost your burden there. Go to Calvary again. Perhaps that very cross which gave you life may give you fruitfulness.

What is my barrenness? It is the platform for His fruit-creating power. What is my desolation? It is the setting for the sapphire of His everlasting love. I will go in poverty, I will go in helplessness, I will go in all my shame and backsliding; I will tell Him that I am still His child, and in confidence in His faithful heart, I will sing and cry aloud.

Sing, believer, for it will cheer your heart and the hearts of other desolate ones. Sing on, for now that you are really ashamed of being barren, you will be fruitful soon; now that God makes you reluctant to be without fruit, He will soon cover you with clusters. The experience of our barrenness is painful, but the Lord's visitations are delightful. A sense of our own poverty drives us to Christ, and that is where we need to be, for in Him is our fruit found.

SIMPLY WAIT

Wait on the LORD.
PSALM 27:14 KJV

There are hours of perplexity when the most willing spirit, anxiously desirous to serve the Lord, does not know which direction to take. Then what should it do? Fly back in cowardice, turn to the right hand in fear, or rush forward in presumption? No, simply wait.

Wait in prayer, however. Call upon God and tell Him your difficulty and plead His promise of aid. In dilemmas between one duty and another, wait with simplicity of soul upon the Lord. It is sure to be well with us when we feel and know our own folly and are heartily willing to be guided by the will of God. But wait in faith. Express your unwavering confidence in Him; for unfaithful, untrusting waiting is but an insult to the Lord. Believe that He will come at the right time. Wait in quiet patience, not rebelling because you are under the affliction but blessing your God for it. Accept the case as it is, and put it as it stands, simply and with your whole heart, without any self-will, into the hand of your covenant God, saying, "Now, Lord, not my will but Yours be done. I do not know what to do; I am brought to extremities, but I will wait until You cleave the floods or drive back my foes. I will wait if You keep me many a day, for my heart is fixed upon You alone, O God; and my spirit waits for You in the full conviction that You will yet be my joy and my salvation, my refuge and my strong tower."

TRUST YOURSELF TO GOD

On mine arm shall they trust.
ISAIAH 51:5 KJV

In seasons of severe trial, the Christian has nothing on earth that he can trust in and is therefore compelled to cast himself on his God alone. When no human deliverance can avail, he must simply and entirely trust himself to the providence and care of God. There is no confiding in God sometimes because of the multitude of our friends; but when a man is so poor, so friendless, so helpless that he has nowhere else to turn, he flies into his Father's arms and is blessedly clasped within them! When he is burdened with troubles so pressing that he cannot tell them to any but his God, he may be thankful for them for he will learn more of his Lord than at any other time.

Now that You have only God to trust in, see that you place your full confidence in Him. Do not dishonor the Lord by unworthy doubts and fears, but be strong in faith, giving glory to God. Now is the time for feats of faith and valiant exploits. Be strong and very courageous, and the Lord your God shall certainly, as surely as He built the heavens and the earth, glorify Himself in your weakness and magnify His might in the midst of your distress. Your faith would lose its glory if it rested on anything discernible by the carnal eye. May the Holy Spirit give you rest in Jesus.

DEPENDENCE ON GOD

Trust in him at all times.
PSALM 62:8 NIV

Faith is as much the rule of temporal as of spiritual life; we ought to have faith in God for our earthly affairs as well as for our heavenly business. It is only as we learn to trust in God for the supply of all our daily needs that we shall live above the world. We are not to be idle; that would show we did not trust in God but in the devil, who is the father of idleness. We are not to be imprudent or rash; that were to trust chance and not the Living God, who is a God of economy and order. Acting in all prudence and uprightness, we are to rely simply and entirely upon the Lord at all times.

Trusting in God, you will not be compelled to mourn because you have used sinful means to grow rich. Serve God with integrity, and if you achieve no success, at least no sin will lie upon your conscience. Trusting God, you will not be guilty of self-contradiction. Be a man with living principles within; never bow to the varying customs of worldly wisdom. Walk in your path of integrity with steadfast steps, and show that you are invincibly strong in the strength which confidence in God alone can confer. Your heart will be fixed, trusting in the Lord.

There is no more blessed way of living than a life of dependence upon a covenant-keeping God. We have no care for He cares for us; we have no troubles because we cast our burdens upon the Lord.

TRIALS OF THE RIGHTEOUS

The LORD trieth the righteous.
PSALM 11:5 KJV

All events are under the control of Providence; consequently all the trials of our outward life are traceable at once to the great First Cause. All providences are doors to trial. Even our mercies, like roses, have their thorns. Men may be drowned in seas of prosperity as well as in rivers of affliction. Our mountains are not too high and our valleys are not too low for temptations: Trials lurk on all roads. We are beset and surrounded with dangers. Yet no shower falls from the threatening cloud without permission; every drop has its order before it hastens to the earth.

The trials which come from God are sent to prove and strengthen our graces, and so at once to illustrate the power of divine grace, to test the genuineness of our virtues, and to add to their energy. You would never have possessed the precious faith that now supports you if the trial of your faith had not been like unto fire. Worldly ease is a great foe to faith; it loosens the joints of holy valor and snaps the sinews of sacred courage. While the wheat sleeps comfortably in the husk, it is useless to man; it must be threshed out of its resting place before its value can be known. Thus it is well that Jehovah tries the righteous, for it causes them to grow rich toward God.

THE TREE THAT
PRODUCES FRUIT

"Your fruitfulness comes from me."
HOSEA 14:8 NIV

The fruit of the branch is directly traceable to the root. Sever the connection, the branch dies, and no fruit is produced. By virtue of our union with Christ, we bring forth fruit. Prize this precious union to Christ, for it must be the source of all the fruitfulness which you can hope to know. If you were not joined to Jesus Christ, you would be a barren bough indeed.

The fruit owes much to the root—that is essential to fruitfulness—but it owes very much also to external influences. How much we owe to God's grace-providence in which He provides us constantly with quickening, teaching, consolation, strength, or whatever else we want. To this we owe our all of usefulness or virtue.

The gardener's sharp-edged knife promotes the fruitfulness of the tree by thinning the clusters and by cutting off superfluous shoots. So is it, Christian, with that pruning by the Lord. "My Father is the Husbandman. Every branch in Me that bears not fruit He takes away; and every branch that bears fruit, He purges it that it may bring forth more fruit." Since our God is the author of our spiritual graces, let us give to Him all the glory of our salvation.

GREAT ANSWER TO PRAYER

I will answer thee, and shew thee great and mighty things, which thou knowest not.
JEREMIAH 33:3 KJV

There are different translations of these words. One version renders it, "I will show you great and fortified things." Another, "great and reserved things." Now there are reserved and special things in Christian experience: All the developments of spiritual life are not alike easy of attainment. There are the common frames and feelings of repentance and faith and joy and hope, which are enjoyed by the entire family; but there is an upper realm of rapture, of communion and conscious union with Christ, which is far from being the common dwelling place of believers.

Prevailing prayer is victorious over the God of mercy, "By his strength he had power with God." Prevailing prayer takes the Christian to Carmel and enables him to cover heaven with clouds of blessing and earth with floods of mercy. Prevailing prayer bears the Christian aloft to Pisgah and shows him the inheritance reserved; it elevates us to Tabor and transfigures us, until in the likeness of his Lord as He is, so are we also in this world. If you would reach to something higher than ordinary groveling experience, look to the Rock that is higher than you and gaze with the eye of faith through the window of importunate prayer. When you open the window on your side, it will not be bolted on the other.

BE GOOD
REPRESENTATIVES
OF CHRIST

*Lead me, LORD, in your righteousness
because of my enemies.*
PSALM 5:8 NIV

Very bitter is the enmity of the world against the people of Christ. Men will forgive a thousand faults in others, but they will magnify the most trivial offense in the followers of Jesus. Instead of vainly regretting this, let this be a special motive for walking very carefully before God. If we live carelessly, the world will soon see it, and with its hundred tongues, it will spread the story, exaggerated and emblazoned by the zeal of slander. They will shout triumphantly, "See how these Christians act! They are hypocrites." Thus will much damage be done to the cause of Christ and much insult offered to His name.

The cross of Christ is in itself an offense to the world; let us take heed that we add no offense of our own. Let us mind that we put no stumbling blocks where there are enough already. Let us not add our folly to give point to the scorn with which the worldly deride the Gospel. In the presence of adversaries who will misrepresent our best deeds and impugn our motives where they cannot censure our actions, how circumspect should we be! Not only are we under surveillance, but there are more spies than we know of. The espionage is everywhere, at home and abroad. O Lord, lead us ever, lest our enemies trip us up!

Day 324

BAD NEWS? DON'T FEAR

He will not be afraid of evil tidings.
PSALM 112:7 NKJV

Christian, you ought not to dread the arrival of evil tidings; because if you are distressed by them, how do you differ from other men? Other men have not your God to fly to; they have never proved His faithfulness as you have done, and it is no wonder if they are bowed down with alarm and cowed with fear. But you profess to be of another spirit; you have been begotten again unto a lively hope, and your heart lives in heaven and not on earthly things. Now if you are seen to be distracted as other men, what is the value of that grace which you profess to have received? Where is the dignity of that new nature which you claim to possess?

If you should be filled with alarm, you would doubtless be led into the sins so common to others under trying circumstances. The ungodly, when they are overtaken by evil tidings, rebel against God; they murmur and think that God deals harshly with them. Will you fall into that same sin? Will you provoke the Lord as they do? Moreover, unconverted men often run to wrong means in order to escape from difficulties, and you will be sure to do the same if your mind yields to the present pressure. Trust in the Lord, and wait patiently for Him. Your wisest course is to do as Moses did at the Red Sea: "Stand still, and see the salvation of God."

ENCOURAGE FELLOW CHRISTIANS

"Encourage him."
DEUTERONOMY 1:38 NASB

God employs His people to encourage one another. He did not say to an angel, "Gabriel, My servant Joshua is about to lead My people into Canaan—go, encourage him." God never works needless miracles; if His purposes can be accomplished by ordinary means, He will not use miraculous agency.

Gabriel would not have been half so well fitted for the work as Moses. A brother's sympathy is more precious than an angel's embassy. The angel, swift of wing, had better known the Master's bidding than the people's temper. An angel had never experienced the hardness of the road nor seen the fiery serpents, nor had he led the stiff-necked multitude in the wilderness as Moses had done.

We should be glad that God usually works for man by man. It forms a bond of brotherhood, and being mutually dependent on one another, we are fused more completely into one family. Labor to help others; especially strive to encourage them. Leave the young believer to discover the roughness of the road by degrees, but tell him of the strength which dwells in God, of the sureness of the promise, and of the charms of communion with Christ. Aim to comfort the sorrowful and to animate the desponding. Speak a word in season to him who is weary, and encourage those who are fearful to go on their way with gladness. God encourages you by His promises, Christ encourages you as He points to the heaven He has won for you, and the Spirit encourages you as He works in you to will and to do of His own will and pleasure.

GOD'S GIFTS

For this child I prayed.
1 SAMUEL 1:27 KJV

Devout souls delight to look upon those mercies that they have obtained in answer to supplication, for they can see God's especial love in them. When we can name our blessings Samuel, that is, "asked of God," they will be as dear to us as her child was to Hannah. Peninnah had many children, but they came as common blessings unsought in prayer; Hannah's one heaven-given child was dearer by far because he was the fruit of earnest pleadings.

Did we pray for the conversion of our children? How doubly sweet when they are saved to see in them our own petitions fulfilled! Better to rejoice over them as the fruit of our pleadings than as the fruit of our bodies. Have we sought of the Lord some choice spiritual gift? When it comes to us, it will be wrapped up in the gold cloth of God's faithfulness and truth, and so be doubly precious. Have we petitioned for success in the Lord's work? How joyful is the prosperity that comes flying upon the wings of prayer!

Even when prayer speeds not, the blessings grow all the richer for the delay. That which we win by prayer, we should dedicate to God, as Hannah dedicated Samuel. The gift came from heaven; let it go to heaven. Prayer brought it, gratitude sang over it, let devotion consecrate it.

THANKSGIVING FOR BLESSINGS

You crown the year with your bounty.
PSALM 65:11 NIV

All the year through, every hour of every day, God is richly blessing us. Like a river, His loving-kindness is always flowing with a fullness inexhaustible as His own nature. Like the atmosphere that constantly surrounds the earth, the benevolence of God surrounds all His creatures; in it, as in their element, they live and move and have their being. Yet as the sun on summer days gladdens us with beams more warm and bright than at other times, so is it with the mercy of God; it has its golden hours, its days of overflow when the Lord magnifies His grace before the sons of men.

The joyous days of harvest are a special season of excessive favor. It is the glory of autumn that the ripe gifts of providence are then abundantly bestowed; it is the mellow season of realization, whereas all before was but hope and expectation. Great is the joy of harvest. Happy are the reapers who fill their arms with the liberality of heaven. The psalmist tells us that the harvest is the crowning of the year. Surely these crowning mercies call for crowning thanksgiving!

Let us render it by the inward emotions of gratitude. Let our hearts be warmed; let our spirits remember, meditate, and think upon this goodness of the Lord. Then let us praise Him with our lips, and laud and magnify His name from whose bounty all this goodness flows. Let us glorify God by yielding our gifts to His cause. A practical proof of our gratitude is a special thank offering to the Lord of the harvest.

RICH IN CHRIST

The unsearchable riches of Christ. . .
EPHESIANS 3:8 NKJV

My Master has riches beyond the count of arithmetic, the measurement of reason, the dream of imagination, or the eloquence of words. They are unsearchable! You may look and study and weigh, but Jesus is a greater Savior than you think Him to be when your thoughts are at the greatest. My Lord is more ready to pardon than you to sin, more able to forgive than you to transgress. My Master is more willing to supply your wants than you are to confess them.

When you put the crown on His head, you will only crown Him with silver when He deserves gold. My Master has riches of happiness to bestow upon you now. He can make you to lie down in green pastures and lead you beside still waters. There is no love like His; neither earth nor heaven can match it. My Master does not treat His servants offensively; He gives to them as a king gives to a king. He gives them two heavens—a heaven below in serving Him here and a heaven above in delighting in Him forever. He will give you on the way to heaven all you need; your bread shall be given you, and your waters shall be sure. There, where you shall hear the song of them who triumph, the shout of them who feast, and shall have a face-to-face view of the glorious and beloved One.

Lord, teach us more and more of Jesus, and we will tell out the good news to others.

Day 329

GOD REJOICES IN US;
WE REJOICE IN GOD

I will rejoice over them to do them good.
JEREMIAH 32:41 KJV

How heart-cheering to the believer is the delight which God has in His saints! We cannot see any reason in ourselves why the Lord should take pleasure in us; we cannot take delight in ourselves, for we often have to groan being burdened, conscious of our sinfulness and deploring our unfaithfulness—and we fear that God's people cannot take much delight in us, for they must perceive so much of our imperfections and our follies that they may rather lament our infirmities than admire our graces. But we love to dwell upon this transcendent truth, this glorious mystery: That as the bridegroom rejoices over the bride, so does the Lord rejoice over us.

In what strong language He expresses His delight in His people! Who could have conceived of the Eternal One as bursting forth into a song? Yet it is written, "He will rejoice over you with joy, He will rest in His love, He will joy over you with singing." As He looked upon the world He had made, He said, "It is very good"; but when He beheld those who are the purchase of Jesus' blood, His own chosen ones, it seemed as if the great heart of the Infinite could restrain itself no longer but overflowed in divine exclamations of joy. Should we not utter our grateful response to such a marvelous declaration of His love, and sing, "I will rejoice in the Lord; I will joy in the God of my salvation"?

Day 330
ACCEPTED IN CHRIST

Blessed be the God and Father of our Lord Jesus Christ,
who hath blessed us with all spiritual blessings in heavenly
places in Christ. . .to the praise of the glory of his grace,
wherein he hath made us accepted in the beloved.
EPHESIANS 1:3, 6 KJV

What a state of privilege! It includes our justification before God, but the term *acceptance* in the Greek means more than that. It signifies that we are the objects of divine complacence—even of divine delight. How marvelous that we mortals, sinners, should be the objects of divine love! But it is only "in the Beloved."

Rejoice then, believer, in this: "There is nothing acceptable here!" But look at Christ, and see if there is not everything acceptable there. Your sins trouble you; but God has cast your sins behind His back, and you are accepted in the Righteous One. You have to fight with corruption and to wrestle with temptation, but you are already accepted in Him who has overcome the powers of evil. The devil tempts you; be of good cheer: He cannot destroy you for you are accepted in Him who has broken Satan's head.

Know by full assurance your glorious standing. Even glorified souls are not more accepted than you are. They are only accepted in heaven "in the Beloved," and you are even now accepted in Christ after the same manner.

THE VIEW FROM GOD'S THRONE

The LORD looks from heaven;
He sees all the sons of men.
PSALM 33:13 NKJV

Perhaps no figure of speech represents God in a more gracious light than when He is spoken of as stooping from His throne and coming down from heaven to attend to the wants and to behold the woes of mankind. We cannot help pouring out our heart in affection for our Lord who inclines His ear from the highest glory and puts it to the lip of the dying sinner whose failing heart longs after reconciliation. How can we but love Him when we know that He numbers the very hairs of our heads, marks our paths, and orders our ways?

Especially is this great truth brought near to our heart when we recollect how attentive He is, not merely to the temporal interests of His creatures but to their spiritual concerns. Though leagues of distance lie between the finite creature and the Infinite Creator, yet there are links uniting both. When a tear is wept by you, do not think that God does not behold; for "Like as a father pities his children, so the Lord pities them who fear Him." Your sigh is able to move the heart of Jehovah, your whisper can incline His ear unto you, your prayer can stay His hand, your faith can move His arm. Do not think that God sits on high taking no account of you. For the eyes of the Lord run to and fro throughout the whole earth to show Himself strong on behalf of those whose heart is perfect toward Him.

Day 332
PRAISE GOD DAILY

Sing the glory of his name; make his praise glorious.
PSALM 66:2 NIV

It is not left to our own option whether we shall praise God or not. Praise is God's most righteous due, and every Christian, as the recipient of His grace, is bound to praise God from day to day.

It is true we have no commandment prescribing certain hours of song and thanksgiving: But the law written upon the heart teaches us that it is right to praise God. Yes, it is the Christian's duty to praise God. It is not only a pleasurable exercise, but it is the absolute obligation of his life.

You who are always mourning, do not think that you are guiltless in this respect or imagine that you can discharge your duty to your God without songs of praise. You are bound by the bonds of His love to bless His name as long as you live, and His praise should continually be in your mouth, for you are blessed in order that you may bless Him. If you do not praise God, you are not bringing forth the fruit which He, as the divine Husbandman, has a right to expect at your hands.

Arise and chant His praise. With every morning's dawn, lift up your notes of thanksgiving, and let every setting sun be followed with your song. Girdle the earth with your praises; surround it with an atmosphere of melody, and God Himself will hearken from heaven and accept your music.

JEHOVAH'S GIFTS

The LORD gives grace and glory.
PSALM 84:11 NASB

Bounteous is Jehovah in His nature; to give is His delight. His gifts are beyond measure precious and are as freely given as the light of the sun. He gives grace to His elect because He wills it, to His redeemed because of His covenant, to the called because of His promise, to believers because they seek it, to sinners because they need it. He gives grace abundantly, seasonably, constantly, readily, sovereignly. Grace in all its forms He freely renders to His people: comforting, preserving, sanctifying, directing, instructing, assisting grace; He generously pours into their souls without ceasing, and He always will do so, whatever may occur. Sickness may befall, but the Lord will give grace; poverty may happen to us, but grace will surely be afforded; death must come, but grace will light a candle at the darkest hour. How blessed it is as the seasons pass and the leaves begin again to fall to enjoy such an unfading promise as this: "The Lord will give grace."

Grace and glory always go together. God has married them, and none can divorce them. The Lord will never deny a soul glory to whom He has freely given to live upon His grace; indeed glory is nothing more than grace in full bloom, grace like autumn fruit, mellow and perfected. Glory, the glory of heaven, the glory of eternity, the glory of Jesus, the glory of the Father, the Lord will surely give to His chosen. Oh, rare promise of a faithful God!

Day 334
THIRST QUENCHED

"Whoever drinks the water I
give them will never thirst."
JOHN 4:14 NIV

He who is a believer in Jesus finds enough in his Lord to satisfy him now and to content him forevermore. The believer is not the man whose days are weary for want of comfort and whose nights are long from absence of heart-cheering thought, for he finds in religion such a spring of joy, such a fountain of consolation that he is content and happy. Put him in a dungeon, and he will find good company; place him in a barren wilderness, he will eat the bread of heaven; drive him away from friendship, he will meet the "Friend who sticks closer than a brother."

The heart is as insatiable as the grave until Jesus enters it, and then it is a cup full to overflowing. There is such a fullness in Christ that He alone is the believer's all. The true saint is so completely satisfied with the all-sufficiency of Jesus that he thirsts no more—except it be for deeper draughts of the living fountain. In that sweet manner shall you thirst, a thirst of loving desire; you will find it a sweet thing to be panting after a fuller enjoyment of Jesus' love.

Do you feel that all your desires are satisfied in Jesus and that you have no want now but to know more of Him and to have closer fellowship with Him? Then come continually and take of the water of life freely. Jesus will never think you take too much but will ever welcome you, saying, "Drink abundantly, beloved."

FUTURE FAULTLESSNESS

Faultless before the presence of his glory. . .
JUDE 1:24 KJV

Revolve in your mind that wondrous word *faultless*! We are far off from it now; but as our Lord never stops short of perfection in His work of love, we shall reach it one day. The Savior who will keep His people to the end will also present them at last to Himself as "a glorious Church, not having spot or wrinkle or any such thing, but holy and without blemish." All the jewels in the Savior's crown are without a single flaw. All the maids of honor who attend the Lamb's wife are pure virgins without spot or stain.

But how will Jesus make us faultless? He will wash us from our sins in His own blood until we are white and fair as God's purest angel; and we shall be clothed in His righteousness, that righteousness which makes the saint who wears it positively faultless, perfect in the sight of God. The work of the Holy Spirit within us will be altogether complete. He will make us so perfectly holy that we shall have no lingering tendency to sin. We shall be holy even as God is holy, and in His presence we shall dwell forever. Saints will not be out of place in heaven; their beauty will be as great as that of the place prepared for them. Sin gone, Satan shut out, temptation past forever, and ourselves "faultless" before God, this will be heaven indeed!

LORD OF THE WINTER

Thou hast made summer and winter.
PSALM 74:17 KJV

Begin this wintry month with your God. The cold snows and the piercing winds all remind you that He keeps His covenant with day and night, and tend to assure you that He will also keep that glorious covenant which He has made with you in the person of Christ Jesus. He who is true to His word in the revolutions of the seasons of this poor, sin-polluted world will not prove unfaithful in His dealings with His own well-beloved Son.

Winter in the soul is by no means a comfortable season, and if it be upon you just now, it will be very painful to you: But there is this comfort, namely that the Lord makes it. He is the great Winter King and rules in the realms of frost, and therefore you cannot murmur. Losses, crosses, heaviness, sickness, poverty, and a thousand other ills are of the Lord's sending and come to us with wise design. Frosts kill noxious insects and put a bound to raging diseases. Oh, that such good results would always follow our winters of affliction!

How we prize the fire just now! How pleasant is its cheerful glow! Let us in the same manner prize our Lord, who is the constant source of warmth and comfort in every time of trouble. Let us draw near to Him, and in Him find joy and peace in believing. Let us wrap ourselves in the warm garments of His promises and go forth to labors which befit the season.

THE IMPORTANCE OF PRAYER

We raise our heart and hands toward God in heaven.
LAMENTATIONS 3:41 NASB

The act of prayer teaches us our unworthiness, which is a very salutary lesson for such proud beings as we are. If God gave us favors without constraining us to pray for them, we should never know how poor we are, but a true prayer is an inventory of wants, a catalogue of necessities, a revelation of hidden poverty. While it is an application to divine wealth, it is a confession of human emptiness. The most healthy state of a Christian is to be always empty in self and constantly depending upon the Lord for supplies, to be always poor in self and rich in Jesus.

Prayer is in itself, apart from the answer that it brings, a great benefit to the Christian. As the runner gains strength for the race by daily exercise, so for the great race of life, we acquire energy by the hallowed labor of prayer. An earnest pleader comes out of his closet, even as the sun rises from the chambers of the east, rejoicing like a strong man to run his race. Prayer girds human weakness with divine strength, turns human folly into heavenly wisdom, and gives to troubled mortals the peace of God. We know not what prayer cannot do!

We thank You, great God, for the mercy seat, a choice proof of Your marvelous loving-kindness. Help us to use it in the right manner throughout this day!

QUIETNESS OF THE SOUL

I will meditate in thy precepts.
PSALM 119:15 KJV

There are times when solitude is better than society and silence is wiser than speech. We should be better Christians if we were more alone, waiting upon God and gathering through meditation on His Word spiritual strength for labor in His service. Our bodies are not supported by merely taking food into the mouth, but the process which really supplies the muscle and the nerve and the sinew and the bone is the process of digestion. It is by digestion that the outward food becomes assimilated with the inner life. Our souls are not nourished merely by listening awhile to this, and then to that, and then to the other part of divine truth. Hearing, reading, marking, and learning all require inward digesting to complete their usefulness, and the inward digesting of the truth lies for the most part in meditating upon it.

Why is it that some Christians, although they hear many sermons, make but slow advances in the divine life? Because they neglect their closets and do not thoughtfully meditate on God's Word. They love the wheat, but they do not grind it; they would have the corn, but they will not go forth into the fields to gather it; the fruit hangs upon the tree, but they will not pluck it; the water flows at their feet, but they will not stoop to drink it. From such folly, deliver us, O Lord, and this be our resolve: "I will meditate on Your precepts."

A PERSONAL RELATIONSHIP

*I count all things but loss for the excellency of the
knowledge of Christ Jesus my Lord.*
PHILIPPIANS 3:8 KJV

Spiritual knowledge of Christ will be a personal knowledge.
I cannot know Jesus through another person's acquaintance
with Him. No, I must know Him myself; I must know Him
on my own account.

It will be an intelligent knowledge—I must know Him,
not as the visionary dreams of Him but as the Word reveals
Him. I must know His natures, divine and human. I must
know His offices, His attributes, His works, His shame,
His glory.

It will be an affectionate knowledge of Him; indeed,
if I know Him at all, I must love Him. An ounce of heart
knowledge is worth a ton of head learning.

Our knowledge of Him will be a satisfying knowledge.
When I know my Savior, my mind will be full to the brim—I
shall feel that I have that which my spirit panted after.

At the same time it will be an exciting knowledge; the
more I know of my Beloved, the more I shall want to know.
I shall want the more as I get the more. This knowledge of
Christ Jesus will be a most happy one.

Come, my soul, sit at Jesus' feet and learn of Him all
this day.

In His arm He will gather the lambs.
ISAIAH 40:11 NASB

Our good Shepherd has in His flock a variety of experiences—some are strong in the Lord, and others are weak in faith—but He is impartial in His care for all His sheep, and the weakest lamb is as dear to Him as the most advanced of the flock. He finds newborn souls, like young lambs, ready to perish—He nourishes them until life becomes vigorous; He finds weak minds ready to faint and die—He consoles them and renews their strength. All the little ones He gathers, for it is not the will of our heavenly Father that one of them should perish.

What a quick eye He must have to see them all! What a tender heart to care for them all! What a far-reaching and potent arm to gather them all! How gently did He gather me to Himself, to His truth, to His blood, to His love, to His Church! With what effectual grace did He compel me to come to Himself! How frequently has He restored me from my wanderings and once again folded me within the circle of His everlasting arm! The best of all is that He does it all Himself personally, not delegating the task of love but condescending Himself to rescue and preserve His most unworthy servant. How shall I love Him enough or serve Him worthily?

Great Shepherd, add to Your mercies this one other: a heart to love You more truly as I ought.

A SONG FOR THE NIGHT

"God my Maker, who gives songs in the night."
JOB 35:10 NIV

Any man can sing in the day. It is easy to sing when we can read the notes by daylight; but he is skillful who sings when there is not a ray of light to read by—who sings from his heart. No man can make a song in the night of himself; he may attempt it, but he will find that a song in the night must be divinely inspired. Let all things go well, I can weave songs, fashioning them wherever I go out of the flowers that grow upon my path; but put me in a desert where no green thing grows, and with what shall I frame a hymn of praise to God? How shall a mortal man make a crown for the Lord where no jewels are? Let but this voice be clear and this body full of health, and I can sing God's praise. Silence my tongue, lay me upon the bed of languishing, and how shall I then chant God's high praises, unless He Himself gives me the song? No, it is not in man's power to sing when all is adverse, unless an altar coal shall touch his lips. Then, since our Maker gives songs in the night, let us wait upon Him for the music.

Oh Chief Musician, let us not remain songless because affliction is upon us, but tune our lips to the melody of thanksgiving.

Day 342
YOU ARE SAFE

---

*If ye were of the world, the world would love
his own: but because ye are not of the world,
but I have chosen you out of the world,
therefore the world hateth you.*

JOHN 15:19 KJV

Here is distinguishing grace and discriminating regard, for
some are made the special objects of divine affection. Do not
be afraid to dwell upon this high doctrine of election. Desire
to have your mind enlarged that you may comprehend more
and more the eternal, everlasting, discriminating love of God.
When you have mounted as high as election, tarry on its
sister mount, the covenant of grace. Covenant engagements
are the munitions of stupendous rock behind which we lie
entrenched; covenant engagements with the surety, Christ
Jesus, are the quiet resting places of trembling spirits.

If Jesus undertook to bring me to glory, and if the Father
promised that He would give me to the Son to be a part of
the infinite reward of the travail of His soul, then, my soul,
until God Himself shall be unfaithful, until Jesus shall cease
to be the truth, you are safe. When David danced before the
ark, he told Michal that election made him do so. Come, my
soul, exult before the God of grace and leap for joy of heart.

PRAISE GOD FOR
ANSWERED PRAYER

I will praise You, O LORD.
PSALM 9:1 NKJV

Praise should always follow answered prayer. Has the Lord been gracious to you and inclined His ear to the voice of your supplication? Then praise Him as long as you live. Deny not a song to Him who has answered your prayer and given you the desire of your heart. To be silent over God's mercies is to incur the guilt of ingratitude. To forget to praise God is to refuse to benefit ourselves; for praise, like prayer, is one great means of promoting the growth of the spiritual life. It helps to remove our burdens, to excite our hope, to increase our faith.

To bless God for mercies received is also the way to benefit our fellowmen. Others who have been in like circumstances will take comfort if we can say, "Oh, magnify the Lord with me, and let us exalt His name together; this poor man cried, and the Lord heard him!" Weak hearts will be strengthened, and drooping saints will be revived as they listen to our "songs of deliverance." Their doubts and fears will be rebuked as we teach and admonish one another in psalms and hymns and spiritual songs. They too shall "sing in the ways of the Lord" when they hear us magnify His holy name.

Praise is the most heavenly of Christian duties. The angels do not pray, but praise both day and night; and the redeemed, clothed in white robes with palm branches in their hands, are never weary of singing the new song "Worthy is the Lamb."

SPIRITUAL RENEWAL

Renew a right spirit within me.
PSALM 51:10 KJV

A backslider, if there be a spark of life left in him, will groan after restoration. In this renewal the same exercise of grace is required as at our conversion. We needed repentance then; we certainly need it now. We wanted faith that we might come to Christ at first; only the like grace can bring us to Jesus now. We wanted a word from the Most High, a word from the lips of the loving One to end our fears then; we shall soon discover, when under a sense of present sin, that we need it now.

No man can be renewed without as real and true a manifestation of the Holy Spirit's energy as he felt at first, because the work is as great, and flesh and blood are as much in the way now as ever they were. Let your personal weakness be an argument to make you pray earnestly to God for help. Oh, that you may have grace to plead with God, as though you pleaded for your very life—"Lord, renew a right spirit within me." He who sincerely prays to God to do this will prove his honesty by using the means through which God works. Be much in prayer, live much upon the Word of God, be careful to watch over the future uprisings of sin. Continue in all those blessed ordinances which will foster and nourish your dying graces; and knowing that all the power must proceed from Him, cease not to cry, "Renew a right spirit within me."

Our Unchanging Lord

I am the Lord, I change not.
MALACHI 3:6 KJV

It is well for us that, amidst all the variableness of life, there is One whom change cannot affect, One whose heart can never alter, and on whose brow mutability can make no furrows. All things else have changed—all things are changing. The sun itself grows dim with age, the heavens and earth must soon pass away—they shall perish, they shall wax old as does a garment; but there is One who only has immortality, of whose years there is no end, and in whose person there is no change. The delight which the mariner feels when, after having been tossed about for many days, he steps again upon the solid shore, is the satisfaction of a Christian when, amidst all the changes of this troublesome life, he rests the foot of his faith upon this truth—"I am the Lord; I change not."

With God "is no variableness, neither shadow of turning." Whatever His attributes were of old, they are now: His power, His wisdom, His justice, His truth are alike unchanged. He has ever been the refuge of His people, their stronghold in the day of trouble, and He is their sure Helper still. He is unchanged in His love. He has loved His people with "an everlasting love"; He loves them now as much as ever He did. Precious is the assurance that He changes not! The wheel of providence revolves, but its axle is eternal love.

GOD'S RESPONSE TO PRAYER

Behold, he prayeth.
ACTS 9:11 KJV

Prayers are instantly noticed in heaven. Here is comfort for the distressed but praying soul. Oftentimes a poor brokenhearted one bends his knee but can only utter his wailing in the language of sighs and tears; yet that groan has made all the harps of heaven thrill with music, that tear has been caught by God and treasured in heaven. "You put my tears into Your bottle" implies that they are caught as they flow.

The suppliant whose fears prevent his words will be well understood by the Most High. He may only look up with misty eye, but "prayer is the falling of a tear." Tears are the diamonds of heaven; sighs are a part of the music of Jehovah's court and are numbered with "the sublimest strains that reach the majesty on high." Think not that your prayer however weak or trembling will be unregarded. Our God not only hears prayer but also loves to hear it.

He regards not high looks and lofty words, He cares not for the pomp and pageantry of kings, He listens not to the swell of martial music, He regards not the triumph and pride of man; but wherever there is a heart big with sorrow or a lip quivering with agony or a deep groan or a penitential sigh, the heart of Jehovah is open. He marks it down in the registry of His memory; He puts our prayers, like rose leaves, between the pages of His book of remembrance, and when the volume is opened at last, there shall be a precious fragrance springing up from it.

THE OPEN DOOR
OF PRAYER

*Their prayer came up to His holy
dwelling place, to heaven.*
2 CHRONICLES 30:27 NKJV

Prayer is the never-failing resort of the Christian in any case, in every plight. When you cannot use your sword, you may take to the weapon of all prayer. Sword and spear need furbishing, but prayer never rusts; and when we think it most blunt, it cuts the best. Prayer is an open door which none can shut. Devils may surround you on all sides, but the way upward is always open; and as long as that road is unobstructed, you will not fall into the enemy's hand. Prayer is never out of season: In summer and in winter, its merchandise is precious. Prayer gains audience with heaven in the dead of night, in the midst of business, in the heat of noonday, in the shades of evening. In every condition, whether of poverty or sickness or obscurity or slander or doubt, your covenant God will welcome your prayer and answer it from His holy place.

Nor is prayer ever futile. True prayer is ever more true power. You may not always get what you ask, but you shall always have your real wants supplied. When God does not answer His children according to the letter, He does so according to the spirit. If you seek bodily health, should you complain if instead He makes your sickness turn to the healing of spiritual maladies? Is it not better to have the cross sanctified than removed? Forget not to offer your petition and request, for the Lord is ready to grant you your desires.

Day 348
ACKNOWLEDGING OUR WEAKNESS

"For my power is made perfect in weakness."
2 CORINTHIANS 12:9 NIV

A primary qualification for serving God with any amount of success, and for doing God's work well and triumphantly, is a sense of our own weakness. When God's warrior marches forth to battle strong in his own might, when he boasts, "I know that I shall conquer; my own right arm and my conquering sword shall get unto me the victory," defeat is not far distant. God will not go forth with that man who marches in his own strength.

Those who serve God must serve Him in His own way and in His strength, or He will never accept their service. That which man does unaided by divine strength God can never own. The mere fruits of the earth He casts away; He will only reap that corn, the seed of which was sown from heaven, watered by grace, and ripened by the sun of divine love. God will empty out all that you have before He will put His own into you. The river of God is full of water, but not one drop of it flows from earthly springs. God will have no strength used in His battles but the strength that He Himself imparts.

Are you mourning over your own weakness? Take courage, for there must be a consciousness of weakness before the Lord will give you victory. Your emptiness is but the preparation for your being filled, and your casting down is but the making ready for your lifting up.

THE LIGHT OF CHRIST

In your light we see light.
PSALM 36:9 NIV

No lips can tell the love of Christ to the heart until Jesus Himself shall speak within. Descriptions all fall flat and tame unless the Holy Spirit fills them with life and power; until our Immanuel reveals Himself within, the soul sees Him not. If you would see the sun, would you gather together the common means of illumination and seek in that way to behold the orb of day? No, the wise man knows that the sun must reveal itself, and only by its own blaze can that mighty lamp be seen. It is so with Christ.

Purify flesh and blood by any educational process you may select, elevate mental faculties to the highest degree of intellectual power, yet none of these can reveal Christ. The Spirit of God must come with power and overshadow the man with His wings, and then in that mystic holy of holies, the Lord Jesus must display Himself to the sanctified eye. Christ must be His own mirror. The great mass of this blear-eyed world can see nothing of the ineffable glories of Immanuel. Only where the Spirit has touched the eye with eye salve, quickened the heart with divine life, and educated the soul to a heavenly taste, only there is He understood.

Happy are those to whom our Lord manifests Himself, for His promise to such is that He will make His abode with them. O Jesus, our Lord, our hearts are open; come in, and go out no more forever. Show Yourself to us now! Favor us with a glimpse of Your all-conquering charms.

Day 350

ETERNAL LIGHT

The night also is Yours.
PSALM 74:16 NKJV

Lord, You do not abdicate Your throne when the sun goes down, nor do You leave the world all through these long wintry nights to be the prey of evil; Your eyes watch us as the stars, and Your arms surround us as the zodiac belts the sky. The dews of kindly sleep and all the influences of the moon are in Your hand, and the alarms and solemnities of night are equally with You. This is very sweet to me when watching through the midnight hours or tossing to and fro in anguish. There are precious fruits put forth by the moon as well as by the sun: May my Lord make me to be a favored partaker in them.

The night of affliction is as much under the arrangement and control of the Lord of Love as the bright summer days when all is bliss. Jesus is in the tempest. His love wraps the night about itself as a mantle, but to the eye of faith, the sable robe is scarce a disguise. From the first watch of the night even unto the break of day, the eternal Watcher observes His saints and overrules the shades and dews of midnight for His people's highest good. We believe in no rival deities of good and evil contending for the mastery, but we hear the voice of Jehovah saying, "I create light, and I create darkness; I, the Lord, do all these things."

EXCELLENT THOUGHTS
OF CHRIST

Give thanks to Him, bless His name.
PSALM 100:4 NASB

Our Lord would have all His people rich in high and happy thoughts concerning His blessed person. Jesus is not content that His brethren should think meanly of Him; it is His pleasure that His espoused ones should be delighted with His beauty. We are not to regard Him as a bare necessity but as a luxurious delicacy, as a rare and ravishing delight. To this end He has revealed Himself as the "pearl of great price" in its peerless beauty, as the "bundle of myrrh" in its refreshing fragrance, as the "rose of Sharon" in its lasting perfume, as the "lily" in its spotless purity.

Consider what the angels think of Him as they count it their highest honor to veil their faces at His feet. Consider what the blood-washed think of Him as day without night they sing His well-deserved praises. High thoughts of Christ will enable us to act consistently with our relations toward Him. Our Lord Jesus desires us to think well of Him, that we may submit cheerfully to His authority. High thoughts of Him increase our love. Love and esteem go together.

Therefore, think much of your Master's excellencies. Study Him in His primeval glory, before He took upon Himself your nature! Think of the mighty love that drew Him from His throne to die upon the cross! Admire Him as He conquers all the powers of hell! See Him risen, crowned, glorified! Bow before Him as the Wonderful Counselor, the Mighty God, for only thus will your love to Him be what it should.

Day 352

WATER FOR THE THIRSTY

I will pour water upon him that is thirsty.
ISAIAH 44:3 KJV

When a believer has fallen into a low, sad state of feeling, he often tries to lift himself out of it by chastening himself with dark and doleful fears. Such is not the way to rise from the dust but to continue in it. It is not the law, but the Gospel which saves the seeking soul at first; and it is not a legal bondage, but Gospel liberty which can restore the fainting believer afterward. Slavish fear does not bring the backslider back to God, but the sweet wooings of love allure him to Jesus' bosom.

Are you this morning thirsting for the Living God and unhappy because you cannot find Him to the delight of your heart? Have you lost the joy of religion, and is this your prayer: "Restore unto me the joy of Your salvation"? Are you conscious also that you are barren, like the dry ground, that you are not bringing forth the fruit unto God which He has a right to expect of you? Then here is exactly the promise that you need: "I will pour water upon him who is thirsty." You shall receive the grace you so much require, and you shall have it to the utmost reach of your needs. Water refreshes the thirsty: You shall be refreshed; your desires shall be gratified. Your life shall be quickened by fresh grace. Whatever good quality there is in divine grace, you shall enjoy it to the full; all the riches of divine grace you shall receive in plenty.

GRAVEN ON HIS PALMS

Behold, I have graven thee upon
the palms of my hands.
ISAIAH 49:16 KJV

No doubt a part of the wonder that is concentrated in the word *behold* is excited by the unbelieving lamentation of the preceding sentence. Zion said, "The Lord has forsaken me, and my God has forgotten me." How amazed the divine mind seems to be at this wicked unbelief! What can be more astounding than the unfounded doubts and fears of God's favored people?

The Lord's loving word of rebuke should make us blush. He cries, "How can I have forgotten thee when I have graven you upon the palms of My hands?" We do not know which to wonder most at: the faithfulness of God or the unbelief of His people. He keeps His promise a thousand times, and yet the next trial makes us doubt Him. He never fails, and yet we are as continually vexed with anxieties, molested with suspicions, and disturbed with fears.

Behold is a word intended to excite admiration. Here, indeed, we have a theme for marveling. Heaven and earth may well be astonished that rebels should obtain so great a nearness to the heart of infinite love as to be written upon the palms of His hands. The name is there, but that is not all: "I have graven your person, your image, your case, your circumstances, your sins, your temptations, your weaknesses, your wants, your works; I have graven you, everything about you, all that concerns you; I have put you altogether there." Will you ever say again that God has forsaken you when He has graven you upon His own palms?

Just as you received Christ Jesus as Lord,
continue to live your lives in him.
Colossians 2:6 niv

The life of faith is represented as receiving—an act which implies the very opposite of anything like merit. It is simply the acceptance of a gift. As the earth drinks in the rain, as the sea receives the streams, as night accepts light from the stars, so we, giving nothing, partake freely of the grace of God.

The saints are not, by nature, wells or streams; they are but cisterns into which the living water flows: They are empty vessels into which God pours His salvation. The idea of receiving implies a sense of realization, making the matter a reality. One cannot very well receive a shadow; we receive that which is substantial: So is it in the life of faith; Christ becomes real to us. While we are without faith, Jesus is a mere name to us—a person who lived a long while ago, so long ago that His life is only a history to us now! By an act of faith, Jesus becomes a real person in the consciousness of our heart.

But receiving also means grasping or getting possession of. The thing which I receive becomes my own: I appropriate to myself that which is given. When I receive Jesus, He becomes my Savior—so mine that neither life nor death shall be able to rob me of Him. All this is to receive Christ—to take Him as God's free gift, to realize Him in my heart, and to appropriate Him as mine.

INVITATION TO BETHLEHEM

For unto us a child is born, unto us a son is given.
ISAIAH 9:6 KJV

Come to the babe of Bethlehem. Come, you little children, boys and girls, come; for He also was a boy. "The holy child Jesus" is the children's Savior and says still, "Suffer the little children to come unto Me, and forbid them not." Come, young women, you who are still in the morning of your beauty, and, like Mary, rejoice in God your Savior. The virgin bore Him on her bosom, so come and bear Him in your hearts, saying, "Unto us a child is born, unto us a son is given." And you men in the plenitude of your strength, remember how Joseph cared for Him and watched with reverent solicitude His tender years: Be for His cause as a father and a helper; sanctify your strength to His service. And you women advanced in years, you matrons and widows, come like Anna and bless the Lord that you have seen the salvation of Israel; and you older men, who like Simeon are ready to depart, come and take the Savior in your arms, adoring Him as your Savior and your all. You shepherds, you simplehearted, you who labor for your daily bread, come and adore the Savior.

Day 356

JESUS IS ALL WE NEED

His name shall be called Wonderful, Counsellor,
The mighty God, The everlasting Father,
The Prince of Peace.
ISAIAH 9:6 KJV

Rejoice, you who feel that you are lost; your Savior comes to seek and save you. Be of good cheer, you who are in prison, for He comes to set you free. You who are famished and ready to die, rejoice that He has consecrated for you a Bethlehem, a house of bread, and He has come to be the bread of life to your souls.

Rejoice, sinners everywhere, for the restorer of the castaways, the Savior of the fallen is born. Join in the joy, you saints, for He is the preserver of the saved ones, delivering them from innumerable perils, and He is the sure prefect of those He preserves. Jesus is no partial Savior, beginning a work and not concluding it; but restoring and upholding, He also perfects and presents the saved ones without spot or wrinkle or any such thing before His Father's throne.

Rejoice aloud, all you people; let your hills and valleys ring with joy, for a Savior who is mighty to save is born among you.

UNKNOWN BY MEN,
BUT KNOWN TO GOD

Behold, I bring you good tidings of great joy,
which shall be to all people. For unto you is born
this day in the city of David a Saviour.
LUKE 2:10–11 KJV

Observe how the angel begins, "Behold, I bring you good tidings of great joy. . .for unto you is born this day. . ." So then the joy began with the first who heard it, the shepherds.

"*To you,*" He says; "for unto *you* is born." Shall the joy begin with you today?—for it profits you little that Christ was born or that Christ died, unless unto *you* a child is born, and for you Jesus bled. A personal interest is the main point. "But I am poor," one says. So were the shepherds. You poor, to you this mysterious child is born. "The poor have the Gospel preached unto them." "He shall judge the poor and needy, and break in pieces the oppressor."

"But I am obscure and unknown," says another. So were the watchers on the midnight plain. Who knew the men who endured hard toil and kept their flocks by night? But you, unknown by men, are known to God: Shall it not be said that "unto you a child is born"? The Lord does not regard the greatness of men but has respect to the lowly.

But you are illiterate, you say; you cannot understand much. Perhaps, but unto the shepherds Christ was born, and their simplicity did not hinder their receiving Him but even helped them to it. Let it be the same with you: Receive gladly the simple truth as it is in Jesus.

Behold, a virgin shall conceive, and bear a son,
and shall call his name Immanuel.

ISAIAH 7:14 KJV

Let us today go down to Bethlehem, and in company with wondering shepherds and adoring Magi, let us see Him who was born King of the Jews. Jesus is Jehovah incarnate, our Lord and our God, and yet our Brother and Friend; let us adore and admire.

Let us notice at the very first glance His miraculous conception. It was a thing unheard of before and unparalleled since, that a virgin should conceive and bear a son. The first promise read thus, "The seed of the woman," not the offspring of the man. Since venturous woman led the way in the sin which brought forth paradise lost, she, and she alone, ushers in the Regainer of paradise.

Our Savior, although truly man, was as to His human nature the Holy One of God. Let us reverently bow before the holy Child whose innocence restores to manhood its ancient glory; and let us pray that He may be formed in us, the hope of glory. Fail not to note His humble parentage. His mother has been described simply as "a virgin"—not a princess or prophetess nor a matron of large estate. True, the blood of kings ran in her veins, nor was her mind a weak and untaught one for she could sing most sweetly a song of praise; but yet how humble her position, how poor the man to whom she stood affianced, and how miserable the accommodation afforded to the newborn King!

GOOD TIDINGS

---

*And the angel said unto them, Fear not: for, behold,
I bring you good tidings of great joy, which shall be to
all people. For unto you is born this day in the city of
David a Saviour, which is Christ the Lord. And this
shall be a sign unto you; Ye shall find the babe wrapped
in swaddling clothes, lying in a manger.*

LUKE 2:10–12 KJV

Earth's joy is small, her mirth is trivial, but heaven has sent
us joy immeasurable, fit for immortal minds. Inasmuch as
no note of time is appended and no intimation is given
that the message will ever be reversed, we may say that it
is a *lasting* joy, a joy which will ring all down the ages, the
echoes of which shall be heard until the trumpet brings the
resurrection; yes, and onward forever and ever. For when
God sent forth the angel in his brightness to say, "I bring
you good tidings of great joy, which shall be to all people,"
He did as much as say, "From this time forward, it shall be
joy to the sons of men; there shall be peace to the human
race and goodwill toward men forever and ever, as long as
there is glory to God in the highest."

What a blessed thought! The Star of Bethlehem shall
never set. Jesus, the fairest among ten thousand, the most
lovely among the beautiful, is a joy forever.

CHRIST THE LORD

---

*For unto you is born this day in the city of David
a Saviour, which is Christ the Lord.*

LUKE 2:11 KJV

"Christ the Lord." The word *Lord*, or *Kurios*, used here is tantamount to "Jehovah." We cannot doubt that because it is the same word used twice in the ninth verse, and in the ninth verse none can question that it means Jehovah. Listen, "And, lo, the angel of the *Lord* came upon them, and the glory of the *Lord* shone round about them." And if this is not enough, read the twenty-third verse: "As it is written in the law of the *Lord*, every male that openeth the womb shall be called holy to the *Lord*." The word "Lord" here assuredly refers to Jehovah, the one God.

Our Savior is Christ, God, Jehovah. No testimony to His divinity could be plainer; it is indisputable. And what joy there is in this, for suppose an angel had been our Savior: He would not have been able to bear the load of my sin or yours; or if anything less than God had been set up as the ground of our salvation, it might have been found too frail a foundation. But if He who undertakes to save is none other than the Infinite and the Almighty, then the load of our guilt can be carried upon such shoulders, the stupendous labor of our salvation can be achieved by such a worker, and that with ease: For all things are possible with God, and He is able to save to the uttermost those who come to God through Him.

PONDER GOD'S GOODNESS

But Mary kept all these things,
and pondered them in her heart.
LUKE 2:19 KJV

There was an exercise on the part of this blessed woman of three powers of her being: her memory—she kept all these things; her affection—she kept them in her heart; her intellect—she pondered them. Memory, affection, and understanding were all exercised in relation to the things which she had heard.

Beloved, remember what you have heard of your Lord Jesus and what He has done for you. Let your memory treasure up everything about Christ that you have either felt or known or believed, and then let your fond affections hold Him fast forevermore. Love the person of your Lord! Let your intellect be exercised concerning the Lord Jesus. Meditate on what you read: Stop not at the surface; dive into the depths. Abide with your Lord: Let Him not be to you as a wayfaring man who lingers for a night, but constrain Him, saying, "Abide with us, for the day is far spent." Hold Him, and do not let Him go. The word *ponder* means "to weigh." Make ready the balances of judgment. Oh, but where are the scales that can weigh the Lord Christ? "He takes up the isles as a very little thing"; who shall take Him up? "He weighs the mountains in scales"; in what scales shall we weigh Him?

If your understanding cannot comprehend, let your affections apprehend; and if your spirit cannot compass the Lord Jesus in the grasp of understanding, let it embrace Him in the arms of affection.

THE SHEPHERD'S PRAISE

---

*And the shepherds returned, glorifying and
praising God for all the things that they had
heard and seen, as it was told unto them.*

LUKE 2:20 KJV

What was the subject of their praise? They praised God for
what they had heard—for the good tidings of great joy that
a Savior was born unto them. Let us copy them; let us also
raise a song of thanksgiving that we have heard of Jesus and
His salvation. They also praised God for what they had seen.

One point for which they praised God was the agreement
between what they had heard and what they had seen. Observe
the last sentence: "As it was told unto them." Have you not
found the Gospel to be in yourselves just what the Bible said
it would be? Jesus said He would give you rest—have you not
enjoyed the sweetest peace in Him? He said you should have
joy and comfort and life through believing in Him—have you
not received all these? Are not His ways, ways of pleasantness,
and His paths, paths of peace?

I have found Christ sweeter than His servants ever said
He was. I looked upon His likeness as they painted it, but it
was merely a daub compared with Himself; for the King in
His beauty outshines all imaginable loveliness. Surely what
we have "seen" keeps pace with, no, far exceeds, what we have
"heard." Let us then glorify and praise God for a Savior so
precious and so satisfying.

Day 363

THE BEAUTY OF JESUS

Your eyes will see the king in his beauty.
ISAIAH 33:17 NIV

The more you know about Christ, the less will you be satisfied with superficial views of Him; and the more deeply you study His transactions in the eternal covenant, His engagements on your behalf as the eternal Surety, and the fullness of His grace which shines in all His offices, the more truly will you see the King in His beauty. Long more and more to see Jesus.

Meditation puts the telescope to the eye and enables us to see Jesus after a better sort than we could have seen Him if we had lived in the days of His flesh. Would that our conversation were more in heaven and that we were more taken up with the person, the work, the beauty of our incarnate Lord. More meditation and the beauty of the King would flash upon us with more resplendence. It is very probable that we shall have such a sight of our glorious King as we never had before when we die. Many saints in dying have looked up from amidst the stormy waters and have seen Jesus walking on the waves of the sea and heard Him say, "It is I; do not be afraid." Thick veils and clouds hang between our souls and their true life: When will the day break and the shadows flee away? Oh long-expected day, begin!

Day 364

GLORY TO
GOD FOREVER

To whom be glory for ever. Amen.
ROMANS 11:36 KJV

"To whom be glory forever." This should be the single desire
of the Christian. All other wishes must be subservient and
tributary to this one. The Christian may wish for prosperity
in his business, but only so far as it may help him to promote
this: "To Him be glory forever." He may desire to attain more
gifts and more graces, but it should only be that "to Him
may be glory forever." You are not acting as you ought to
do when you are moved by any other motive than a single
eye to your Lord's glory. As a Christian, you are "of God
and through God"; then live "to God." Let nothing ever
set your heart beating so mightily as love for Him. Let this
ambition fire your soul; be this the foundation of every
enterprise upon which you enter and this your sustaining
motive whenever your zeal would grow cold: Make God
your only object.

Let your desire for God's glory be a growing desire. Has
God prospered you in business? Give Him more as He has
given you more. Has God given you experience? Praise Him by
stronger faith than you exercised at first. Does your knowledge
grow? Then sing more sweetly. Do you enjoy happier times
than you once had? Have you been restored from sickness,
and has your sorrow been turned into peace and joy? Then
give Him more music. Give Him honor, putting the "Amen"
to this doxology to your great and gracious Lord, by your own
individual service and increasing holiness.

CHRIST
IS EVERLASTING

You are from everlasting.
PSALM 93:2 NKJV

Christ is everlasting. Of Him we may sing with David, "Thy throne, O God, is forever and ever." Rejoice in Jesus Christ, the same yesterday, today, and forever. Jesus always was. The Babe born in Bethlehem was united to the Word, which was in the beginning, by whom all things were made. If He were not God from everlasting, we could not so devoutly love Him; but since He was from all eternity with the Father, we trace the stream of divine love to Himself equally with His Father and the blessed Spirit. As our Lord always was, so also He is forevermore. Jesus is not dead; "He ever liveth to make intercession for us." Resort to Him in all your times of need for He is waiting to bless you.

Furthermore, Jesus our Lord ever shall be. When only your last battle remains to be fought, you shall find that the hand of your conquering Captain has not grown feeble—the living Savior shall cheer the dying saint. When you enter heaven, you shall find Him there bearing the dew of His youth, and through eternity the Lord Jesus shall still remain the perennial spring of joy and life and glory to His people. Living waters may you draw from this sacred well! Jesus always was, He always is, He always shall be. He is eternal in all His attributes, in all His offices, in all His might and willingness to bless, comfort, guard, and crown His chosen people.

A BENEDICTION
OF PEACE

Peace I leave with you, my peace I give unto you.
JOHN 14:27 KJV

Beloved friends, as you go to your families, as you go through life, as you go into eternity, I pray that you "go in peace." It is heaven here on earth to possess "the peace of God which passeth all understanding." Peace should be the continual portion of all believers. This is what the angels sang when our Lord Jesus appeared on earth: "Glory to God in the highest, and on earth peace, goodwill toward men." And as it was at the beginning of our Savior's life, it was also at the end, for this was our Lord's legacy to all His disciples: "Peace I leave with you, my peace I give unto you." He who is called "the God of peace" should be very precious to your soul.

Peace is the result of what the Savior has done for you. Has He forgiven you? Then you have peace. Has He saved you? Then feel an inward peace that no one can take from you! Did He die for you? Then you can never die in the full meaning of the word. Has He risen for you? Then because He lives, you will live also; so do not let your heart be troubled, but be at peace. Will He come again to receive you to Himself? Then let your peace be like a river flowing from the very throne of God!

SCRIPTURE INDEX

MORE CLASSIC DEVOTIONS FROM BARBOUR PUBLISHING

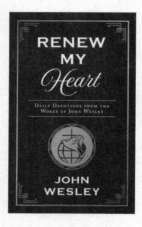

Barbour's classic devotionals offer time-tested insights into God, scripture, and the Christian experience. In *Renew My Heart*, you'll find 365 powerful readings drawn from the sermons and notes of English theologian and evangelist John Wesley (1703–1791), founder of the "Methodist" movement in pursuit of holy living.

Paperback / 978-1-64352-794-9 / $9.99